THE PRACTICE OF QUIXOTISM

Postmodern Theory and Eighteenth-Century Women's Writing

by

Scott Paul Gordon

THE PRACTICE OF QUIXOTISM
© Scott Paul Gordon, 2006.

All rights reserved. No part of this book may be used or reproduced in any manner whatsoever without written permission except in the case of brief quotations embodied in critical articles or reviews.

First published in 2006 by
PALGRAVE MACMILLAN™
175 Fifth Avenue, New York, N.Y. 10010 and
Houndmills, Basingstoke, Hampshire, England RG21 6XS
Companies and representatives throughout the world.

PALGRAVE MACMILLAN is the global academic imprint of the Palgrave Macmillan division of St. Martin's Press, LLC and of Palgrave Macmillan Ltd. Macmillan® is a registered trademark in the United States, United Kingdom and other countries. Palgrave is a registered trademark in the European Union and other countries.

ISBN-13: 978–1–4039–7444–0
ISBN-10: 1–4039–7444–6

Library of Congress Cataloging-in-Publication Data

Gordon, Scott Paul, 1965–
   The practice of quixotism : Postmodern theory and
eighteenth-century women's writing / by Scott Paul Gordon.
     p. cm.
   Includes bibliographical references and index.
   ISBN 1–4039–7444–6 (alk. paper)
   1. English literature—Women authors—History and criticism.
2. English literature—18th century—History and criticism. 3. Cervantes Saavedra, Miguel de, 1547–1616—Influence. 4. Don Quixote (Fictitious character). 5. Reality in literature. 6. Delusions in literature. I.Title.

PR113.G67 2006
820.9′928709033—dc22   2006041564

A catalogue record for this book is available from the British Library.

Design by Newgen Imaging Systems (P) Ltd., Chennai, India.

First edition: October 2006

10 9 8 7 6 5 4 3 2 1

Printed in the United States of America.

To my parents

Contents

Acknowledgments		vii
Introduction	The Quixote Trope	1
Chapter 1	Historicizing Quixote and the Scandal of Quixotism	11
Chapter 2	Charlotte Lennox's *Female Quixote* and Orthodox Quixotism	41
Chapter 3	Suspicion and Experience in Sarah Fielding's *David Simple*	67
Chapter 4	Mary Wortley Montagu and the Quixotic Dream of Objectivity	93
Chapter 5	Quixotic Perception in Sophia Lee's *The Recess*	117
Chapter 6	Ann Radcliffe's *The Mysteries of Udolpho* and the Practice of Quixotism	141
Epilogue	Beyond Quixotism?: Quixotism and Contemporary Theory	167
Notes		187
Index		233

Acknowledgments

This book began as a job talk on Lennox's *Female Quixote* delivered at Lehigh University, where I have taught ever since. This project would have been impossible without the personal and institutional support, as well as the intellectual stimulation, I have been lucky to find at Lehigh. For this I am grateful to Pete Beidler, Bobb Carson, Kate Crassons, Beth Dolan, Alex Doty, Betsy Fifer, Ed Gallagher, Stephannie Gearhart, Barry Kroll, Rita Kurtz, Ed Lotto, Carol Laub, Rosemary Mundhenk, Barbara Pavlock, Deep Singh, Barbara Traister, Bob Watts, Stephanie Watts, and Ed Whitley. The absence from Lehigh of Patty Ingham, witty in herself and cause of wit in others, occasions daily disappointments. I am thankful to have had Jan Fergus's help during most of the writing of this book, and the book would have been better if she were still able to extend such help. I regret that I cannot thank Jim Frakes for the support he gave me for so many years.

My deepest thanks go to Dawn Keetley, who, I think, read more versions of more pages than anybody and who always offered generous and careful readings; to David Hawkes and Seth Moglen, who, despite (or because of) their distrust of the postmodern and neopragmatist writers on whom I draw, helped me think through many theoretical issues; to Tracey Cummings, Bob Wilson, Tom O'Connor, and especially Chris Litman, who endured many conversations that forced me to better conceive (or abandon) my arguments; and to James Dinh for always alerting me when I am thinking too much.

The final manuscript benefited from classroom conversations during spring 2005 with a superb group of graduate students: Wes Atkinson, Kate Cartwright, Kurt Douglass, Kelli Gorski, Duane Graner, Karen Manahan, Sam Norwood, Tom O'Connor, Kim Robertson, Paul Sisko, Minh Trinh, and Heather Urbanski. It has benefited, as well, from conversations with the scholars who participated in a lecture series, sponsored by Lehigh's Lawrence Henry Gipson Institute for Eighteenth-Century Studies, on the "(Pre)History of Objectivity": Peter Dear, Adrian Johns, Mary Poovey, Harriet Ritvo, Londa Schiebinger, and Julie Solomon.

The Lawrence Henry Gipson Institute for Eighteenth-Century Studies provided financial assistance, as did Lehigh University in the form of a two-year Class of 1961 Professorship. This book could not have been written without the help of the staff of Lehigh's libraries, in particular the Interlibrary Loan office. I am grateful, as well, to the editorial staff at Palgrave Macmillan, especially Farideh Koohi-Kamali, for offering excellent and timely advice on matters of all sorts.

Portions of chapters 2 and 5 rework material that has appeared in *Studies in English Literature* (38.3: 1998), in *Eighteenth-Century Women: Studies in their Lives, Works, and Culture* (4: 2006), and in *Cervantes in the English-Speaking World: New Essays* (ed. Darío Fernández-Morera and Michael Hanke (Edition Reichenberger, 2005) and I thank the editors of each for permission to reprint.

Finally, and most importantly, I thank my family—my parents, my brothers and their families, all the Baksts, and, of course, Gus—for offering support of all kinds, large and small, during the many years I was writing this book.

Introduction: The Quixote Trope

Nobody wants to be a quixote. We invoke quixotes—deploying what I call the "quixote trope," a depiction of another's deluded perceptions that implies the objectivity of one's own—precisely to dismiss others' beliefs. Viewing the world through a generic lens that their reading has deposited in their heads, quixotes see what is not really there: they mistake their imagination's own products as real phenomena available to everyone else's senses. Let me introduce a pair of terms, useful in discussing quixotism, that I will employ throughout this study: quixotes think they simply *find* the world that, as others can see, their quixotic imagination *makes* or calls into existence.[1] So a recent send-up of literary theory, ridiculing "a generation of scholarly knights riding off in quest of image patterns, paradoxes, and mythic parallels," accuses theoretically minded critics of "finding" in texts not what is "actually" there but rather objects from their own deluded imaginations; a review of a reading of Genesis charges the author with quixotically "find[ing] there what he already believes," the "coherence" he "discovers (actually, puts) in Genesis" proving only his "folly" and "zeal"; and Roger Kimball's recent *Rape of the Masters* (2004) berates recent art historians for " 'projecting' merely subjective fantasies into paintings" instead of just "registering what is before [their] eyes."[2] According to their critics, these "over-readers"—like quixotes—misrecognize things they have themselves created (patterns, paradoxes, parallels, coherences) as actually present in the reality, in this case the texts, they encounter.[3]

Both ostensibly rational individuals and deluded quixotes are convinced, of course, that their perceptions simply register without mediation the "reality" that exists outside. As Wendy Motooka says, a quixote "attempts to universalize his or her own peculiar way of thinking," which seems to the quixote as self-evident and reasonable as ostensibly rational subjects' perceptions seem to them.[4] Neither the quixote nor the rationalist admits the traces of the other within their own vision. Although one who observes a quixote can recognize that the presence of a genre produces the quixote's world, quixotes believe they simply encounter a world of facts and objects that preexists them. Both quixotes and their rational opposites, then, consider their own perceptions as universally valid. The quixote trope or the discourse of quixotism, as I discuss more fully in chapter 1, functions to disguise this resemblance by positioning one belief as deluded (produced by an individual's errant imagination) and the other as objective (registering the "real" without distortion). To paraphrase Jonathan Swift, the quixote trope is the "*Racket*" that "every Man carrie[s] about Him" to "strike" awareness of his own quixotism "from himself."[5]

Quixotism, that is, is a discourse that describes—or establishes—a stark difference between an "us" and a "them." No matter how persuasively current critical discourses may dismantle prevailing oppositions to show that what appears to be a difference *between* categories (us vs. them, objectivity vs. subjectivity, inclusivity vs. exclusivity, tolerance vs. intolerance, rationality vs. irrationality) actually disguises a difference *within* a category,[6] those who use these categories deploy them to insist on the very differences that our deconstructive analyses aim to collapse. The term "quixotism," in effect, functions as a performative utterance that marks off an "other." To identify a behavior or belief as quixotic does not name a preexisting phenomenon as much as it produces the distinction itself as a reality for users. Just as to utter the words " 'I name this ship *Queen Elizabeth*' has the effect of naming . . . the ship," so for me to call another a "quixote" has the effect of creating *for me* a real distinction between my own beliefs and the (now) utterly different (and ridiculous) beliefs to which I apply the label.[7] Individuals do not deliberately use the quixote trope with this strategy in mind: for users, the quixote trope describes a real difference, and the trope functions effectively only when subjects blind themselves to its role in establishing certain beliefs or perceptions as the perceptions that all, were all rational, would share immediately. The quixote trope enables us to dismiss others' beliefs (as partial, distorted, deluded, biased, perverse) and to validate our own. In 1720 Bernard Mandeville's *Free Thoughts on Religion, The Church and National Happiness* argued that the "generality of Men are so wedded to and so obstinately fond of their own Opinion, and a Doctrine they have been imbued with from their Cradle, that they cannot think any one sincere, who being acquainted with it, refuses to embrace it"[8]; two hundred years later John Dewey claimed in *Human Nature and Conduct: An Introduction to Social Psychology* (1922) that each subject is "rigidly sure of the rightness" of his or her own beliefs and "thinks the other the creature of personal desire, whim or obstinacy."[9] The quixote trope is one strategy by which subjects preserve this configuration, affirming their own beliefs as rational, clear-sighted, and in touch with a "real" to which quixotes might return if they could abandon the fictions inside their heads.

This demand, indeed confidence, that one can eliminate one's prejudices lies at the heart of Enlightenment thought and of what I call in chapters 1 and 2 "orthodox" quixote narratives, which are profoundly normative. This is evident, for instance, in Richard Graves's *Spiritual Quixote, or The Summer's Ramble of Mr. Geoffrey Wildgoose: A Comic Romance* (1773), where Mr. Wildgoose's "romantic and irregular undertaking," his quest for "primitive Christianity," begins after he reads too many seventeenth-century Puritan tracts. The novel ends with Wildgoose "cured" and "reclaim[ed] . . . from his erroneous opinions," confessing that he "find[s] my head much clearer than it has been for some months" and that "many things appear to me in a very different light from what they have lately done." His friend Greville rejoices that Wildgoose can now "see things in their proper light" and that "the mist was dispelled from his mind," phrases so crucial to the text's project that Greville repeats them ten chapters later when he notes that Wildgoose had "been for some time under the influence of a deluded imagination: but . . . the mists, which had clouded his reason, seemed now to be dispelled." Wildgoose himself, in the novel's last chapter, testifies that "it had pleased God lately to open his eyes" and that "a weight of gloom had . . . been removed from his mind."[10] Wildgoose and his companion, Jerry, rejoin the very community from which, Graves's text suggests, they had alienated themselves: emerging from the mists that benighted them, the travelers want nothing more than to settle into the community they should never have left.

Graves's language reveals how effortlessly the quixote story embodies the Enlightenment dream. The language of "clouded . . . reason," of "mists . . . dispelled," of "open[ing] . . . eyes" is routine in quixote narratives: the two quixotes in Elizabeth Hamilton's *Memoirs of Modern Philosophers* (1800), which I discuss in chapter 2, prove that "Imagination is for ever raising a bewildering mist, which distorts every object."[11] This rhetoric reproduces the key elements of the Enlightenment belief that if one could only remove the barriers that impede proper perception, each subject would be able to see things as they truly are. "It is by shaking off all Clogs of Prejudice, and Fetters of humane Authority, by thinking freely," Mandeville wrote, "that Men can only mount to Wisdom."[12] The disintegration of these barriers—typically conceived of as religious, philosophical, and scientific authorities—was the primary aim of what Hans-Georg Gadamer has called the "emancipatory Enlightenment." The "heritage of the Enlightenment," Gadamer argues, has always contended that "a progressive process of clarification" can "set man, the actor and agent, free": "undertak[ing] to free us of outer and inner social forces and compulsions simply by making us aware of them," the "customary Enlightenment formula" requires us to "see through pretexts or unmask pretensions," a "demagicification of the world" that will leave subjects perceptually acute and free. Modern science, whose pretensions to objectivity have enticed other disciplines to adopt its model as theirs, "stands or falls," Gadamer summarizes, on this "principle of being unbiased and prejudiceless." "The rapid progress of knowledge," Joseph Priestley wrote in his preface to *Experiments and Observations on Different Kinds of Air* (1774), "which like the progress of . . . light from the sun, extends itself not in this way or that way only, but in all directions, will, I doubt not, be the means, under God, of extirpating all terror and prejudice." Above all, Enlightenment discourse promises that if individuals struggle to "see through prejudices or tear away the pretenses that hide reality," a day will arrive when (in Graves's terms) all the "mists" will have disappeared and individuals will be able to "see things in their proper light."[13] The quixote story, I argue here, has been the principal literary means to further this agenda.

As it reached its four-hundredth anniversary in 2005, however, the story of Quixote seems to have reversed its cultural currency. We are still, it is true, familiar with the story of Don Quixote himself: an extravagant TV-movie on TNT (2000) cast John Lithgow as Don Quixote and Vanessa Williams as Dulcinea, Brian Stokes Mitchell played Quixote on Broadway in a 2002–2003 revival of the 1965 musical "The Man of la Mancha," the critically acclaimed *Lost in La Mancha* (2003) documented Terry Gilliam's failed attempt to turn Cervantes's tale into a major motion picture, and Edith Grossman's new translation of *Don Quixote* (2003) received widespread attention. But the Quixote story no longer performs the work that, I argue in chapters 1 and 2, it once did. Teaching readers how to make sense of strikingly divergent perspectives on "the way things are," *El ingenioso hidalgo Don Quixote de le Mancha* (1605) and its many retellings positioned such alternate accounts as aberrant or deluded and insisted on their cure. We no longer look for this story, however, our postmodern sensibilities preferring to celebrate—rather than to police, dismiss, or ridicule—different, isolated, or unique points of view. In the stories we now tell, ostensibly mistaken "readers" of reality—paranoids, amateur detectives, children with overactive imaginations—inevitably turn out to be more perceptive, creative, and brave than the doubting realists who surround them.

The line that divides quixotes from nonquixotes has never seemed so invisible. In 1920 Georg Lukács separated those whose perceptions of objects "appear to be unmediated" only because "the awareness of mediation is lacking" from others who are capable of "comprehending reality . . . without any preconceptions,"[14] but much recent theory refuses to posit a space "beyond quixotism" from which we might see how things really are, free from prejudice, bias, or presuppositions. Indeed, as I argue at greater length in my Epilogue, much recent theoretical writing portrays all subjects as fundamentally and irremediably quixotic, encountering "reality" only as shaped or organized by the assumptions and stories that our culture has deposited in our minds. Each of our current critical buzzwords, as Fred Parker has recently noted, reveals a "hyperalterness to thinking as a lens or filter or reconfiguring matrix, rather than a window onto the world."[15] Postmodern theory, however, is not the first to notice that culture-bound assumptions shape one's encounters with "reality": *Don Quixote* portrays that very phenomenon. Four centuries ago the quixote embodied the charge often lodged against our postmodern world, in which, it is said, subjects "now inhabit a real of purely fictive or illusory appearances" and cannot differentiate "between truth and the various true-seeming images."[16] *Don Quixote* exposes the genres or stories that haunt our perception in order to dispel them and to restore a properly unmediated encounter with the real; much recent theory, undermining the fundamental *telos* of the typical quixote tale, suspects the impossibility of this project. *The Practice of Quixotism* focuses on a series of eighteenth-century quixote tales that also undermine the quixote tale's deep commitment to common sense, to a "real" that all properly configured subjects share, to a clear demarcation between those who see clearly and those whose vision suffers distortions because of internalized lenses, filters, or presuppositions.

These texts are unusual in that many eighteenth-century quixote narratives continue to use the figure of quixote in normative ways. These orthodox tales prohibit epistemological uncertainty: encouraging readers to distance themselves from the quixote figure, they reinforce readers' confidence in the clarity and objectivity of their own perceptions and clearly mark the "real" from its distortions. Most quixote narratives, even those whose quixote figures may embody ideals that subvert dominant culture, never allow the reader to be confused about the reality, or unreality, of events or objects. Anthony Close's account of *Don Quixote* holds for most of its imitators: Cervantes's text offers a "split perspective on events, one sane, the other deluded . . . [W]e are encouraged to adopt the first in a spirit of sardonic detachment from the second . . . By implication, we are included in that knot of spectators gazing in astonishment at the self-absorbed figure." Critics of *Quixote* since Leo Spitzer have explored the text's "perspectivism," but while *Quixote* reveals to readers how particular objects, such as the washing basin that Quixote sees as a helmet, appear to the quixote, the text permits no uncertainty about the "real" status of this object: "there is no one else in the world of the novel to whom [the object] appears to be 'something else again,' nor is there anyone but Don Quixote to whom it appears to be a helmet."[17] This clarity characterizes, as well, most eighteenth-century quixote texts: in *The Female Quixote, or The Adventures of Arabella* (1752), as Debra Malina says, Charlotte Lennox "situate[s] her implied readers outside the satire, where they can judge, along with the author, the 'extravagance' of Arabella's expectations, the absurdity of her 'Foible,' and the outlandishness of her speech and behavior."[18] Most quixote narratives, in short, allow readers to reaffirm the stark distinction between reality and delusion and to rest comfortably with—indeed to strengthen their confidence in—the validity of their own vision.

The quixote narratives on which this study focuses, however, disrupt this project, often by featuring innovative formal strategies that prevent readers from using the quixote figure, as these orthodox narratives encourage, to reaffirm their own epistemological superiority. Chapters 3 through 6, each centering on one of these less-than-orthodox quixote narratives, proceed primarily thematically, uncovering in very different texts a shared interest in the unorthodox implications of the practice of quixotism. Instead of allowing readers to differentiate themselves from an evidently deluded quixote figure, these narratives trick readers into seeing things as the quixote does; instead of offering multiple perspectives on objects or events only to authorize one and ridicule others, they leave readers unable to choose among alternatives; instead of offering readers a vantage point from which they can confidently know the "real," they deny readers any reliable ground from which to gain clear sight. In blurring the boundaries between the real and the illusory, by fooling and refooling readers, these texts prompt readers to recognize the genres that may shape their own vision. Above all, these texts depict quixotes without demanding that "errant" imaginations that view reality differently must be cured so that they can rejoin the community or consensus from which they should never have wandered. In allowing quixote figures to expose competing construals of reality, these tales embrace or, at the very least, tolerate (rather than attempt to cure) a model of perception that acknowledges the subject's *activity* in making the very world he or she seems to find.

This study, then, does not trace the changing attitudes toward the quixote figure over the centuries. That story, which usually identifies the eighteenth century as the moment when readers and writers began to admire rather than ridicule quixote figures, has been often told, and I discuss it briefly in chapter 1.[19] Here, indeed, I am not telling a chronological story at all: orthodox quixote narratives continue to appear alongside the texts I analyze in chapters 3 through 6, each of which challenges such normative uses of the quixote story. Each of these texts contests the quixote story's traditional use by refusing to reaffirm the polar opposites of "real" and "delusion" on which these traditional narratives depend. The texts I discuss here offer readers a position—an awareness of the relativity and contingency of one's own way of seeing—that may be unavailable in ordinary interaction either to the quixote or to its (supposedly) rational "other," both of whom, as I have mentioned above, believe their perceptions to be universally valid. And if these texts do provoke readers to recognize themselves *as* quixotes, they do not imply that such recognition enables them to enact the Enlightenment fantasy of occupying a position "beyond quixotism" where, having shed these filters that distort vision, they can finally see things "as they are." Indeed, these texts are no more univocal about the difference that such recognition or reflection makes than the recent theory I explore in my Epilogue.

By appropriating a traditional narrative (the quixote story) to undermine its fundamental prop (the clear distinction between the "real" and the "deluded"), these texts subvert a literary tradition; and these texts are epistemologically radical, too, in that they imply the inevitable presence of "prepossessions" that determine what and how we know and moreover, suggest, that one's own perceptions may not register the "real." But I do not suggest that the unorthodox appropriations of the quixote I explore in the following chapters serve an oppositional politics. Like the quixote trope itself, which (as the next chapter shows) may be appropriated by any writer to solidify his or her own claim and present that of an opponent as delusory, these unorthodox appropriations serve writers with varied political affiliations. I do not find that these texts are politically radical, or at least not consistently so: the epistemological and literary subversions, that is, do not translate easily into cultural or political subversions (attempted or accomplished).

I do not claim a space "beyond quixotism" for my own study, either, and I suspect that I find what I look for. While I do not claim to find a full-formed postmodernism, a commitment to social construction and situated knowledges, in the eighteenth-century texts I discuss here, I do find these texts interested in the failure of "reason" or "rationality" to explain all it claims to explain, in the role internalized genres play in producing ostensibly "immediate" experience, in the unreliability of that experience itself, in the incommensurability of genres or "paradigms," and in the power that objects created *by* subjects exercise *over* subjects. I find that several of these texts deploy strategies that effectively frustrate readers' desire to assume the mantle of objective vision with which they might comfortably observe a deluded quixote, and in so doing they seem to imply that we are all quixotes. These texts do not invoke our language—Mary Wortley Montagu (in chapter 4) does not speak of the contingency of paradigms, Ann Radcliffe (in chapter 6) does not call Emily St. Aubert a fetishist—and they often approach these questions from different directions, and for different reasons, than we might. It feels to me that I have found these positions *in* the texts themselves, that the questions my contemporary context has led me to ask have enabled me to see aspects of these texts that heretofore have not been seen. This conviction may be as inevitable as it is unjustified, and Stanley Fish (like Nelson Goodman) might suggest that these phenomena that I have found waiting for me in the text were placed there—made—by my own reading practices.[20] That I find this very sort of epistemological doubt in several of the texts I read only intensifies the sort of *mise en abîme* that quixote narratives seem so easily to expose. I can respond to these doubts only by embracing Donna Haraway's argument that as critics, as construers, we are accountable less to a text itself than to our readings and their consequences.[21]

The Epilogue to this study examines such contemporary critical and cultural theory, which, I argue, tends to depict all subjects as inevitably and ineradicably quixotic: in this sense, contemporary theory continues to work out questions about objectivity, and the possibility of prejudice-free perception, made prominent by seventeenth- and eighteenth-century quixote narratives. The study begins in chapter 1 with an exploration of the seventeenth-century origins of the quixote figure that emerges to manage the problems that arise with the privileging of individual judgment or perception. Chapter 1 also analyzes why eighteenth-century quixote narratives, designed to expose the dangers of individual imagination and solitary reading, paradigmatically feature *female* quixotes. Chapter 2, then, discusses the "normative" work performed by a series of orthodox eighteenth-century narratives about female quixotes, some little known (Maria Edgeworth's *Angelina; or, L'Amie Inconnue*, Tabitha Gilman Tenney's *Female Quixotism: Exhibited in the Romantic Opinions and Extravagant Adventures of Dorcasina Sheldon*, and Elizabeth Hamilton's *Memoirs of Modern Philosophers*, each published between 1800–1801, and Eaton Stannard Barrett's *The Heroine: Or, Adventures of Cherubina* [1813]), and one famous, Charlotte Lennox's *Female Quixote*. My description of Lennox's text as orthodox counters much recent criticism that sees in Arabella's quixotism a subversion of the patriarchal culture that surrounds her.

Chapters 3 through 6 focus on female quixote narratives that disrupt this normative work. Chapter 3 centers on Sarah Fielding's *The Adventures of David Simple* (1744) and *The Adventures of David Simple: Volume the Last, in which his History is Concluded* (1753), which seem to follow orthodox quixote narratives by dismissing (as a form of quixotism) "suspicion": suspicious subjects, who believe they detect (or "find") malice in others, actually project (or "make") these qualities onto others as a result of a set of internalized assumptions they do not recognize. Fielding's text tries to claim that suspicion is justified only when it follows, or is anchored in, an accurate reading of another's behavior. But the text, I show, cannot sustain this effort. It shows, instead, that accurately reading the "real" is impossible because "prepossessions" occupy every subject's mind, shaping what one sees and how one understands it. Chapter 4 analyzes Mary Wortley Montagu's *Reasons that Induced Dr S[wift] to write a Poem call'd the Lady's Dressing room* (1732), which cleverly deposits Swift himself in a genre: the disappointment poem. This effort shows that Swift's way of seeing the world (evident in his misogynist poem, "The Lady's Dressing Room" [1730], to which Montagu's responds) depends on the genre in which, unawares, he acts. Above all, this poem (as well as others by Montagu) shows that the same event placed within different genres comes to signify differently.

Chapter 5 explores a text that struggles to resist the "quixote cured" model: Sophia Lee's *The Recess, or a Tale of Other Times* (1783–1785) repeatedly deposits readers in consciousnesses that seem quixotic only long after we have comfortably seen the world as these quixotes see it. This text demonstrates the genres that "prepare" or haunt perception without positing a space "beyond quixotism" to which all subjects must aspire. Chapter 6 suggests that, although critics have tended to treat Emily St. Aubert, the heroine of Ann Radcliffe's *Mysteries of Udolpho: A Romance* (1794), as a female quixote who needs to be cured of her imaginative distortions of reality, *Udolpho* itself is less committed than its critics to a "real" that is purged of imagination or subjectivity. While the novel tries to "cure" Emily of one quixotism, it tries to install another; Emily ends up, at the close of the text, not in the "real" but in a mode of quixotism that, it is crucial, the narrative itself acknowledges, endorses, and tries to produce. Far from curing quixotes, then, this narrative aims to create them.

CHAPTER 1

Historicizing Quixote and the Scandal of Quixotism

I. Quixotism: Ideal or Ridiculous?

The scandal of quixotism is the quixote's claim to valid perception. A quixote's "consciousness," as Susan Staves writes, is "formed by the reading of some particular kind of literature" and he "then goes forth into the world, assuming the world's reality will match the literary reality he knows."[1] We need to broaden this definition beyond the "literary," since as early as the 1640s English writers began to liken those whose expectations seemed too dependent on a wide range of texts—political and religious as well as literary—to Cervantes's knight errant. But Staves's focus on the conflict between the quixote's reality and the "world's reality," held in common (presumably) by all but the quixote, identifies the central provocation of quixote narratives. The quixote narrative, in what I call throughout this study its "orthodox" form, tells the story of the restoration of common perceptions. The friends of the female quixote in Maria Edgeworth's *Angelina; or, L'Amie Inconnue* (1801) hope to "bring her back to . . . common sense," while those concerned about Bridgetina Botherim, one of several quixotes in Elizabeth Hamilton's *Memoirs of Modern Philosophers* (1800), worry that she "has gone too far astray in the fields of imagination to be easily brought back to the plain path of common sense."[2] These quixotes come to accept that their vision *is* aberrant and, cured of what Samuel Johnson called the "false representations" that had improperly interposed between them and reality, finally view the world precisely the way those around them have always viewed it.[3] Orthodox quixote narratives, as I suggest more fully in the next chapter, participate in the "optimism of the Enlightenment, with its conviction that human reason, properly freed and illuminated, could find . . . the truth"⁴: as typically deployed, such narratives are deeply committed to "common sense."⁵

This claim differs from a general understanding that *El ingenioso hidalgo Don Quixote de le Mancha* (1605) bequeathed to subsequent literature an "adversary" or "subversive" force located in Quixote's "attack" on "social assumptions," his "adversariness to bourgeois values," his "radical distaste" for "existing society."⁶ This emphasis on Quixote's idealism, which runs deep in popular and scholarly accounts of quixote narratives, emerged in eighteenth-century writing, where, critics agree, attitudes toward Don Quixote "changed from ridicule to veneration." Eighteenth-century texts increasingly deploy quixotes less to satirize them than to indict the society that mistreats them. By challenging the values of those who surround him, the quixote, in Homer Goldberg's phrase, "earn[s] the readers affection and admiration." "If Quixote is a dangerous deluded fool," Ronald Paulson argues, "the people he meets are as dangerously *un*deluded: *his* impossibly high standards illuminate *their* crassly prudential ones."⁷ Such readings that idealize quixotes (typically called the "Romantic" approach to the text) have, in turn, frustrated critics who believe that they distort a text that ridicules, satirizes, or burlesques its knight errant and what he stands for. In the half century since Oscar Mandel criticized readings in which Quixote's "delusions were promoted to ideals and their impracticability was blamed on the drabness of the real world," many critics have come to consider such readings as themselves quixotic. That is, they transform the seventeenth-century Cervantes, as Anthony Close puts it, into a "novelist of the realist or the naturalist schools" and thus ignore "the questions" that *Don Quixote* "most obviously and naturally prompts." This claim deploys a version of the quixote trope: Close positions his own account as non-ideological, attending only to "*Don Quixote*'s essential nature," and insists that in other accounts "ideological commitments warp interpretation" (and lead critics to find Cervantes "simultaneously attuned to a Spanish Baroque and a postmodernist wavelength" or to detect an "extraordinary coincidence between his outlook, despite its antique context, and our contemporary, postmodern preoccupations").⁸ *Don Quixote*'s reception history paradoxically records not only competing readings of Cervantes's text but also critics' efforts to establish *their* accounts' validity by depicting competing accounts as quixotic.

Rather than debate the proper response to Cervantes's hero, I want to note here that this picture of the subversively idealistic Quixote depends on a focus on the *content* of particular quixotisms, the ideals (justice, compassion, love, religion) that the quixote embodies and practices despite an inhospitable environment. So Eric Ziolkowski, likening Quixote's attempt to revive the antique ideal of chivalry to the effort to preserve religious faith in a predominantly secular world, exalts Quixote for "trying to sustain his faith in his illusions once he starts to be confronted and thwarted by the harsh contingencies of reality," while Alexander Welsh embraces what he calls Quixote's "quest for justice." These recent examples only extend the celebrations in eighteenth-century writing of Quixote as a person "of great Innocence, Integrity and Honour, and of highest Benevolence."[9] All these critics celebrate Quixote for the content of his quixotism, the ideals, preserved from the past, that affront prevailing norms.

But orthodox quixote narratives, even when offering in the *content* of the quixote's ideals an affront to dominant culture, carry a counterweight that stabilizes rather than subverts norms: these texts reject the *structure* of quixotism, the quixote's tendency to substitute the figments of his imagination for the "real" itself. The practice of quixotism involves (to reintroduce terms I will use throughout this study) *making* rather than *finding* the real, and orthodox quixote narratives are built to reject this practice by representing it as misinterpretation, misconstrual, overreading. If "genre," as Rosalie Colie says, is Quixote's "fix on the world," orthodox quixote narratives critique this practice of filtering the "world" through any such lens.[10] Hamilton captures this practice when she describes Bridgetina as "translating every sentence" others utter "into [her] own language" (2: 34): once Bridgetina "determined in her own mind" that a certain young man loved her, "she interpreted every part of his conduct in her own favour" (2: 234).[11] Some contexts, of course, present such activity as admirable: the "strong misreading" of one (male) writer by another (male) writer, theorized by Harold Bloom, positions such "translation" as creativity itself.[12] But the discourse of quixotism casts such translations not as creative but as deluded. Orthodox quixotes narratives, even if quixotes embody attractive ideals, consistently chastise the practice of quixotism and cure it. As John Richetti notes, eighteenth-century novels based on the "example of Cervantes' *Don Quixote*" typically "feature the deflation or cancellation of eccentric individual perspectives by social norms or by the brute factual force of the physical world."[13] The subversive content of quixote narratives, that is, typically resides within an epistemologically conservative narrative structure.

The most familiar modern descendent of the quixote is the paranoid, who shares Quixote's "ingenuity in adapting reality to his preconceptions."[14] The paranoid "logically weaves all events, all persons, all chance remarks and happenings, into his system," but he cannot see this "weav[ing]" as his own activity: the paranoid claims to merely find the objects and connections that others cannot, or will not, see. The paranoid cannot own the "viewed world" as "actually its own product," as Paul Smith suggests, and this "dual ability to objectify or *realize* a reality and yet to proclaim the 'subject's' innocence of its formation" defines paranoia.[15] Quixotes share with paranoids this "innocence," this inability to see themselves as actively construing the reality they consider simply given. No matter how obvious it is to observers (the position that orthodox quixote narratives offer to readers) that the quixote's vision is distorted, quixotes themselves harbor no such suspicions. It occurs no more frequently to quixotes to reflect on the reality or accuracy of their perceptions than it occurs to us to do so. The quixote encounters a world filled with objects and values, and this reality feels to the quixote precisely the way our reality feels to us.

It is this unself-conscious confidence that differentiates the quixote from the seventeenth- or eighteenth-century skeptic. As Michael McKeon writes, "Don Quixote himself can[not] be said to live by [the] creed of the skeptic. The delicate contingency of his belief is perceptible only to others . . . There is no element of provisionality in Don Quixote's credence; he is simply mad."[16] The discourse of quixotism, it is true, can provoke questions similar to those pursued by skeptics—Where does our knowledge come from? What can we know? How certain is our knowledge?—and the innovative quixote narratives that I discuss in chapters 3 through 6 resemble the "skeptical consciousness" recently explored by Fred Parker that emphasizes the unreliability of human senses and the inevitable conflict of opinions on any subject.[17] But, unlike skeptics, quixotes themselves are blissfully unaware of such epistemological uncertainties and remain stubbornly confident in the validity of their perceptions. And orthodox quixote narratives portray a "real" that is embraced unproblematically by all—all but the quixote, of course.

II. Quixotism and Objectivity

The normative work performed by orthodox quixote narratives resembles the epistemological promises offered by the writings of Cervantes's contemporary Francis Bacon. Although few have explored the relations between Cervantes's prose romance and Bacon's scientific writings (except the journal *Baconiana*, whose claim in 1916 that Bacon "was the real author" of *Don Quixote* enacts its own quixotic capacity to translate any verbal phenomenon into a sign of Bacon's presence[18]), both circulate a common proto-Enlightenment obsession with distinguishing the "real" from its distortions. Both focus on figures whose perceptions have been shaped by the fictions they have consumed but who, unaware of these mediations, are naively confident that they perceive the "real" itself. And both posit unmediated vision as an attainable ideal. Its central metaphor promising that illumination can dispel the dark shadows that previously obscured things, Enlightenment thought contends that, according to Peter Hulme and Ludmilla Jordanova, "[t]o look well and carefully, sufficient light is required, and looking in this way was deemed the only route to secure knowledge."[19] But the notion implicit in this metaphor that the impediment to accurate vision is the lack of light on the objects one tries to understand obscures the internal barriers that impede accurate knowledge of objects. Bacon focused on these barriers, which he famously called "idols," a term, developed from the Latin "idola," that refers not to false gods but to phantoms or delusive images. The *Advancement of Learning, Divine and Humane* (1605) calls them "false appearances," while *Valerius Terminus, or The Interpretation of Nature* (1603) prefers "idols" and "fictions."[20] Each variant, however, identifies the same phenomenon: the internalized fictions that prevent the mind from gaining real knowledge of the nature of things.

In *New Organon, or True Directions Concerning the Interpretation of Nature* (1620), Bacon lists four types of Idols, each emanating from a different source. The "Idols of the Tribe," rooted in "human nature itself," lead men to "measure . . . things" according to the "measure of the individual": we "suppose the existence of more order and regularity in the world" than actually exists, we stubbornly preserve any opinion we have adopted by neglecting contrary evidence and embracing "all things" that "support and agree with it," we are so captivated by the nearby and familiar that our mind "feigns and supposes all other things to be somehow, though it cannot see how, similar to those few things by which it is surrounded." The "Idols of the Cave," Bacon's second category, arise from each individual's "peculiar constitution" and vary depending on one's education, conversations, reading, accepted authorities, or occupation. "Every one," Bacon notes ruefully, "has a cave or den of his own, which refracts and discolours the light of nature." The "Idols of the Marketplace," the "most troublesome of all," have "crept into the understanding through the alliances of words and names"; the "ill and unfit choice of words wonderfully obstructs the understanding." Finally, the "Idols of the Theater" are "impressed and received into the mind from the play-books of philosophical systems," a problem that, Bacon's *Natural and Experimental History for the Foundation of Philosophy* (1622) asserts, is particularly dire in his own culture that "confined" the "sciences... to certain and prescribed authors" who are "imposed on the old and instilled in the young."[21] Each of these Idols, Bacon warns, prevents the understanding from encountering things themselves.

Individuals, however, believe that their perceptions deliver to them things themselves. They are unaware that Idols mediate their perceptions, and as a consequence they misrecognize a confused mixture—"things" blending with their own imagination—as the "nature of things" themselves. The mind, Bacon warns in his *Great Instauration* (1620), "in forming its notions mixes up its own nature with the nature of things."[22] Most troublesome, the mind's captivity to these Idols ensures that this mixture occurs not intermittently but persistently. As Bacon argues in *De dignitate et augmentis scientiarum* (1623, a Latin expansion of his own *Advancement*):

> False Appearances or Idols . . . do not deceive in particulars, as others do, by clouding and snaring the judgment; but by a corrupt and ill-ordered predisposition of mind, which as it were perverts and infects all the anticipations of the intellect. For the mind of man (dimmed and clouded as it is by the covering of the body), far from being a smooth, clear, and equal glass (wherein the beams of things reflect according to their true incidence), is rather like an enchanted glass, full of superstition and imposture.[23]

These Idols, Bacon suggests, shape (in his view, "pervert") *all* perception, "predisposi[ng]" the mind to see "things" improperly. By insisting that it is not the "judgment" that Idols infect, Bacon rejects the possibility that the mind *first* encounters "things" themselves and *then* wrongly evaluates them. The errors of the understanding do not result from a failed second step in a two-step process. On the contrary, Idols ensure that the very objects that the mind receives—to observe, judge, analyze, assess—are already reshaped by cultural or personal forms.

Bacon reiterated his theory of Idols in each of his scientific works. The description in *De Augmentis* of the mind as "an enchanted glass, full of superstition and imposture" had, in the *Advancement*, concluded with the phrase "if it be not delivered and reduced"—and the promise of "deliver[y]" runs through all of Bacon's work. Bacon's *Great Instauration* does warn that some Idols "are hard to eradicate" and others "cannot be eradicated at all," and James Bono is right to note that for Bacon "the real weaknesses of human knowledge are nearly intractable" and "cannot simply be bracketed by, for example, attempting to remove the biases and distortions that individuals bring to sense perception." But Bacon believes that instruments and experiment *can* solve this problem by, as Donna Haraway writes, "factor[ing] out human agency from the product."[24] The validity of this solution is, for my purposes here, less important than the consistency of his promise that the mind can be corrected so that it no longer functions like "an uneven mirror [that] distorts the rays of objects according to its own figure and section." Proper "interpretation of nature" depends, as the *New Organon* insists, on Bacon's texts having first "performed these expiations and purgings of the mind." If men would "discard, or at least set apart for a while, these volatile and preposterous philosophies" that have "led experience captive," if they could achieve "minds washed clean from opinions," men could then "study" the "works of God" in "purity and integrity." Bacon's model, then, insists that only the mind that is "washed clean" can encounter the "works of God" without impediment. His *De Augmentis* defines "true philosophy" as that which "echoes most faithfully the voices of the world itself, and is written as it were at the world's own dictation; being nothing else than the image and reflexion thereof, to which it adds nothing of its own, but only iterates and gives it back."[25]

Bacon's demand that the mind must "[add] nothing of its own" suggests that in proper perception "things" control the process by depositing their "true" image in the mind (as if through a "smooth, clear, and equal glass"). This assumption persists through the eighteenth century: John Locke's influential *Essay Concerning Human Understanding* (1690) theorizes that objects "obtrude their particular *Ideas* upon our minds, whether we will or no." "The mind can no more refuse" these impressions, Locke added, "than a mirror can refuse, alter, or obliterate the Images or *Ideas*, which, the Objects set before it, do therein produce." William Congreve's *The Mourning Bride* (1697) offers an identical account, describing "Sight" as a "Mechanick Sense" in which "our Eyes, like common Mirrours / Successively reflect succeeding Images; / Not what they would, but must." This image of perception's passivity also organizes Edmund Burke's *Philosophical Enquiry into the Origin of our Ideas of the Sublime and the Beautiful* (1757), which describes how different types of objects produce different responses in passive spectators. Rebuking those who "attribute the cause of feelings which merely arise from the mechanical structure of our bodies, or from the natural frame and constitution of our minds, to certain conclusions of the reasoning faculty on the objects presented to us," Burke positions observers at the mercy of external objects, whose particular features necessarily produce sensations that comprise the experiences we call "sublime" or "beautiful."[26] Some have claimed that Burke's aesthetic theory marks a "transitional moment when speculation withdrew from the search for sublimity in the object and began to be centered in the emotions of the subject," but actually Burke's account preserves the focus on the object by proposing that its particular structure generates the perceiver's subsequent response. As Frances Ferguson notes, Burke's account "relies on the absolute reality of objects and upon the immutable reality of differences among them," and Thomas Weiskel's description of Burke's model—objects " 'occasion' sensations, and sensations quite automatically produce reflections, which may in turn be recognized by consciousness"—reveals how thoroughly objects remain in control. These accounts depict the proper mind as passive, "mak[ing] no conscious or voluntary contribution" to perception.[27] A mind captured by Idols, on the other hand, imposes on things its own images, and it is such illicit activity that Bacon consistently attacks: "We clearly impress the stamp of our own image on the creatures and works of God, instead of carefully examining and recognising in them the stamp of the Creator himself." "God Forbid," Bacon wrote in the "Plan" to his *Great Instauration*, "that we should give out a dream of our own imagination for a pattern of the world."[28]

Bacon's objection to system and system-making, embraced and elaborated on by many seventeenth- and eighteenth-century writers, taps this suspicion of minds that *make* rather than *find* the "real." System-makers, like quixotes, allow the ideas, patterns, or genres in their minds to distort their perception of objects themselves. In his posthumously published *General Scheme, or Idea, of the Present State of Natural Philosophy* (1705), Robert Hooke, frequent spokesman for the Royal Society, faulted most philosophers for construing the entire world through the lens of their systems. "Just as a Man that is troubled with the Jaundice, supposes all things to be Yellow," Hooke complained, "Or a melancholy Person, that thinks he meets with nothing but frightful Apparitions, does convert all things he either sees or hears into dreadful Representations, and makes use of them to strengthen his Phant'sy . . . so is it in Constitutions of Mind as to Philosophy." "Every one," Hooke summarizes, "according to the things he most fancies naturally . . . endeavours to make all things he meets with, agreeable or subservient thereto."[29] A similar denunciation of system-making surfaces in Jonathan Swift's *Tale of a Tub: Written for the Universal Improvement of Mankind* (1704), which claims that those who "advance new Systems" in philosophy attempt to "reduce the Notions of all Mankind, exactly to the same Length, and Breadth, and Height of his own": such "*Romantick* System[s]" reveal only "*Madness* or *Phrenzy*."[30] We have seen that this indictment of the mind's activity in transforming the real also organizes Hamilton's *Memoirs* (Bridgetina improperly "translat[es]" one thing into another), which describes "one of the prime advantages of *system*" as the mind's "ab[ility] to twist, and turn, and construe every thing to its own advantage" (3: 107). Bridgetina's "mind was so completely occupied in discussion and investigation of abstract theory," that she was "totally lost to the perception of all that was obvious to common observation. Just as those whose opticks, by being constantly employed on distant objects, lose the power of seeing whatever comes close to the eye" (2: 147). These texts offer a shared critique of system-making. Each rejects the active (and unrecognized) agency of quixotic minds, which, rather than passively registering the "real" itself, actively remake it ("twist, and turn, and construe," "[endeavour]" and "convert," "reduce") into something it is not. Moreover, each emphasizes that such quixotic minds, enthralled to particular "Idols," patterns, or stories, convert a diversity of things ("all things," "every thing") into "one" thing. The consequence of this improper making is that, like the quixotic Bridgetina, system-makers cannot see what actually lies before their eyes, what should be "obvious to common observation." The jaundiced mind that "supposes all things" to be like itself, the melancholy mind that "convert[s] all things" into confirmation of its fears, the idolatrous mind that functions like an "enchanted glass," the system-making mind that "construe[s]" everything into what it expects or hopes to find: All these metaphors of lenses that distort perception align such system-makers with quixotes, all mistaking the products of the lens for the real itself.

It is crucial for Bacon to create minds that can see things "in themselves" because, as Bono has argued, Bacon felt that "God's marks and traces *are* his creatures and works." In this Bacon departed from a Paracelsian tradition that saw in things "signatures" or "symbols," a tradition that required observers to convert observed things into the larger network of which they are part. For Bacon, however, the mind must *not* redescribe, through a hermenuetic exercise, the "thing" itself into "complex webs of signification whose nodes, through resemblance, reverberate sympathetically, if occultly." These conversion operations only reveal the Idols that hold minds captive. Bacon contrasts what the mind "suppose[s]" with what it would "find" if such "predispositions" did not distort its perceptions such that the understanding accepts as "real" those things that "do not exist." For Bacon, then, only a mind purged—only such "cleansed" minds—can encounter the "thing" itself (and the knowledge of God that such a thing may enable). This belief functions to minimize the significance of the interpreter of nature. What Bono calls "the regime of 'facts' " effectively "efface[s] the role of the individual scientist," once again rejecting the Paracelsian "enterprise" at the center of which "were not facts, but rather the individual investigator's mind and imagination" whose "actual role as producer of this knowledge was at the forefront of *scientia*."[31] For Bacon, the individual scientist must disappear so that things can speak for themselves. Only then, according to Baconian science, could one gain knowledge about the reality that preexists and remains untouched by observers and their theories.

The invention of *pure facts,* present and waiting to be discovered, was one product of this seventeenth-century empiricist discourse. Such writing contended that the "facts" seen through the new scientific instruments "were not of one's own making," as Stephen Shapin and Simon Schaffer demonstrate, but "were, in the empiricist language-game, discovered rather than invented." Lorraine Daston concurs, arguing that during the seventeenth century " 'fact' shed its associations with 'doing' and 'making' . . . and migrated toward 'datum,' that which is given rather than made." Despite their shared etymology, " 'fact' and 'manufacture' were nearly antonyms by the late eighteenth century," and in the sciences "that which is made edged closer to that which is made up, to fabrication or invention in the pejorative sense." "The solidity and permanence of matters of fact," Shapin and Schaffer continue, "reside in the absence of human agency in their coming to be. Human agents make theories and interpretations, and human agents may therefore unmake them. But matters of fact are regarded as the very 'mirror of nature.' "[32] Bacon establishes his "regime of 'facts,' " as we have seen, on a brutal purge that leaves the mind cleansed of all fictions whatsoever. As the "Plan" to the *Great Instauration* puts it, "the expurgation of the intellect . . . qualif[ies] it for dealing with truth."[33]

Don Quixote embodies an *un*purged mind. If Bacon likens a proper intellect, one capable of discovering the "nature of things," to "a fair sheet of paper with no writing on it," then Quixote's mind is disabled from finding the "nature of things" because it *already* has "writing on it."[34] Don Quixote's mind has been inscribed by the romances he has consumed, and his perceptual problems—taking windmills for giants, flocks of sheep for threatening armies—confirm Bacon's theory that the fictions inside our heads control not only our response to what we see but also what we see itself. Indeed, the figure of quixote has long been our primary image of perception gone awry, and quixote tales an important imaginative apparatus to affirm the binary opposition between fact and interpretation so central to Bacon. Hamilton's *Memoirs* captures this precisely when it states, in Baconian language, of a female quixote that "wild and ungoverned imagination reigned paramount in her breast. The investigation of truth had no longer any charm . . . and the mind, instead of deducing inferences from facts, was now solely occupied in the invention of extravagant and chimerical situations" (1: 146–47). This opposition takes many forms—questions of fact versus questions of meaning, objective versus subjective, primary versus secondary qualities—but in all its forms it separates and privileges (in John Dewey's phrases) "objects already empirically given or presented, existentially vouched for" from subsequent "conceptions" of such objects.[35] This opposition underlies, as well, Wendy Motooka's study of eighteenth-century quixote figures, *The Age of Reasons* (1998). Motooka suggests that "the senses of English quixotes are always reliable. Their unusual views cannot be dismissed as the raving results of faulty perception. Rather, English quixotes are characterized by their uncommon ways of *interpreting* the findings of common sense." It is a "consistent fact," Motooka repeats, "that eighteenth-century English quixotes, unlike Cervantes' own Don Quixote, never err in their senses (they never mistake burlap for silk, or garlicky breath for Arabian perfume); they err only in their judgments about the empirical evidence before them."[36] *The Practice of Quixotism* offers ample evidence that eighteenth-century quixotes *do* "err in their senses," mistaking one thing for another just as Don Quixote himself mistakes "burlap for silk, or garlicky breath for Arabian perfume." But my point here is that, while Motooka distinguishes between "judgment" and perception, between "misperceiving" and "misinterpreting," between interpretation and "the findings of common sense," it is precisely these distinctions that quixote figures can problematize. Motooka, like Bacon, describes these activities as if they follow a two-step process—first everyone perceives the identical object, then different subjects interpret it differently—but quixote figures may suggest, to the contrary, the collapse of these stages into each other. Quixote figures can be deployed to place in doubt, as my subsequent chapters will show, the givenness of "empirical evidence" and to expose instead the subject's role in constructing the very objects that powerfully affect him or her as "givens."

In its orthodox mode, however, the story of a quixote cured provides the classic staging of this binary opposition: a man who misperceives reality because he has consumed too many chivalric romances comes to see the "real" itself only when the lens that had distorted his vision is dissolved. As in Bacon's scientific texts, the quixote narrative defines the "real"—the fact, the objective, the primary, the "given"—as that which is left after subjects' illusory projections have been dispelled. Cervantes's text, Mandel argues, "unequivocally discredit[s]" Quixote's "private reality" in favor of an "immovable reality" that is "indivisible, solid, and incapable of being new-created by a romantic imagination."[37] Displaying the inversion of proper perception, orthodox quixote tales demonstrate the danger of "changing 'reality' into appearance, of introducing 'relativities' into things as they are in themselves—in short, of infecting real things with subjectivity."[38] It is the active contribution that Quixote's imagination makes that marks him as an *il*legitimate perceiver, since in proper perception the subject contributes nothing.

III. Managing Competing Perceptions

Orthodox quixote narratives, then, like Bacon's scientific writing, insist on the absolute difference between proper or accurate perceptions of the real and the many possible misconstruals of it. Although it focuses on narratives that resist this orthodox mode, this study will encounter many such narratives that deploy the quixote trope to position one set of perceptions (usually one's own) as objective and others as distorted. Sarah Fyge Egerton's "The Liberty" (1703), for instance, offers competing perceptions of women's experience, marking one as quixotic, the other as accurate.[39] The poem describes most women as "obsequious Fools" who "square there lives, by Customs scanty Rules, / Condemn'd for ever, to the puny Curse, / Of Precepts taught, at Boarding-school, or nurse" (1–4). For Egerton, these rule-bound fools exist within a magic circle of their own making: such women are "Confin'd to a strict Magick complaisance, / And round a Circle, of nice visits Dance, / Nor . . . beyond the Chalk advance" (7–9). Significant for our purposes is that Egerton imagines that these "Fools" misrecognize their confinement within the chalk circle as pleasure: "Some boast their Fetters, of Formality, / Fancy they ornamental Bracelets be" (26–27). By adding that "I'm sure the[y're] Gyves, and Manacles to me" (28), Egerton distinguishes her perceptions from those of other women, whose contentment only proves that the "Precepts taught, at Boarding-school, or nurse" have effectively colonized their minds. Egerton sees these "Rules" as "Manacles"; her contemporaries, trapped within the "Magick . . . Circle," misperceive them as pleasures. The poem's closing lines hint that Egerton's contemporaries are as aware as she is of their confinement and endure it only reluctantly: "I'll appeal," she says, "to all the formal Saints" to ask "With what reluctance they indure restraints" (51–52). But most of the poem implies not only that the manacled women (unlike herself) do not see themselves as confined, but also that, if they did see it, the magic that confines them would dissolve. This imaginary force initially appears as "The Devil Censure" (10) and later as "That dreaded Censure . . . / Which has no Terror, if we did not fear" (19–20), but this suggestion that these "Fetters" are imaginary does not minimize their efficacy. Egerton's poem insists that, when these internalized texts ("Precepts") are experienced as real, they shape conduct. But by implication, her poem also displays optimism that recognizing these texts *as* imposed—as she herself has—can free women from their constraints: Censure "has no Terror, if we did not fear." Her poem looks forward to, and tries to produce, the sort of cure—the cleansing of a too-active imagination—crucial to orthodox quixote narratives. Egerton's poem exemplifies a typical use of the quixote trope, in which a narrative authority (and the reader) stands outside the supposedly quixotic figures and can see others' delusions objectively. Outside the "Magick . . . Circle" that confines others and causes them to misperceive their own experience, Egerton perceives the reality that is unavailable to those within the circle. Egerton's poem reveals how it is in competition with a rival set of perceptions that quixotism surfaces as such.

One purpose of this book is to suggest that the word "quixote" functions like the term "paranoid": it is a term of abuse one applies to distance oneself from another's perceptions and to position these perceptions as faulty, as excessive, as invalid, as making rather than discovering sense. Any perceptions identified as those of a quixote, then, have always already been marked as aberrant. Our own perceptions (or any that still have a chance at being valid) never seem quixotic. When Edgeworth's Angelina suddenly recognizes her servant's resemblance to Sancho Panza (" 'She's actually a female Sancho Panza,' thought Angelina"), she cannot apply this recognition to herself: "Her own more striking resemblance to the female Quixote never occurred to our heroine—so blind are we to our own failings."[40] "Quixote" is a label, in effect, that one group uses to describe another. Raymond Williams has written that "[t]here are no masses; there are only ways of seeing [other] people as masses." Stanley Fish's

Trouble With Principle (1999) similarly analyzes the word "personal":

> No party to any conflict will accept the adjective "personal," because to have a conviction is to believe that what it commits you to is true not only for you but for everyone, including those who, for whatever reasons (blindness, error, perversity) are not presently persuaded of it ... "[P]ersonal" is the label you give to agendas and systems of value of the other fellow, while reserving the labels "public" and "general" ... for your own.[41]

The application of the label "quixote" denies the labeled figure what Paul Hammond, in a different context, calls "a plausible subjectivity, moving him out of the kind of narrative or social space which readers could imagine themselves inhabiting." What Leo Bersani writes about the paranoid holds true for the quixote: "paranoids [do not] label themselves paranoid ... 'I' can never be the subject of 'I am paranoid' as an uncontested, undivided judgment": such a sentence imagines how others view us.[42] The successful application of the label "quixote" marks the moment when this competition has ended, when certain perceptions (now marked as "quixotic") have been invalidated and others established as routine, obvious, or commonsensical.

Quixotism is, in this account, a strategy to dismiss differing experience. Orthodox quixote narratives are defensive, compensatory narratives designed precisely to enable readers to blind themselves to the existence of competing construals of reality. In most quixote narratives, the very presence of a quixote marks the completion of a process that has ended with the devaluation and dismissal of a certain set of perceptions; readers join this story too late to see the quixote's perceptions as anything but deluded. Don Quixote may ascribe what happens to him to magicians, but "readers of Cervantes' novel," as Alexander Welsh notes, "understand that the blows come from windmills or from people trying to go about their ordinary business." Richard Predmore concurs: "If the characters of *Don Quixote* are frequently confused or mistaken in the presence of the deceptive appearances of reality, the narrator is not confused nor does he permit the reader to be confused." He always "relat[es] the adventures in such a way that the reader always knows what objective reality is."[43] What I call the scandal of quixotism in the text above, the exposure that others construe reality differently than oneself, is, then, rarely experienced as such in orthodox quixote narratives. This scandal never surfaces at all if the quixote narrative, in which the evidently disturbed quixote figure is "cured" by the narrative's end, does its work. That is to say, by delivering to readers a central figure comfortably positioned as deluded, mad, aberrant, unnatural, sick, ridiculous, even dangerous, most quixote narratives refuse to let the quixote's perceptions attain the validity they would need to rival the reader's own.[44] The efficacy of the quixote trope depends on ensuring that the space from which one speaks is uncontaminated by quixotism. The consequences of not preserving this structure are disquieting, as Fish implies:

> From the outside we are all Gullivers, wondering at the foolishness of those who would destroy each other over the issue of which end is the best for the cracking of an egg, remarking on the insanity of those who will go to war over the presence or absence of altar rails. But in some other configuration of battle we will be insiders, and it will then be *our* lot to be derided by those who cannot see for the life of them why supposedly rational people should be so excited by the trifles we are willing to fight for.[45]

Orthodox quixote narratives, demanding the cure of an evidently deluded quixote, are organized to prevent the reversal of perspective that Fish describes. Such narratives are one means to police—to reaffirm, to maintain, to preserve—the fiction that we all share a common reality.[46]

This discourse of quixotism develops only in a context that demands that individuals test truths for themselves before they accept them: only here need writers frown on the erratic individual mind embodied by the quixote and demand the cures that restore these errant individuals to the "reality" everybody else (presumably) shares. George M. Fredrickson's *Racism: A Short History* (2002) argues that racism was most fully elaborated in the West because the presence of another contradictory ideology—of equality—drove racist ideology to justify or defend the exploitation and elimination accomplished elsewhere without such discursive supports. Mary Poovey has argued, similarly, that "conceptualizing subjectivity did not seem politically important until the demise of the sovereign mode of government, for only when individuals were allowed to govern themselves did it seem necessary to theorize how they did so."[47] We might say, analogously, that only when contemporary discourses began to emphasize individual reason did it seem necessary to generate a discourse, quixotism, that aims to manage misconstrual. In 1690 John Locke wrote that we can no more "know with other Mens Understandings" than we can "see with other Mens Eyes." "So much as we our selves consider and comprehend of Truth and Reason," Locke declared, "so much we possess of real and true Knowledge." He added that "the floating of other Mens Opinions in our brains makes us not a jot more knowing, though they happen to be true. What in them was Science, is in us but Opinatrety, whilst we give up our Assent only to reverend Names, and do not, as they did, employ our own Reason to *understand* those Truths." John Milton's *Areopagitica: A Speech . . . for the Liberty of Unlicenc'd Printing* (1644) had argued similarly that "a man may be a heretick in the truth; and if he beleeve things only because his Pastor says so, or the Assembly so determins, without knowing other reason, though his belief be true, yet the very truth he holds, becomes his heresie."[48] This demand that we "employ our own Reason" imagines optimistically that all properly regulated minds will arrive at the same "Truths": Locke's epistemology, in which, as Joel Weinsheimer writes, each "isolated being . . . judges things in freedom, independently of others' opinions," did not aim to theorize or endorse social chaos. Although Locke spends considerable time describing the prevalence of error and ignorance, he offers a "normative epistemology" that describes the "positive conditions in the mind which lead us toward knowledge and rational belief."[49] Shared truths and common beliefs will fail to emerge only when illegitimate authorities ("other mens Opinions," the "Pastor" or "the Assembly") interpose certain beliefs in place of each individual's unfettered judgment.

Typical quixote narratives invoke, similarly, a common or shared reality, a reality affirmed all the more solidly by the mad quixote's refusal to accept it. Quixote narratives, like Locke's epistemological writings, reaffirm common sense after showing it endangered by errant individual reasoning. "Ultimately," Gillian Brown notes, "quixotic mimeticism leads to social mimeticism, with the quixotes joining and affirming a common reality."[50] My next chapter explores further the quixote narrative's commitment to "common sense"; here, I aim only to note that while these narratives explore the failure of one individual to arrive where he or she should have, they do so not to undermine or subvert common sense. These narratives do not focus on these particular failures to reject the principle of individual reasoning or to license differing views: instead, they explain away the presence of different views and avoid calling into question the confidence that individual judgments could arrive at common beliefs. Quixote narratives work to manage this problem by marking *different* perceptions as *aberrant* ones. The ultimate truth of orthodox quixote narratives is the common reality in which all but the quixote believe and to which the quixote returns, chastened and cured, by narrative's end. As Mandel writes, Don Quixote "belongs to the family of error-stricken comic heroes whose destiny is to re-enter the company of the sound and the normal."[51] Quixote narratives suggest that seventeenth-century culture, the moment of the "rise of individualism," had little tolerance for perceptions that conflicted with common sense.

IV: Varieties of Seventeenth-Century Quixotism

The usefulness of the figure of quixote in positioning differing perceptions as aberrant ones is evident as early as the English Civil War. Less than thirty-five years after the first volume of Cervantes's *El ingenioso hidalgo Don Quixote de le Mancha* had been "Englished" as *The history of the valorous and wittie knight-errant Don Quixote of the Mancha* (1612), English writers had begun to describe as "*Quixotes*" any individual whose perceptions diverged from the larger community's.[52] Isolated by his mistaken acceptance as real of the imaginary creations of his own mind, the quixote figure helped mid-seventeenth-century English writers understand what had gone wrong in their own polity. Edmund Gayton's *Pleasant Notes Upon Don Quixot* (1654) contains an introductory poem, identified as composed by an "Itinerant Minister" "Banisht" from his living, that notes wryly that "I scarce have laught, but with a sullen smile, / To see your *Quixot* acted in our Ile." Sectaries were not always figured as deluded quixotes, since that image defuses the charge—also polemically useful—that they are self-interested hypocrites. Portraying sectaries as cunningly self-interested, their enthusiasm cloaking devious plots, John Taylor's *Swarme of Sectaries* (1641) defined the "Knave Puritan" as "He whose best good, is only good to seeme, / And seeming holy, gets some false esteeme: / Who makes Religion hide Hypocrisie, / And zeale to cover cheating Villany." Seventy years later Bernard Mandeville would remark wryly that a "National Church seldom acknowledges the Sincerity of Schismaticks."[53]

But many Civil War polemicists did depict Commonwealth leaders as quixotes who fought enemies of their own imaginations.[54] Henry More's *Enthusiasmus Triumphatus, or A Discourse of the Nature, Causes, Kinds, and Cure, of Enthusiasme* (1656), written to counter the charge that enthusiasts were cunning Machiavels, explicitly distinguishes "*shrewd Politician[s]*" from "mere *Enthusiast[s]*," who "can neither keep out nor distinguish betwixt [their] own Fancies and reall Truths."[55] *A Breife Description or Character of the Religion and Manners of the Phanatiques in Generall* (1660) agreed that such sectaries, "like Don Quixotes and Knights-Errant, have so many

Romances, forms, and idæa's of Religion in their heads," while John Philips's *Montelion, 1660, or, The Prophetical Almanack* (1660) contends that "Those they call Saints have many windmils in their heads."[56] These polemics insist that something "in their heads"—deposits left by reading—prevents these misguided sectaries from perceiving what is in front of their eyes. The odd *Midsummer Moon, Or, Lunacy Rampant* (1654) complains that Francis Cheynell's attempts to reform Oxford reveal only that "he's *Don Quixoted*" and "takes the Colledge for an Enchanted Castle, the fellows for Gyants, W. W. Ink—and L. L. for three distressed damsels." The anonymous *We have Brought our Hoggs to a Fair Market* (1660) ridicules the commonwealth leaders as "*Quixots* of our late times" who "fought with the Windmills of their own Heads," lines that this pamphlet lifted from John Cleveland's more famous attack in *Character of London-Diurnall* (1647): "The *Quixotes* of this Age fight with the Wind-mills of their owne heads; quell Monsters of their owne creation, make plots, and then discover them."[57] Cleveland's distinction between "mak[ing]" and "discover[ing]" is, as we have seen, crucial to quixote narratives: all who write about quixotes struggle to find a language to describe quixotes' acceptance of fantasies that have no "reality" outside their heads *as if* the "real" itself. The quixote "makes" the windmills—they are minted by his imagination—but he feels as though he "discovers" them.

Both royalist and parliamentary newspapers repeatedly deployed the quixote trope to insist that the other side mistook imaginary phenomenon as "realities" and fought against imaginary enemies. That the charge was leveled by all sides indicates the availability of the quixote trope for partisans of all stripes. As significantly, it reveals its usefulness in making sense of a situation in which the "same" objects seemed so different to different people: *Mercurius Britanicus* complained in March 1645 that its opponents "*spell* the Parliament *Rebels*; Popery, the *Protestant Religion*; Idolatrie and Superstition, *Decencie*; Episcopacie, *Iure Divina*; Reformation, *Schisme*." Each side charged the other with viewing events through an inappropriate lens. Cleveland suggests that the newspaper form itself encourages quixotism by forcing events, whose issue remained yet uncertain, into a romance plot: "The *Diurnall* as yet hath not talk't much of his Victories; but there is the more behind: For the Knight must always beat the Gyant." In May 1648 the Parliamentary *Britanicus* charged that the royalist *Elenticus* was suffering so severely from "*Knight-Errantry*" that it "mistakes . . . Sheep and Armies, Bel-weathers and Captains"; the royalists, *Britanicus* charged, "think they attempt great castles" that will eventually "be found some little encounter with a Windemill." As Joad Raymond has noted, John Hall (*Britanicus*'s writer) repeatedly invoked "Quixote's distorted vision" to explain royalist perception.[58] In his *Character of a Diurnal-Maker* (1654), Cleveland offered an interesting metaphor for this distortion: to call a newsbook-writer a historian is to "[K]Night a Man-drake; 'tis to view him through a Perspective, and by that grosse Hyperbole to give the reputation of an Engineer, to a Maker of Mouse-traps."[59] Cleveland's "Perspective" glass literalizes the metaphor, central to quixotism, of a filter that stands between one's mind and reality and produces perceptions that, unknown to the perceiver, have been inappropriately mediated.

The quixote figure is one of several figures available to help seventeenth-century writers think through the phenomenon of competing accounts of reality: its cousins are the sectary, the enthusiast, the native. Suffering from similar delusions and posing a similar threat to communal life, these figures gather at the same place in the cultural imaginary. Each of these figures requires policing because each idolizes the productions of his own mind, refusing to check these imaginary creations against common belief or, if they do perform such "reality checks," stubbornly privileging their peculiar way of seeing over common sense. The native fetishist, first depicted in the anthropological and travel literature that grew out of cross-cultural encounters between seventeenth-century European and African traders, seemed to suffer from a familiar form of delusion. The "essential problem" of the fetish, as William Pietz has argued, is "the problem of the social and personal value of material objects"[60]: European traders discovered that African natives valued objects entirely differently than they did. These traders solved this scandal posed by competing accounts or valuations of the same object by deploying the discourse of fetishism that dismissed one code of values (the Africans') as mistaken, illusory, or deluded. The discourse of fetishism, that is, functions identically to the discourse of quixotism: the European traders believed that the Africans were unable to see what lay in front of their faces, the "real" object in all its objective ordinariness. Thomas Astley's *New General Collection of Voyages and Travels* (1746) contended that the African natives (like "the *Romish* Church and Priests") believe that "the supreme Deity, for the Benefit of his Creatures" has endowed certain "material Objects" (*Fetishes*) "with certain Virtues and Powers."[61] From Astley's perspective, of course, neither "the supreme Deity" nor nature itself creates these *Fetishes*: the natives' imaginations do, illegitimately transforming simple objects into divine things. Fetishists, like quixotes, make the objects they think they merely find. The same phenomenon is evident in Eliza Haywood's ridicule in the *Female Spectator* (1744–1746) of politicians, who, like South Sea natives, "idolize, and in a Manner worship, what has no other Merit than *themselves have given it*," or in Daniel Defoe's debunking in *The Compleat English Gentleman* (1728/1729) of those who, by imagining that some difference in "Constitution" or in "the very Fluids of Nature," establish the "*Gentleman*" as "a different Species from the rest of Mankind" and in effect "ma[k]e an Idol" of him.[62] Like those who deploy the quixote trope, these users of the discourse of fetishism believe that others simply lack their ability to see the "real." If they could only shed the Idols that block true sight, they could rejoin the community of common sense.

The great nineteenth-century theorists who appropriate this eighteenth-century discourse—Karl Marx and Sigmund Freud—preserve its emphasis on individuals (or cultures) who misrecognize as essential to an object qualities or values with which they themselves have endowed it. Marx (who annotated de Brosses's *Du culte des dieux fétiches* [1760], which coined the word "fetish") suggests in *Capital: A Critique of Political Economy* (1867) that it is not only in the "mist-enveloped regions of the religious world" that "productions of the human brain appear as independent beings endowed with life" but also in the modern world. In this "world of commodities," the "social character of men's labour appears . . . as an objective character stamped on the product of that labour." Enveloped in this "mist," "the social relation between men . . . assumes, in their eyes, the fantastic form of a relation between things." Marx expects his "scientific discovery" to dispel these "fantastic" forms, to "*dissipate the mist* through which the social character of labour appears to us to be an objective character of the products themselves." The metaphor of dispelling the "mist," which my Introduction noted in Richard Graves's *Spiritual Quixote, or The Summer's Ramble of Mr. Geoffrey Wildgoose: A Comic Romance* (1773), allies Marx's aim with the Enlightenment project to reduce objects that have been "overvalued" (Sigmund Freud's term) to their proper value or size. An object takes one real and many distorted forms, each generated by a deluded, mistaken, irrational, superstitious, or traumatized subject: for Freud, subjects "endow" or "appoint" objects to play powerful roles in their erotic life.[63] Both Marx and Freud deploy this discourse of fetishism to denounce the subject's role in creating the very object he takes to be "given." Were it not for such factors that lead subjects to misconstrue objects, this discourse insists, we would all see the same "real." The ultimate product of the discourse on fetishism (as of traditional quixote tales) *is* the "real" as something that preexists our encounter with it.[64]

Because they mistake figments of their imagination for real objects in the world, neither quixote nor sectary nor fetishist can participate in the culture that all members of the polity should hold in common.[65] The suspicion that quixotism, in its varied forms, leads to a dangerous social isolation is perhaps most visible in the anxiety surrounding the seventeenth- and eighteenth-century "enthusiast," whose mind, in Lawrence Klein's words, "magnified and inflated its own workings into ontological realities." This concern about eighteenth-century enthusiasts repeats denunciations of seventeenth-century sectaries, whose "radical claims of spiritual independence," as Kristin Poole has argued, "conflicted with older notions of communality."[66] Contemporaries particularly worried about the "unsociability" of enthusiasts, their "hypertropic egoism in which the interior life of the self stood uncorrected and undisciplined by social institutions or intercourse." Enthusiasm, Klein summarizes, "was an expression of the solitary frame of mind." Seventeenth- and eighteenth-century texts return often to this suspicion of solitude, in which individual imaginations, it was thought, might wander away from perceptions or beliefs held in common. Jan Goldstein has shown how eighteenth-century sensationalist psychology, aiming to "identity the environments and practices most liable to cause imagination to go astray," consistently focused on "solitary" environments "where, in the absence of the consensual force of community, the distinction between a publicly ratified reality and a personal imaginative fiction might easily be blurred."[67] Isolation and solitude, then, seem to simultaneously be both cause and consequence of quixotism: separation from others produces quixotic minds that, once formed, isolate quixotes from their communities and the beliefs and perceptions others (supposedly) share in common.

The magnitude of the scandal posed by the quixote's unsociability is exposed by Peter Dear's contention that seventeenth-century scientific practice depended on communal knowledge: "the world," Dear notes, "was construed through communal eyes."[68] Dear argues that most knowledge production, including knowledge about the natural world, preserved an Aristotelian ideal that demanded "principles, or premises, that were *evident* and therefore immediately conceded by all" (42). Knowledge with pretensions to be accepted as scientific, that is, began not with individual experiments but with evident truths agreed upon (it was thought) by all. Problems arose only when this expectation was not met, when knowledge seemed to derive from contestable or "singular experiences." Thus Pascal strives to turn accounts "of particular contrived events . . . into publicly available, and in that sense, evident experiences. His accounts needed . . . to function *as if* they were evident, to enable them to undergird demonstrations" (185). Galileo, too, expected others to credit his observations only if he could convince them that "the phenomenon was not novel and was apparently uncontroversial" (147)—that it was knowledge already held in common. This model of knowledge rules out "singular experiences" (experiments), which, since "known only to a privileged few," were "not suitable elements of scientific discussion" (44). The "specifiable singular propositions regarding individual instances" (30) embraced by English experimental philosophy "could not play a role in scientific discourse unless they were universal; if they were not, they could never be evident" (43). (Dear considers English experimentalism, which relied on such "singular, contrived events" as the "foundational elements in making natural knowledge," as a "detour" and unrepresentative of early modern science [3, 13]). Such singular experiences provoked difficult questions: "how could 'experiences' be established as common property if most people lacked direct access to them?" (59). Stephen Shapin and others have helped answer this question, analyzing the strategies (virtual witnessing, methods to dismiss differing experience) devised to make particular observations credible. But this effort, Dear points out, is necessary only "for a kind of natural philosophy that rested on discrete, singular experiences presented historically—the hallmark of the new English philosophy of the period." In most seventeenth-century science, this "reliance on isolated testimony" was "irrelevant because prepackaged philosophic universality was the norm" (149). Dear's account of the communal nature of seventeenth-century knowledge helps us see how seriously the quixote threatens this community based on knowledge held in common. Quixotes refuse to see the world through "communal eyes": their perceptions stubbornly resist sharing others' vision.

It is not entirely correct, however, to say that quixotes see the world through "individual"—in contrast to the others' "communal"—"eyes." I earlier quoted depictions of sectaries and enthusiasts as "private" and "individual" figures "undisciplined by social institutions." But while enthusiasts or sectaries are undisciplined by *dominant* social institutions, they act well within the discipline of the small society that is the sect. The persistent description of quixotes as those who elevate their private and individual mental creations ignores—or deliberately mistakes—the fact that the quixote's vision derives from a shared way of seeing: a genre. We risk merely repeating (rather than analyzing) seventeenth- and eighteenth-century representations when we portray the field divided between (on the one hand) communal vision shared by most and (on the other) private vision maintained by the lone sectary or quixote. Instead, we might see a dominant communal vision competing against a minority communal vision. Certainly the phenomenon of quixotism endorses the latter view, since the quixote processes reality through a lens that is generic—romance, religion, satire—and thus available to all. Quixotes, too, "construe" the world "through communal eyes," although the dominant culture refuses to recognize it as such. The persistence with which writers position quixotes as isolated individuals demands more attention: for it is this anxiety about what to do with those who seemed solitary or isolated in their private worlds—whether sectaries, enthusiasts, or, as I discuss later in this chapter, novel readers—that fuels typical quixote narratives. Indeed, a primary ideological effort of typical deployments of the quixote trope is precisely to position dissenting perspectives *as* isolated—as queer beliefs of one misguided individual rather than shared attitudes of groups. The discourse of quixotism, that is, offers simultaneously (1) a strategy to deal with differing perspectives at a time when perceptions were expected to be communal, and (2) a means to portray any differing perceptions as isolated rather than communal. And if this desire to see dissent or aberrant perspectives as solitary collides with or precipitates an anxiety about things done in privacy, isolation, and solitariness, then all these matters converge on anxiety about reading and readers.

V. Female Quixotes

At the heart of the quixote figure, of course, lies anxiety about reading: Don Quixote himself suffers from reading too many chivalric romances.[69] Blanford Parker notes that with Locke's "notion of thinking for oneself comes a fear of imaginative literature, which may use its gorgeous rhetoric to confuse the uncritical mind."[70] It is a short step from Locke's image of "other Mens Opinions" "floating . . . in our brains" to full-blown quixotism in which a text's way of seeing (its genre) comes to shape perceptions: both imagine that other texts have illegitimately colonized what ought to be (the discourse of quixotism insists) a free mind. Quixotism reveals the fear not merely that literature's rhetoric will confuse the mind but that the mind will swallow literature whole and come to view the world through a generic lens. Thomas Laqueur speculates that a series of apparently unlike objects—credit, masturbation, and fiction—caused similar anxiety in the eighteenth century because each so deeply involves "imagining" that it "remove[s] one from 'reality' ": what is not there turns out to be more desirable than what is.[71]

In the eighteenth century, the "fiction" problem—the danger that readers will come to prefer, indeed believe in, an imagined world rather than the real one—was largely construed as a female problem. There are, of course, eighteenth-century male quixotes: the "projector" in Swift's *Tale of a Tub*, Strephon in Swift's "Lady's Dressing Room" (1730), Parson Adams in Henry Fielding's *The History of the Adventures of Joseph Andrews* (1742), Uncle Toby and Walter Shandy in Laurence Sterne's *The Life and Opinions of Tristram Shandy, Gentleman* (1759–1767), Wildgoose in Graves's *Spiritual Quixote*. Many writers, it is true, avoid gendering quixotism and imply the presence of quixotism in *all* minds. A character in Henry Fielding's *The Coffee-House Politician, or The Justice Caught in His Own Trap* (1730) proposes that "The greatest Part of Mankind labour under one Delirium or other: And *Don Quixotte* differed from the rest, not in Madness, but the Species of it. The Covetous, the Prodigal, the Superstitious, the Libertine, and the Coffee-house Politician, are all *Quixottes* in their several Ways." Twenty years earlier Richard Steele's *Tatler* (1710) made a similar point that while "all the Readers of his History" tend to "receive" Quixote's story as "ridiculous," "it is very certain that we have Crowds among us far gone in as visible a Madness as his, tho' they are not observed to be in that Condition." Peter Motteux's preface to his translation of *The History of the Renowned Don Quixote de la Mancha* (1712) proposed that "Every man has something of *Don Quixote* in his Humour, some darling *Dulcinea* of his thoughts." Each of these claims, I should note, invokes pervasive quixotism to demand its cure: Motteux insists that these invisible quixotes "themselves need the chiefest Amendment," while Fielding's *Coffee-House Politician* praises "that Man alone from Madness free . . . / Who, by no wild unruly Passion blind, / To Reason gives the Conduct of his Mind."[72] Even John Locke's *Conduct of the Understanding*, begun in 1697 but published only in *The Posthumous Works of Mr. John Locke* (1706), that wryly notes that "every one is forward to complain of the *Prejudices* that mislead other Men or Parties, as if he were free, and had none of his own," insists as well that each individual can "Cure" this "hindrance to Knowledge" if one will only "let alone other's *Prejudices* and examine [one's] own."[73]

Despite this recognition that all individuals might become quixotes, many writers assumed that susceptibility to quixotism—as with other cultural problems such as nerves or hysteria—affected the population unevenly. Eighteenth-century literary discourse discussed the dangers of reading and of imagination in gendered terms. (Laqueur finds similarly that in seventeenth-century Dutch art, while "men were rarely depicted in . . . absorbed reading," women were "depicted exclusively as lost to the world in their little books.") Many writers contended that errant imaginations, whether made visible in their susceptibility to the promises of fiction or of financial schemes, were more likely to afflict women. Exploring cultural representations of both finance and fiction, Catherine Ingrassia reports that "criticism of women's financial interests echoes contemporaneous criticism of their fascination with popular fiction; both depict women transfixed and aroused by imaginatively based pursuits that divert them from their appropriate activities." "Women were thought by men—and by some women—to be the prototypical absorbed readers," Laqueur summarizes, "ready to give themselves over to the imaginative flights of fiction": the woman reader "was the misguided reader par excellence, the enthralled reader, the prototypical victim of imaginative excess."[74] If earlier critics seemed to accept uncritically the eighteenth-century assumption that the typical reader "swayed by the novelist, would be a woman,"[75] more recent critics carefully identify these claims of women's susceptibility as a popular *representation* that may not correspond to actual reading practices. "According to popular opinion in the eighteenth century," Debra Malina argues, the reader "who could not distinguish fiction from reality . . . tended to be female." "Misreading," Jacqueline Pearson concurs, "tends to be gendered as feminine."[76]

This claim that women were overly susceptible to imagination and fiction was reinforced by a related, but distinct, tendency to associate women *with* imagination, both being potentially unruly forces that required, writers contended, the government of masculine reason. As William Warner writes: "the pejorative terms applied to romance (*fanciful, wishful, out of touch with reality*, etc.) are also applied to women," while "the favorable terms applied to novels (*realistic, rational, improving*) are congruent with those that describe the male as a politically responsible member of the public sphere."[77] Such claims that aimed to disable women from *ever* triumphing over this problem were pervasive, and they persist even today. Recent critics continue to treat the interested, exaggerated, and often hysterical claims of eighteenth-century writers, who forged this association of women with fiction, as accurate indications of actual reading practices. Each time we repeat the unsubstantiated assumption that women largely wrote and read the novel, we give new life to an eighteenth-century myth.[78] Jan Fergus's work on what readers actually read explodes such myths,[79] but (as Fergus acknowledges) the fact that actual eighteenth-century reading practices contradict contemporaries' beliefs about who read what demands that we explore further why this myth was so persuasive and prevalent among eighteenth-century readers and writers. The association of women with fiction functioned, on the one hand, to demean the novel itself and to position other literary genres as more masculine forms; on the other, it functioned to ridicule women themselves, who, critics repeatedly asserted, devoured fiction obsessively and could hardly tell the real from the fictional. The reduction in the satires of Pope and Swift of women to ornament, to paint and patches, as in the many accounts of "Lady Credit," only literalizes this association of women with falsehood, with imagination, and with fiction.[80]

This gendered difference relied on the long-standing and frequently reasserted notion that women were plagued by excessive or uncontrolled imaginations. Much medical writing, as Mary Sheriff shows, insisted that "in comparison to the equilibrium that marked man's body, women's organs (both sense and sex organs) received livelier impressions and were more easily stimulated."[81] English writing does begin in the mid- and late-eighteenth century to associate imagination with genius and creativity,[82] a recuperation that may have been energized by the emergent consumer revolution that needed individual consumers to invest objects with personal fantasies. Modern consumers, as Colin Campbell argues, "do not so much seek satisfaction from products, as pleasure from the self-illusory experiences which they construct from their associated meanings": by "substitut[ing] illusory for real stimuli, and by creating and manipulating illusions," such consumers use "the faculty of the imagination" to "construct [their] own pleasurable environment."[83] Campbell's depiction of a gender-neutral consumer, however, disables him from analyzing whether both men and women could lay claim to this rehabilitated imagination. While some critics, including E. J. Clery, contend that eighteenth-century women writers, emboldened by the actress Sarah Siddons, "laid claim to visionary powers of the imagination," most critics insist that eighteenth-century discourse refused to treat women's imagination as a "positive . . . creative force." Instead, dominant discourse worried that women's imagination, in Mary Sheriff's words, led "not to cultural production but to convulsions, nymphomania, religious hysteria, transgressive sexuality, and social disorder." The claim that romanticism revalued the imagination, Adriana Craciun concurs, "neglects to gender" this "new Romantic ideology of the visionary imagination, for the diseased imagination remained feminized."[84]

Claudia Johnson shows more generally that, at the end of the eighteenth century, men appropriate behaviors traditionally associated with women—weeping, blushing, being overpowered by sensations—a process that revalues such behaviors so that men who display such traits are seen not as effeminate but as "estimable m[e]n of feeling." This appropriation by men of traditionally feminine traits, however, does not leave (or produce) tears and blushes as positive attributes for both genders. Instead, after "sentimental man" has "taken over once-feminine attributes," women who display these attributes come to look "excessively delicate, morbidly *over*sensitive": women's affective displays seem "inferior, unconscious, unruly, or even criminal."[85] The same process occurs when a less pejorative account of imagination emerges but leaves attitudes toward women's imagination largely untouched. What Samuel Johnson's *The History of Rasselas, Prince of Abissinia* (1759) called the "dangerous prevalence" of the imagination would, it was thought, affect women disproportionately.[86] Eighteenth-century writing returned often to the problem of mothers' imaginations, even locating the cause for a child's physical deformity in its mother's errant imagination, a belief parodied in the opening volume of Sterne's *Tristram Shandy* and in Hamilton's *Memoirs of Modern Philosophers*, where Bridgetina Botherim locates the source of her peculiar character in her mother: "With her milk I greedily absorbed the delicious poison which circulated through every vein; and love of literature, and *importunate sensibility*, became from thenceforth the predominant features of my character" (2: 85).[87]

This unequal development of the meanings of the term *imagination* helps us understand the increasing prominence and prevalence of female quixotes. Once powerful male imaginations have come to signify genius, eighteenth-century writers interested in disciplining aberrant points of view tend to focus on female imaginations, which continue to signify aberration. Increasingly, that is, stories designed to discipline the errant imagination, the mission of the orthodox quixote tale, work this plot out with *female quixotes*. In 1752 Henry Fielding noted that while both Charlotte Lennox's *The Female Quixote, or The Adventures of Arabella* (1752) and Cervantes's text show "the Head of a very sensible Person . . . entirely subverted by reading Romances," this phenomenon "seems to me more easy to be granted in the case of a young Lady than of an old Gentleman."[88] By installing young women as the readers most likely to practice quixotism, eighteenth-century critics and moralists placed the larger problem—the potency of imaginations to shape what we take to be the "real"—in a place where it could be clearly seen, decried, and disavowed in the "rest." The repeated focus on a subordinate group's proclivities to quixotism implies its absence everywhere else. The fact that quixotism is increasingly associated with women, to the extent that male critics imply that it is almost inevitable that women will succumb to the texts they read (in Eliza Haywood's *Love in Excess, or The Fatal Enquiry* [1719–1720], D'elmont doubts that it is "possible for *woman*, so much stronger in her fancy, and weaker in her judgment, to suppress the influence of [the] powerful passion" of love[89]), indicates that quixotism continues to carry pejorative connotations throughout the very century when, we have been assured, writers began to venerate the errant knight.[90] Eighteenth-century quixotism puts women on stage, demanding that they practice quixotism, both to initiate a cure (and thus reaffirm the "reality" to which they return) and to enable the rest of the culture to disavow their own quixotism.

The "reality" to which cured female quixotes return involves courtship, marriage, and a productive domestic life: orthodox quixote narratives treat courtship and marriage as the trajectory that all young women would follow naturally had their weak imaginations, enthralled by fictions, not embraced mistaken expectations and (mis)perceived the world. This account of female quixote narratives differs from most recent readings of this genre that depict the practice of quixotism as a strategy that enables young women to voice their resistance to eighteenth-century patriarchy. But these recent accounts, as I argue fully in chapter 2, celebrate what these texts try (perhaps unsuccessfully) to disown. While in Lennox's *Female Quixote*, for instance, Arabella's quixotism leads her for a while to elude the marital match prescribed by her uncle, the text does not embrace this divergence from expected practice as a creative solution or a clever strategy: on the contrary, her refusal exposes the dangerous consequences of novel-reading and delusion, and the novel ends with Arabella married to the very man her uncle had chosen and from whom her quixotism had alienated her. Most female quixote tales, such as *The Female Quixote*, insist that it is only an unhinged mind, disordered by reading too many romances, that leads young women to fail (if not resist) the expected practices of courtship and marriage.

It is hardly surprising, then, that quixote narratives look to the register of sexuality for the problematic consequences of the practice of quixotism.[91] Delia in Delarivier Manley's *Secret Memoirs and Manners of Several Persons of Quality of Both Sexes. From the New Atalantis, an Island in the Mediterranean* (1709) is initiated into quixotism by an "out-of-fashion aunt" who "read books of chivalry and romances with her spectacles." The aunt's books "infected me and made me fancy every stranger that I saw, in what habit so ever, some disguised prince or lover": "those books," Delia adds, "poisoned and deluded my dawning reason."[92] In Johnson's *Rambler* (1751), the quixotic "Imperia," who "spent the early part of her life in the perusal of romances," "expected nothing less than vows, altars, and sacrifices" and "thought her charms dishonoured, and her power infringed, by the softest opposition to her sentiments, or the smallest transgression of her commands."[93] These quixote narratives insist that young women who read too many romances will mistake unfit men as promising suitors, will expect all suitors to behave in ways that few actually will, and will refuse promising suitors as unfit: these behaviors form the basis of most female quixote plots. Such consequences are evident as early as Jane Barker's *The Lining of the Patch Work Screen; Design'd for the Farther Entertainment of the Ladies* (1726), in which the character Dorinda reports that it was "Romantic Whimsies that brought upon me . . . Ruin and Distress; I had read Plays, Novels, and Romances, till I began to think my self a Heroine . . . and all Men that flatter'd, or ogled, me were Heroes; and that a pretty well-behaved Foot-man must needs be the Son of some Lord or great Gentleman." Sixty years later, a speaker in Clara Reeve's *The Progress of Romance, through Times, Countries, and Manners* (1785) charges similarly that from romance "a young woman is taught to expect adventures and intrigues." If a "plain man addresses her in rational terms and pays her the greatest of compliments,—that of desiring to spend his life with her,—that is not sufficient, her vanity is disappointed, she expects to meet a Hero in Romance."[94] (The same fictions that, writers worry, will colonize young women's imaginations and thus cripple their courtships also endanger women's capacity to be proper mothers: a favorite target of antinovel discourse was "mothers, in miserable garrets, *crying for the imaginary distress of an heroine*, while their children were *crying for bread*."[95]) Most quixote narratives cure their female quixotes early enough to leave them marriageable, and in such narratives quixotism functions as a blocking agent that prevents the sort of easy marriages about which no narrative need be told. But some narratives, none more poignant than Tabitha Gilman Tenney's *Female Quixotism: Exhibited in the Romantic Opinions and Extravagant Adventures of Dorcasina Sheldon* (1801), predict more devastating consequences of female quixotism. Tenney's novel warns that quixotism, which roots deep in young women's minds, permanently damages them and leaves them unable to participate in the marriage economy that, for so many, gave them their only positive value.

Orthodox quixote narratives, then, are not only epistemologically conservative (in that they carefully distinguish the "real" from its distortions) but typically socially as well: the "real" that they demand all share is the culture's dominant social order, in which women gain value only by allowing themselves to be passed from a father to a son, from "the nest to [the] cage," as Alithea says in William Wycherley's *The Country Wife* (1675).[96] The quixote trope strives to position any young woman who perceives herself differently—who considers herself not an "object" for exchange but a "subject" who commands—as dangerously deluded, misled by the romances she has read. But I am not suggesting that the quixote narrative is essentially or inevitably conservative, available only to demand that women accommodate themselves to the dominant order that oppresses them. Egerton's "The Liberty" (discussed above) deploys the quixote trope, quite differently, to position women who conform to the social order as deluded. Curing women of quixotism, Egerton suggests, would not insert them into their prescribed place; rather, it would free them from the false consciousness society imposes on them and return them to a "real" that offers different possibilities. Mary Wollstonecraft deployed the quixote trope similarly for feminist projects: encouraging women to "see things as they really are," she insists that this possibility depends on curing the "imagination" from "dwell[ing] on pleasing illusions." She indicts the "lying, yet constantly trusted guide, the imagination" in her *Vindication of the Rights of Woman* (1792), whose "survey [of] the world stripped of all its false delusive charms" depends on (the rhetoric here is, by now, familiar) "the mists, slowly dispersing" and leaving a "clear atmosphere [that] enables [one] to see each object in its true point of view."[97] Far from necessarily serving a particular politics, then, the quixote trope is available for appropriation by any writer who aims to authorize his or her own vision and invalidate others'.

I have described in this chapter—and I continue to describe in the next—"orthodox" quixote narratives that insist on the stark difference between delusion and the "real" that all subjects must share. The eighteenth-century texts that this study explores in chapters 3 through 6, however, resist the tendency to deploy the quixote trope in this orthodox mode. This is no easy task: the history that I trace here primes or "prepossesses" (a term I return to later in this book) readers to receive quixote figures as ridiculous. This study's later chapters attempt to hear the ways in which a series of eighteenth-century women writers, so vulnerable to the charge of quixotism, appropriated the very discourse typically used to subject them.

CHAPTER 2

Charlotte Lennox's *Female Quixote* and Orthodox Quixotism

I. Orthodox Quixote Narratives

Chapters 3 through 6 focus on texts that deploy the quixote trope in ways that subvert its orthodox use. But before investigating these texts, I will use this chapter to flesh out my argument about orthodox quixote narratives that reject the practice of quixotism. I focus here on Charlotte Lennox's *Female Quixote, or The Adventures of Arabella* (1752), now the most widely read eighteenth-century female quixote narrative, in part to question the current critical consensus that celebrates Arabella's quixotism as a strategy to subvert patriarchal oppression. I begin, however, with a series of female quixote narratives written fifty years later: Maria Edgeworth's *Angelina; or, L'Amie Inconnue* (1801), Elizabeth Hamilton's *Memoirs of Modern Philosophers* (1800), Tabitha Gilman Tenney's *Female Quixotism: Exhibited in the Romantic Opinions and Extravagant Adventures of Dorcasina Sheldon* (1801), and Eaton Stannard Barrett's *The Heroine: Or, Adventures of Cherubina* (1813). These novels differ from one another in many ways. They imagine different audiences (Edgeworth's text aims at adolescents[1]), their female quixotes suffer different fates, one was written for an American readership (Tenney published her novel in Boston), and, most significantly, the early nineteenth-century narratives participate in an Anglo-American culture significantly changed from that in which Lennox's text appeared.[2] These later texts are concerned to label "quixotic" types of writing, and forms of thought, quite different from those on which *The Female Quixote* focuses: in particular, the French Revolution provoked in Britain a conservative reaction that stirred up widespread anxiety over what women read and thought, and many texts, including

Hamilton's *Memoirs*, mobilize female quixotes to manage this new, or newly fraught, "problem."[3] But while these later texts deploy female quixotes to manage problems of which Lennox's text is unaware, their return to Lennox's formula (at times even referring to *The Female Quixote*) both testifies to the continued usefulness of the quixote trope in demonizing threatening beliefs and helps us see clearly the structure of quixotism itself, abstracted from the content of particular quixotisms. Written at different historical moments, on different continents, and for different readerships, these texts share a commitment to "common sense" and aim to position the quixote's active role in making her world as delusion. While each of these novels levels a critique at the world that surrounds the quixote, none portrays the practice of quixotism as a "creative" reformation or escape from that sordid reality; instead, these texts insist above all that quixotism, far from being creative, disables women from understanding either their own nature or the world around them.

Most orthodox quixote narratives begin, as Tenney's *Female Quixotism* does, by describing the loss of a mother. This loss deprives the young girl of the figure "whose advice," the narrator insists, "would have pointed out" to the protagonist, Dorcas Sheldon,

> the plain rational path of life; and prevented her imagination from being filled with the airy delusions and visionary dreams of love and raptures, darts, fire and flames, with which the indiscreet writers of that fascinating kind of books, denominated Novels, fill the heads of artless young girls, to their great injury, and sometimes to their utter ruin.[4]

Quixote narratives regularly posit a mother's absence as a crucial problem that has led to the production of female quixotes[5]: in Lennox's *Female Quixote*, Arabella's mother "died in Three Days after her Delivery," while the heroine of Mary Hays's *Memoirs of Emma Courtney* (1796), who "sigh[s] for a romance that would never end" after reading "the Arabian Nights, Turkish Tales, and other works of like marvellous import," lost her mother "in child-bed the twelfth month of her marriage, after having given birth to a daughter." The first letter of Barrett's *The Heroine* describes the quixotic Cherubina as "Motherless" (and "bereft of more than [her] mother," her "good Governess," at the "sensitive age of fifteen"). Jane Austen's *Northanger Abbey* (1818) diverges from the convention only to satirize it, noting of Catherine Morland's mother that, "instead of dying in bringing her into the world, as any body might expect, she still lived on."[6] By explicitly crediting mothers with the capacity to introduce daughters to the "rational path of life," these novels counter a long tradition that held mothers responsible for their daughters' frivolous and excessive imaginations. Although these statements occur in narratives of failed nurturance, they offer some of the century's boldest affirmations of the importance of mothers and mothering.

The opening of Tenney's novel also identifies the culprit ("that fascinating kind of books, denominated Novels") that captures young women's imagination and leads them to mistake fictions for "reality." Dorcasina's father's denunciation of "those pernicious books, from which she had evidently imbibed the fatal poison, that seemed to have, beyond cure, disordered her mind" (50) recurs in all these texts: "Those romances," a character in Barrett's *Heroine* insists, "have turned her brain inside out" (333). Elizabeth Hamilton's novel offers two quixotes to show that novels are not the only sort of texts that can produce a disabling quixotism. Julia Delmond so "devour[s] the pages of a novel or romance in her own apartment" that

> she felt a void in her breast when not under the influence of strong emotions. In vain did her reason revolt at the absurdities which abounded in these motley tales . . . Imagination, wild and ungoverned imagination reigned paramount in her breast. The investigation of truth had no longer any charm. Sentiment usurped the place of judgment, and the mind, instead of deducing inferences from facts, was now solely occupied in the invention of extravagant and chimerical situations.[7]

When Julia suspects (wrongly) that her father wants to marry her off, the novelistic framework (here, derived from Samuel Richardson's *Clarissa, or The History of a Young Lady* [1748]) through which her experience passes becomes clear: "Already did she behold Major Minden, with the determined and selfish obstinacy of the hateful Solmes, persisting in seizing her reluctant hand; while her father, with all the cruelty of all the Harlowes, attempted to force her to the hateful union" (2: 265). But for Hamilton it is not only novels that prevent the mind from seeing the "facts" that lie before it. Another quixote, Bridgetina Botherim, demonstrates that the same consequences can result from reading philosophical texts, which encourage readers to direct their "researches" into "the wild and fruitless regions of idle speculation, where the chimeras of fancy are mistaken for realities, and bold conjecture assumes the authoritative tone of truth" (3: 113–14). In both cases, readers "mistake" the inventions of their minds, deposited or prompted by texts, for "realities."

It is this distinction between "the plain rational path of life" and the "airy delusions" peddled by novels and absorbed by the "imagination" that drives orthodox quixote narratives. Julia Delmond suffers a problem identical to Dorcasina's:

> While following the course of an unreined imagination, [Julia] experienced that deluding species of delight, which rather intoxicates than exhilerates, and which, by its inebriating quality, gives to the sanguine votary of fancy a disrelish for the common enjoyments of life . . . Still she pursued the flattering dream of fancy, and kept her mind's eye so fixt upon its airy visions, that she at length believed their reality, and what appeared at first the mere suggestion of imagination, seemed in the sequel the certain dictates of truth. (1: 114)

Julia's "unreined imagination" prevents her "mind's eye" from perceiving the very things that everybody else holds in "common"; indeed, as Hamilton makes clear, her imagination's "airy visions" come to substitute for "reality." "Julia became," as Hamilton's narrator later asserts, "the dupe of her own romantic imagination" (2: 170). But these novels do not only display the difference between "airy vision" and "reality"; they also insist on the clarity of the distinction. Neither allows a moment's confusion about the status of these two ways of seeing that are starkly distinguished into accurate and delusory. From its opening pages, when it describes Dorcasina's mind as "warped" (11), "perverted" (11; cf. 144, 292, 324–25), and "infect[ed]" (16), Tenney's novel never allows this clarity to lapse. The narrator reports without qualification other characters' diagnosis of Dorcasina's "insanity" (237, 285), a phenomenon that recurs in Hamilton's novel, where other characters describe Bridgetina as fit for "Bedlam" (2: 359) and worry that Julia "has certainly lost her senses" (1: 289), and in Edgeworth's *Angelina*, where every person Angelina encounters recognizes that she is "touched in her brain" and "not in her right understanding."[8] These moments, as well as others that refrain from explicitly invoking the language of insanity, ensure that no uncertainty surfaces about the delusory status of the quixote's perceptions.

Readers of orthodox quixote tales, that is, are never permitted to share the quixote's perceptions of the people or objects with which she comes into contact, since the narrative always reveals the "real" facts before it portrays the quixote's misapprehensions. What Gary Kelly writes of Barrett's *The Heroine* is true of most quixote narratives: "things and people turn out to be not what they seem to the heroine but what the reader knows they must be."[9] In *Female Quixotism*, readers know that the men, whom Dorcas believes love her, tolerate her presence only out of politeness or because they aim to steal her fortune. When, for instance, she meets Captain Barry, who, she wrongly believes, loves and wishes to marry her, their conversation remains at the level of small-talk. Dorcas construes this diffidence as Barry's "modesty in not declaring his passion at once," which, she contends, testifies that it is "sufficiently evident" that "he is violently in love with me": "It is a proof that his love is pure and unfeigned. A true lover is always diffident in the presence of the mistress of his affections" (159).[10] In an identical moment in Hamilton's *Memoirs*, Bridgetina also converts silence into devotion:

> Having determined in her own mind that Henry should be her lover, she interpreted every part of his conduct in her own favour; and persisted in believing, that notwithstanding his saying so little in favour of the new philosophy, its profound principles had made a sufficient impression upon his mind, which he was only deterred from acknowledging by the circumstances of his present situation. (2: 34)

A chapter later Bridgetina itemizes the "thousand instances" of Henry's "particular attention" to her (2: 94), all of which, readers know, she has misinterpreted. The narrator explicitly and consistently undermines Bridgetina's account by revealing that Henry's silences signify *lack* of interest (she so embarrasses him that he desires to be rid of her company). Indeed, to avoid any risk that readers might credit Bridgetina's vision, the narrator prefaces the above account with this sentence: "Happy for Bridgetina her perception was not very acute!" Not once, that is, do these novels neglect to package their quixote's perceptions as delusory. At one point Dorcas's best friend, Mrs. Stanly, wonders aloud that "it is strange that people should see so differently" (254), but Tenney's *Female Quixotism* is interested in competing views of reality only to resolve this "differen[ce]" into clearly identified visions, one accurate, the other deluded. As Gillian Brown notes, Dorcas's "community" must "deprogram" her so that she "affirm[s] her community's standard of reality."[11] These novels demonstrate the *process* by which the quixote makes sense of (indeed, *makes*) her world, but they do so only within a framework that relentlessly reminds readers that this process is flawed.

Quixote narratives might use such interpretive moments to unsettle our confidence in the notion of what is "evident." After all, the evidence that Dorcas's senses deliver seems as solidly real to her as the evidence delivered to our (supposedly) nonquixotic perception: how can we know that we are not as quixotic as she? Other texts, such as Sophia Lee's *The Recess, or a Tale of Other Times* (1783–1785), in which, similarly, a quixote construes lack of interest as silent devotion, encourage such questions by disabling readers from recognizing the quixote's misperceptions, which strike readers (as they do the quixote) as routine. But orthodox quixote narratives prevent this possibility from surfacing by informing readers repeatedly of the "truth": both the narrator and Captain Barry settle the issue long before Dorcas's mistake. These novels display the way in which romantic conventions enable quixotes to translate every object or event into "proof" of what they want to believe, the way they assemble the world they experience, but they do so only after alerting the reader to the invalidity of these accounts.

These accounts show, above all, that the internalized filters, deposited by romance in each quixote's head, simultaneously prevent these figures from seeing the "reality" before their eyes (and what all others see "in common") and ensure that they see, instead, a reality of their own making. Immediately after Dorcas fails to see emotions written clearly on one of her "suitors" faces, the narrator notes that "An indifferent spectator would have there read ill nature and vexation; but Dorcasina saw nothing but tender sorrow, occasioned by the excess of his love, and his unexpected disappointment" (71). Despite Motooka's claim that "eighteenth-century English quixotes . . . never err in their senses" but only in "their judgments about the empirical evidence before them," Tenney's text shows that Dorcas *perceives* differently than those around her. She does not merely misinterpret "the findings of common sense"; indeed, the text refuses to describe the two-step process in which a common or shared perception of an object is followed by divergent "judgments" about that object. Dorcas's "perception" itself is "faulty" or, more precisely, is shaped by the patterns in her head such that, like Don Quixote himself, she sees what is not present.[12] Quixote narratives, and (at their end) quixotes themselves, often deploy language that implies that a state of "blindness" has transformed suddenly to a state of "sight": *Female Quixotism*, for instance, describes Dorcas's steps toward accurate vision as a matter of her opening her eyes ("her eyes were at length opened" [147], "Her eyes seemed to be opened" [317]). But, more complexly, these novels separate blindness (having closed eyes) from quixotism: quixotes see what (and only what) their internalized genre registers. Dorcas perceives, that is, precisely what her presuppositions encourage her to expect (sorrow occasioned by excessive love).

Hamilton's *Memoirs* explores this phenomenon in great detail. When Julia convinces herself that she has discovered the true parents of her ostensibly lower-class lover, Vallaton, she begins to perceive what, the narrative assures us, is not there in "reality":

> [Julia] now began attentively to compare the physiognomy of the General with that of his supposed son. Their eyes then were of the same colour. Their noses too both approached the Roman; though the General's was somewhat more prominent, the similarity was still sufficient for a family likeness. She had before observed a similar degree of resemblance in the mouth of Mrs. Villers; and that making a proper allowance for the alterations produced by time, their foreheads had exactly the same characteristics. These casual resemblances were to her prepossessed imagination, 'confirmation strong as proofs of holy writ.' (1: 277)

The final quotation, from Shakespeare's *Othello*, invokes a famous instance of a figure who takes as certain evidence that is thoroughly unreliable.[13] By identifying Julia's "imagination" as "prepossessed," a phrase this study explores more fully later, the narrator marks her imagination as shaping, rather than merely registering, the "real." A chapter earlier, as Julia first began to speculate on Vallaton's parents, the narrator warns: "Imagination was now at liberty to run its wild career" (1: 251). Crucial here is that the quixote's "prepossessions" lead her to see what is not there and to assemble what she sees into narratives that differ from common sense. When she becomes (wrongly) convinced of Henry's love for her, Bridgetina marvels that she could have been so "blind" to the "proofs" of his "affection" (2: 94), but she speaks these lines, the reader knows, from within a genre of which she's unaware. Her quixotism does leave her "blind" to (or unable to see) certain things; but, more significantly, the genre through which she sees *produces* other "evidence" that she takes to be "real." The practice of quixotism produces an alternate "reality" that seems every bit as real as the world the rest of us encounter. Some objects are invisible to the quixote, but others that seem entirely real are visible only to them.

The primary object invisible to these female quixotes—but visible to other characters, and to readers as well—is their own deluded mind. Dorcas blinds herself to her own quixotism, the novel shows, by deploying the quixote trope itself: when she finds her perceptions to be in conflict or in competition with others', she identifies those around her as deluded so as to protect her own perceptions from challenge. She describes her father as "blinded by prejudice" (78, 94) and "error" (78, 9), and she hopes aloud that Betty, her servant, will be "cured of [her] foolish fears" (243), in order to insulate her own perceptions from the charge of quixotism. The ability to see quixotism in others and to ignore its presence in one's own mind is a universal feature of the female quixote. Julia Delmond, too, can see Bridgetina Botherim's delusions but, tragically, not her own:

> Here Bridgetina ceased; and Julia (bewildered, as she often was, by the illusions of her own imagination) was struck with astonishment at the effects of a similar illusion on the mind of her friend. With regard to Bridgetina, she very quickly perceived the fatal consequences of yielding to the suggestions of a distempered fancy. She saw, that under the idea of cultivating *mind*, [Bridgetina] had only been encouraging the mischievous chimeras of a teeming imagination; but never once did it occur to Julia, that she was herself the victim of the very same species of folly. So much easier is it for the mind's eye to pierce the faults of others, than to cast a retrospective glance upon its own. (2: 97)

The ridicule these novels direct at quixote figures answers—indeed, reverses—the ridicule these quixotes direct at others. Ultimately, these novels critique the quixotes for failing to recognize the status of their own vision and for misrecognizing the sort of "objects" that they are in "reality."

These orthodox quixote narratives locate the consequences of this misrecognition in each female quixote's sexual life. The practice of quixotism, it seems, prevents young women's "natures" from unfolding according to their proper trajectory. Like the "bourgeois sexual ideology" that, in Ellen Pollak's words, "mythologizes female destiny in exclusively sexual terms as a natural continuum between virginity and defloration," these tales, too, define women in entirely sexualized terms by showing that it is only this aspect of their lives that quixotism disrupts.[14] Quixotism does not leave young women less intelligent (most novels emphasize the female quixote's intelligence) or less able to negotiate the difficulties of economic life. If (as Tenney's *Female Quixotism* argues) novels "inspire illusory expectations" (325) and produce minds "fixed in [their] expectations," these "expectations" relate entirely to courtship practice: how suitors should behave, how to interpret suitors' actions and words, the range of experiences that are proper or improper, how long the courtship process should take, whether a young woman can, or should, control her suitor. Rather than specifying or explicitly focusing on this fact, these tales simply assume (and show in the narratives) that it is the romantic life of a young woman that suffers "great injury, and sometimes . . . utter ruin" as a result of quixotism (9). In insisting that the practice of quixotism poses these particular dangers, these tales reaffirm marriage to a proper suitor as the natural *telos* for all young women. Typically quixote narratives cure the female quixote early enough to leave her marriageable and enlist her suitor as the cure's agent: in *The Heroine*, Stuart helps Cherubina become "an altered being" who "look[s] back upon my past delusions, with horror and disgust" (348), while in *The Female Quixote*, Glanville, who had realized early that it is "his Business to produce a Reformation in her" (64) because "his Happiness depended upon curing her of her romantic Notions" (117), reaffirms near the novel's end that "he could not think of marrying *Arabella*, till the Whims her Romances had put into her Head, were eraz'd by a better Knowledge of Life and Manners" (339–40).[15] In curing their quixotes while young, these tales blunt the consequences of quixotism by implying that novel reading need not cause permanent disability.

Other texts intensify this lesson by exposing more severe dangers from the practice of quixotism. The choice to follow Dorcas (still unmarried) into old age—*Female Quixotism*'s most startling innovation—implies that women who read romances may be permanently disabled from participating productively in their communities (where, unfortunately, women's productive roles demanded that they be married). Those who believe that Dorcas has been "cured of her romantic turn of mind" (152) or "cured of all her follies" (236) are always wrong, since her delusions are remarkably resilient, capable of accommodating any sort of experience, no matter how obviously (to us) it contradicts her beliefs. Other characters often wonder that Dorcas will not "credit the evidence of her senses" (194, 216, 317)—Dorcas uses this phrase herself—but the novel shows that, as in all quixotic practice, her "senses" process all "evidence" by means of the filter that novels have deposited in her head. Quixotism, here, seems resistant to any "cure," and the only solution the novel can offer is to prevent quixotism *before* it is generated, a proposal Dorcas offers in her closing letter: "Withhold from [daughters'] eye the pernicious volumes, which . . . inspire illusory expectations" (325). The quixotism that so easily takes root in young women's minds, the novel warns, permanently mars the exchange value of these most important objects. Hamilton's *Memoirs* imagines even more tragic consequences of avoiding this advice: the quixotic Julia Delmond, who has read so many novels that her imagination reshapes the sinister Vallaton into a romantic lover, dies as the result of the affair that her misperceptions enabled. On her deathbed she offers the expected testimony of the quixote's reform: "Those prejudices, against which we have been accustomed so bitterly to rail, I now behold as a salutary fence, which, if I had never dared to overleap, would have secured my peace" (3: 345).

Julia recognizes, albeit too late, that the consequences of abandoning commonly held beliefs ("prejudices") may extend beyond social ridicule or even ostracism to actual death.

Most quixote narratives conclude with such confessions to testify to the thoroughness of the quixote's cure. Edgeworth's Angelina, for instance, reassures her friends repeatedly in the novel's final pages that "I am fully sensible of my folly" (10: 296) or that "I am perfectly in my senses *now*" (10: 302), while the tale's final sentence "assure[s]" readers that "it is possible for a young lady of sixteen, to cure herself of the affectation of sensibility, and the folly of romance" (10: 302). Dorcas, too, repeatedly testifies to her return to common sense (once, thanks to her friends, "truth flashed upon her mind" [322]): "I have been totally wrong" (320), "My own conduct will not bear reflecting upon; I cannot look back without blushing on my follies" (322), she "wondered she was so blinded" (322). Indeed, Tenney's *Female Quixotism* ends with an extended letter in which Dorcas identifies "novels" as "the cause of my ruin," asserts that though she has "passed my life in a dream" that "spell is now broken," and "curse[s] . . . the authors of the writings" that "perverted my judgment" (323–25). The "spell" that had "blinded" these quixotes, as we have seen, never entices readers, in part because these quixote narratives never risk the sort of seductive narrators that, as in Stanley Fish's account of *Paradise Lost* (1667), tempt readers to embrace what they ought to disown.[16] Instead, readers of orthodox quixote narratives gaze *at* the quixote, aware that the quixote's vision is aberrant and anticipating the inevitable cure. Far from portraying the quixotic imagination as admirable, creative, or seductive, each of these novels portrays the quixote as dangerously deluded. The only solution, anticipated by each novel's structure and delivered (although at times too late for the novel's protagonist) by each novel's end, is a cure. Eradication (not celebration) of errant imaginations is the "promis'd end" of each orthodox quixote narrative.[17]

II. Arabella's Quixotism

Charlotte Lennox's *The Female Quixote*, the most studied and celebrated eighteenth-century female quixote narrative, tells a story that justifies the disciplining of an active—and therefore errant or excessive—female imagination. Arabella is not only cured at the novel's close (a cure so awkwardly abrupt that many think that Lennox did not write it[18]) but she herself begs the Doctor to assert his authority over her, to "discover me to myself" (370): she recognizes that her practice of quixotism has disabled her from understanding not just the external world but also her "self." Like Dorcas, Arabella spends the novel's final pages "wholly absorb'd in the most disagreeable Reflections on the Absurdity of her past Behavior, and the Contempt and Ridicule to which she now saw plainly she had exposed herself," and she apologizes to Glanville, her lover, for "the Follies [that] her vitiated Judgment had led her into" (383) soon after she confess her earlier faults: "my Heart yields to the Force of Truth . . . I begin to perceive that I have hitherto . . . trifled away my Time" (381). This language—romances had "vitiated" her "Judgment," her quixotic behavior is absurd and ridiculous, she can "s[ee] plainly" after her "Cure"—reproduces the rhetoric that, as we have seen above, organizes orthodox quixote narratives.

The now-extensive critical tradition that Lennox's text has generated, however, tells a very different story. *The Female Quixote*'s recent readers, treating Arabella's embrace of romance as a strategy to preserve female power, have heroized Arabella for acting and speaking in ways the dominant culture aims to suppress. George Haggerty, for instance, contends that Arabella's romance fantasies enable her not only to "surviv[e] a brutally stifling life" but also to "resist her father" and to "embarrass, if not subvert, the patriarchal energy that is being expended to contain her," while Laurie Langbauer argues, succinctly, that (for Arabella) romance is "empowering, not imprisoning . . . The conventions of romance . . . give women voice."[19] These readings build on Michel Foucault's *Madness and Civilization: A History of Insanity in the Age of Reason* (trans. 1965), which figures madness as a category that a dominant culture constructs to "confine" those values it disowns—a "banishment" that "protects" that culture from having to admit "a proximity, a relation, a quasi-resemblance between itself" and those banished forms—and ends by heroizing those who have managed to speak what the dominant culture rejects.[20] The *locus classicus* for this reading of Arabella is Margaret Doody's influential introduction (1989) to the Oxford University Press paperback edition of *The Female Quixote*: "It is through assuming the powers the romances offer that Arabella can command a space, assert a woman's right to 'a room of one's own', and take upon herself the power to control the movements and behaviour of others . . . she has given herself full leave to speak."[21] Doody celebrates not only Arabella's willingness to "speak" transgressively but also her use of quixotism to assume a "power" ("to control . . . others" as well as her own actions and words) that is typically denied to women. Indeed this contention that Arabella desires the power her society forbids her to possess or exercise has become a critical commonplace, evident in David Marshall's summary that "Arabella's investment in romance is related to her preoccupation with power" or Langbauer's proposal that Arabella "is obsessed with . . . romance" because "she yearns for power." Most critics agree, it seems, that through Arabella's romancing *The Female Quixote* "articulate[s] a fantasy of female power."[22]

One problem with this reading, I argue below, is that it equates Arabella with the strategic coquet from whom the text struggles to distinguish her. Deborah Ross makes this explicit: "[l]ike Arabella, the [coquet] uses chivalric conventions to satisfy the feminine will to power."[23] But before exploring this point, I will note a different implication of the recent consensus that Arabella cleverly practices quixotism to find a "power" or voice typically denied to women. This reading, which enacts the tendency (discussed in chapter 1) to recuperate quixote figures, viewing them as admirable rather than ridiculous, focuses on the *content* of Arabella's quixotism. Such readings celebrate the tradition of romance for enabling Arabella to discover a quality—female agency—that the surrounding culture has abandoned or denounced. The larger culture's ridicule of the romance tradition secures the heroic subversiveness of the very thing, female agency, she finds in romance. It is the content of the form Arabella embraces, the female agency she finds in romance (a close anticipation of recent feminist projects), that earns praise for her quixotism. These readings treat her as a hero, that is, to the extent that she reactivates a value that we embrace (but one that dominant eighteenth-century culture found subversive).

Perhaps all would agree that were Arabella to use romance to escape her subordinate status and to resist the structures that aim to keep her there, she would be justified. And it is clearly true that the novel uses Arabella's quixotism, in ways I describe below, to critique the scheming, frivolous, and self-interested world around her. This distaste for the characters around Arabella, however, does not imply that the novel embraces her quixotism, as if to reject the former requires the embrace of the latter. Indeed, much of the critical debate over *The Female Quixote* has been provoked by the fact that the novel levels (at least) two critiques: it critiques *both* the characters who circle around Arabella (and the values they embody) *and* Arabella's own quixotism. It can do this because there is a third entity here: Arabella separated from her quixotism, an entity implied throughout the novel and produced at its end. It is the character of Arabella herself—not the agency her quixotism leads her to assume—that the novel admires and that stands in contrast to or rebukes those around her. Her quixotism itself remains a constant source of derision, and in heroizing Arabella to recover a subversive text, recent readings necessarily ignore or obscure the steady ridicule that the novel directs at this quixotism. This ridicule attaches not to who Arabella is (she is, as we will see below, admirably generous) but rather to what she does (she makes, rather than finds, the world she thinks she merely experiences). The novel expends enormous energy detailing—and ridiculing—the process by which Arabella's imagination assembles and preserves an alternate reality.

Arabella's imaginative transformations are unacceptable to the extent that they violate what orthodox quixote narratives call "common sense." As George Haggerty writes, "the isolation of [Arabella's] imagination is a measure of her disgrace." Kate Levin notes that Arabella "flout[s] the social consensus" by refusing to "conform to her society's strictures for female behavior," while Elizabeth Kraft argues that Arabella's interpretations of reality, in that they stand "*against* communal interpretation," are "suspect" and fail to gain the "communal sanction" that could establish them as "reality" itself.[24] Arabella violates "social consensus," as Kraft implies, most fundamentally by refusing to perceive as—or what—others perceive. She sees differently; and *The Female Quixote*, like the quixote narratives I explored above, aims to restore a situation in which all perceive alike (or in which competing perceptions have been successfully positioned as aberrant or deviant). The novel's obsessive labeling of Arabella's vision as distorted, misguised, exaggerated, excessive, dangerous, and above all "mad"—she is "fit for a Mad-house," Hervey says, a judgment that others often assert (157, cf. 55, 60, 102, 201, 259, 301, 302, 308, 339, 352)—tries to ensure that readers never doubt that Arabella's quixotism improperly makes the "real" into something it is not. Her quixotism, the internalized filter that romance-reading has deposited in her head, disables her from knowing what Bacon calls "the nature of things" themselves, since her mind has "mixe[d] up its own nature with the nature of things."[25] It is this *activity* of Arabella's imagination that the text portrays and chastises; her mind intrudes in a process that ought to be passive. Like the cluster of female quixote texts written in the early nineteenth century, Lennox's *Female Quixote* severely disapproves of the active (female) imagination and consistently rejects this practice of quixotism.

Like other orthodox quixote narratives, *The Female Quixote* never allows the reader a moment's uncertainty as to the status of Arabella's alternative perceptions of reality. One can see in miniature the novel's care at positioning her perceptions as aberrant in almost any sentence that introduces how Arabella see things: Arabella "saw several Men come towards them, who she took to be the Assistants of her Ravisher, though they were, in reality Haymakers" (157). The distinction between what Arabella "took" an object "to be" and what this object is "in reality" remains as clear throughout the novel as it is in this simple sentence. Later, when Arabella and others travel in a coach attended by servants, they see in the distance three men mounted on horseback. Arabella immediately understands them to be "Knights" who, she is convinced, believe that she and her cousin are being kidnapped and have come to "fight for our Deliverance." The rest of the company recognize them as "Highwaymen." Neither Arabella nor the rest of her company, it is true, have unassailable proof of their perceptions, and so both must interpret these men according to the way they understand the world operates. But to equalize these "ways of seeing" is to ignore that, from the moment the incident begins, the narrator leaves no doubt as to the "real" nature of these objects in the distance ("toward the Close of the Second [day], they were alarmed by the Appearance of three Highwaymen, well mounted, at a small Distance" [257]) and continues throughout the narration to refer to these men as "Highwaymen" (258). Arabella, however, refuses to be convinced, insisting that "it cannot be doubted, but that their Birth is illustrious" (259), an inflexibility that only intensifies the text's ridicule of her. This chapter, like so many others, ends with Glanville's despairing recognition that Arabella is "out of her Senses" (259).

The novel's steady attention to the way in which Arabella's imagination elaborately remakes the real serves to protect the reader from confusing the "real" with its distortions. Quixote narratives, as Amy Pawl notes, characteristically display how "the protagonists sift and twist their literary sources in order to come up with an explanation that accommodates their romantic vision and prevents reality from obtruding itself upon their notice," a phenomenon modeled on what Michael McKeon calls Don Quixote's "exegetical energy."[26] Such "exegetical energy" is clearly visible in an early instance of Arabella's quixotism, when, in the novel's sixth chapter, her imagination transforms a gardener into a man of quality (disguised, she thinks, to court her). The narrator notes that Arabella "had frequent Opportunities of seeing this young Man, whom she observed with a very particular Attention": far from depicting Arabella as "blind," then, the text describes her as extremely active, so active that she "adapt[s] reality to [her] preconceptions."[27] Arabella notes that "His Person and Air had something, she thought, very distinguishing," and that his speech was "framed in a Language vastly superior to his Condition"; she notices, too, that he treats her with a "Respect" beyond the "aukward Civility of the other Servants." The text lays out in such detail the process by which Arabella assembles "evidence" of this individual's nature that I quote the passage at length:

> Having discerned so many Marks of a Birth far from being Mean, she easily passed from an Opinion that he was a Gentleman, to a belief that he was something more; and every new Sight of him adding Strength to her Suspicions, she remained, in a little time, perfectly convinced that he was some Person of Quality, who, disguised in the Habit of a Gardener, had introduced himself into her Father's Service, in order to have an Opportunity of declaring a Passion to her, which must certainly be very great, since it had forced him to assume an Appearance so unworthy of his noble Extraction.
>   Wholly possessed with this Thought, she set herself to observe him more narrowly; and soon found out, that he went very aukwardly about his Work; that he sought Opportunities of being alone; that he threw himself in her Way as often as he could, and gazed on her very attentively: she sometimes fansied she saw him endeavour to suppress a Sigh when he answered her any Question about his Work; once saw him leaning against a Tree with his Hands crossed upon his Breast; and, having lost a String of small Pearls, which she remembered he had seen her threading as she sat in one of the Arbours, was persuaded he had taken it up, and kept it for the Object of his secret Adorations. (22)

A different narrative, perhaps, might celebrate Arabella's active detective work as creative or ingenious. This narrative, however, ensures that her constructions never earn credit by inserting qualifiers ("she thought") that separate her perceptions from that of others, by exposing the alacrity with which Arabella moves from opinion to absolute certainty ("perfectly convinced," "certainly"), and by invoking language that signals Arabella's delusion ("fancy," "possession"). As important, the narrative prepares readers to disbelieve Arabella's perceptions by promising, at the close of chapter V, that chapter VI will show how Arabella's "Imagination, always prepossessed with the same fantastic Ideas, made her stumble upon another Mistake, equally absurd and ridiculous" (21), and then by providing, at the start of chapter VI, the "true" account of the gardener's "nature": the gardener possessed unusual language and bearing because he had "lived in several Families of Distinction," while his "*secondhand* Politeness . . . he had contracted while he lived at *London*" (22).

The narrative does more, however, than insist on the delusory status of Arabella's perceptions. Its method of itemizing the clues that

Arabella "found out," presenting them (in the passage above) to the reader in a list, each item separated by a colon or semicolon, foregrounds the disparate sorts of things that Arabella jumbles together as she assembles her misconstruction. It displays, that is, the process by which she puts together her perceptions. This activity becomes even more visible when Arabella, having been presented with the accurate account of the gardener (he frequented the fish pond, she is told, not to "make away with himself" but "to make away with some of the Carp" [25]), refuses to change her mind, and the text shows her active struggle to see things as she wants to:

> it was some Time before [Arabella] even reconciled Appearances to herself; but, as she had a most happy Facility in accommodating every Incident to her own Wishes and Conceptions, she examined this Matter so many different Ways, drew so many Conclusions, and fansied so many Mysteries in the most indifferent Actions of the supposed noble Unknown, that she remained, at last, more than ever confirmed in the Opinion, that he was some great Personage, whom her Beauty had forced to assume an Appearance unworthy of himself. (25)

The emphasis here, as before, falls on Arabella's activity, the repetition of "so many" stressing the great lengths to which her examinations, drawing of conclusions, and fancying must go. Arabella's tendency to make nothing into something, to ascribe significance or value to insignificant objects or actions, is captured in the stark distinction between "the most indifferent Actions" and "Mysteries." The narrative focuses on the way in which Arabella (like the fetishists I discuss at greater length in chapter 6) makes or invests objects with significances that they do not really possess. The things she imagines to be real, as her uncle says later, "are to be found no-where else, except in [her] Imagination" (63).

The passage's sharpest moment occurs when it defines the activity in which Arabella's mind engages: "She had a most happy Facility in accommodating every Incident to her own Wishes and Conceptions." This "Facility" defines improper perception, which should passively register the true nature of objects, not actively "accommodat[e]" them to what one desires or believes, to a preconception or pattern embraced beforehand. The narrative repeats this description of Arabella's improper activity, this time spoken by Glanville rather than offered by the narrator, near the novel's end. Arabella "had such a strange Facility in reconciling every Incident to her own fantastick Ideas," Glanville worries, "that every new Object added Strength to the fatal Deception she laboured under" (340). Glanville's worry identifies quite precisely the problem with Arabella's quixotism: it disables her from encountering any "Object" as it is. Instead, she converts objects into something else. The problem with this practice of quixotism is that there seems to be no way to dispute a system so capable of "reconciling" or "accommodating" anything to itself, since any "Object" or evidence presented turns out to (or is made to) reconfirm what the individual already believes. Arabella's quixotism, her "strange Facility" of transforming any "Object" according to her system, anticipates Thomas Kuhn's account of "normal science," in which, he contends, scientists typically "force" whatever they encounter into "the conceptual boxes" that they accept as true. Normal science, Kuhn argues, functions by "forc[ing] nature into the preformed and relatively inflexible box that [a] paradigm supplies . . . Those [phenomena] that will not fit the box are often not seen at all." What may, in retrospect, appear "anomalous" or contradictory evidence is initially "almost always identified, without apparent hesitation or puzzlement, as normal": facts are "immediately fitted to one of the conceptual categories prepared by prior experience."[28]

The object Arabella misunderstands most, of course, is herself. The text shows that she consistently *mis*values herself, having learned from romance to see herself as a "heroine" rather than, as the story eventually teaches her, as a "wife." At one level, this means that Arabella believes that she controls a lot more than she actually does. "Most of [Arabella's] adventures," David Marshall remarks, "reiterate her insistence on the authority of her own *commands*, especially over men," which has led some, such as Ronald Paulson, to describe her as a "monster of egotism" who "orders," "commands," and "banishes" as imperiously as an absolute monarch.[29] Indeed when Glanville complains that "you carry your Power farther then ever any Beauty did before you; since you pretend to make People sick and well, whenever you please," Arabella confirms that she thinks of herself as an "absolute Power" (146; cf. 320) upon whom depend others' fates. From her lovers Arabella requires "a more unlimited Obedience . . . than any other Monarch can expect from his Subjects; an Obedience which is circumscrib'd by no Laws whatever" (321). But *The Female Quixote* often reminds readers how "circumscrib'd" Arabella's "Power" is, in part by repeatedly showing her positioned as a pawn in others' "Designs," a term used by the men who aim to possess or trade her. Arabella, who sees imaginary plots everywhere, never perceives the actual plots in which others involve her. As Pawl notes, both

Don Quixote and Arabella are "vulnerable" to others who ask them "to play to their script," a phenomenon that "assaults . . . the agency of the quixote."[30] This economy in which a series of men allow Arabella's "Pow'r" is exposed when an unnamed "Gentleman" gives Arabella control that is explicitly portrayed as illusory: "being extremely glad at having so beautiful a Creature in his Power, [he] told her she might command him in all she pleased" (100). Arabella believes herself to be an "Absolute Power," but the text ridicules Arabella's ideas by showing that she is a different sort of object than she imagines, one controlled more than controlling, an object moved by others, not moving others.

There is another way to construe Arabella's confusion. When Arabella misunderstands her "Powers," she misunderstands the *effects* her body has on the bodies around her. In the eighteenth century, "Power" referred to one body's capacity to cause an effect in or on other bodies: Locke glossed "Power" as "the effects . . . that natural Bodies are able to produce in one another."[31] When Arabella insists that her "Powers" have produced Sir George's apparent resolution to die, she speaks like an unskilled scientist who mistakes accidents for essences: "'Tis very certain, my Beauty has produced very deplorable Effects . . . but you must observe, that my Will has no Part in the Miseries, that unfortunate Beauty occasions . . . by a fatal Necessity, all these Things will happen whether I would or no" (175). Her "Beauty" functions, for Arabella, mechanically (a contemporary gloss for "unavoidable Necessity" [316]), rather than instrumentally (for some purpose). Arabella does not *choose* to follow the "Laws of Romance," which she considers inescapable, any more than we choose to follow the laws of gravity. She considers herself subject to, not in control of, the operation of such laws, and she believes that others respond to her "Beauty" as they must, due to the constitution of her body and theirs. "The Mischief I have done . . . was not voluntary, I assure you," Arabella insists. "My Power is confined by certain unavoidable Laws" (182). The text ridicules these remarks, since her "Beauty," which she insists *had* to have produced certain phenomena, has caused nothing. Arabella has been duped: the phenomena for which she so desperately disowns responsibility have not even occurred. Claiming that she has not deliberately done anything—her nature has simply produced the effects it necessarily must—Arabella positions herself as a natural object that necessarily produces effects on other natural objects. But such claims to possess certain "Powers" demonstrate above all, that Arabella's quixotism has disabled her from understanding the sort of object she really is.

III. CRITICAL QUIXOTISM?

This stark epistemological difference between the reader and Arabella (we know things unproblematically, she cannot; we understand her, she cannot understand herself) is crucial, and critics' disregard of this aspect of the text marks, it seems to me, the power of our desire to recuperate Arabella as a feminist heroine. As Elizabeth Kraft admits, "We *like to see* in the ending of *The Female Quixote* a wistfulness in Lennox's portrayal of the capitulation of a woman whose soul is significant enough to men that they will debate her, whose claim that things happen to her has to be admitted, and whose voice, speaking or silent, has been so dominant throughout the novel."[32] Critics who invoke Arabella's "will to power," in effect, engage in a practice that resembles that within the text itself: just as Arabella sees herself as identical to the objects (heroines) that populate the texts that give her pleasure (seventeenth-century romances), so too recent critics see Arabella as identical to the objects (feminist heroines) that populate the texts that give us pleasure. "Arabella's quixotism," as Motooka writes, "may thus be seen as her feminism."[33] The cost of this account is that we celebrate the very things the novel treats as problems: by describing Arabella as a young woman who "yearns for power," these readings collapse her into the coquet from which the novel distinguishes her. One symptom, that is, of the distortions produced by the desire to recuperate this text as subversively feminist is that it requires critics to transform Arabella into the very object that the text most sharply critiques.

Lennox's earliest works focused on this figure of the coquet, the young woman who, like the heroine of *The Life of Harriot Stuart, Written by Herself* (1751), thinks herself "of prodigious importance."[34] What Harriot calls a "career of coquettry" (64) was one expected result of romance-reading. Critics worried, as Patricia Meyer Spacks notes, that "a young woman who read about heroines might acquire too exalted an idea of her own potential importance."[35] This expectation Lennox's first heroine fulfills: "born" with "latent seeds of coquetry in [her] heart," Harriot begins at the age of three to "appl[y herself] to reading with . . . eager sollicitude." Her reading list becomes evident when, upon meeting her first beaux, Harriot fancies herself "nothing less than a Clelia or Statira"; she mirrors another character who "being deeply read in romances, had her head filled with adventures of gallantry" (64–67). But romances turn Harriet less into a victim, vulnerable like Arabella because of her romance fantasies, than into a coquet who, valuing power and knowing how to gain it, "not only knew the full value of a smile, a sigh, or a blush, but could practise them all upon occasion" (66). This romance-reader-turned-coquet resembles the addressee of Lennox's "Art of Coquetry" (1747), who aims to colonize the entire world of men: "Such by these arts their empire may improve, / And unsubdu'd controul the world by love."[36] The coquet embodies the fear that from romance others learn how to *use* the "arts" of love to control others.

The Female Quixote offers Charlotte Glanville, who has "a large Share of Coquetry in her Composition" and who "coquetted" with Sir George (80, 91), as Arabella's most significant "Other." Mirroring Harriot Stuart's favorite activity (120, 142, 144), Charlotte Glanville fashions herself for public consumption (she "adjust[s]" herself "at the Glass" [282]), always targeting anticipated audiences. She shares Harriot's tendency to practice smiles, sighs, and blushes and, above all, cannot think beyond a model in which every attention paid to Arabella deprives her. Because she "could not think it possible, one Woman could praise another with any Sincerity" (91), Charlotte distrusts Arabella's compliments, but these constant suspicions that Arabella's odd language cloaks secret attacks reveal only Charlotte's narrow mind. When Arabella likens Charlotte to the "fair and virtuous *Antonia*," Charlotte "could not imagine *Arabella* spoke this seriously" and believes her words to have been "designed to sneer at her great Eagerness to make Conquests" (89). Charlotte's failure of imagination (she "could not imagine" and "could not think it possible") perfectly describes her inability to credit any motivation other than self-love or self-interest. The text's disapproval of this coquet reaches its height when it uses her name to epitomize an entire category of egotistically affected women: "[I]nstead of *Clelia*s, *Statira*s, *Mandana*s, &c.," the narrator remarks, Arabella "found only Miss *Glanville*s among all she knew" (341).[37] The text's admiration for romance heroines (or, perhaps, only Arabella's admiration for them) appears no where more clearly than in this sentence that celebrates these romance figures simply by opposing them to coquets such as Charlotte Glanville.

The novel's critique of coquets, then, poses a problem for the recent critical consensus about the novel, since the very things for which we praise Arabella (her willingness to "take upon herself the power to control the movements and behaviour of others") appear in the novel as the typical behavior of a coquet. Were Arabella indistinguishable from the coquet, the novel could not have admired her as lavishly as it does: her *distance* from the coquet earns her praise. Arabella consistently articulates an ethos of generosity, an ethos that she finds modeled in romance: one must "do Good for the sake of Good," she contends, rather than "for the Praise that generally follows it" (304). At the novel's end the Doctor who cures Arabella condemns romances as "contemptible Volumes" or "empty Fictions" composed of "philosophical Absurdities" (374, 377, 378) and charges that "it is impossible to read" romances "without lessening part of that Humility, which keeps us awake to Tenderness and Sympathy, or without impairing that Compassion which is implanted in us as an Incentive to Acts of Kindness"; instead readers are "taught the Arts of Intrigue" (381). This is, as we have seen, a commonplace charge leveled against romance-readers, one that *Harriot Stuart* confirmed. But *The Female Quixote* refutes it: most of its characters that practice "the Arts of Intrigue" have never read romances, while Arabella, who has read romances, remains, almost uniquely in the novel, "awake" to the "Tenderness and Sympathy" that the Doctor claims is "impossible" to preserve after exposure to romance. Arabella's "Compassion" is not "impair[ed]," which is more than can be said for those (Hervey, Charlotte, Selvin, Tinsel) who have never read romances. Arabella possesses all the virtues—"Generosity . . . Disinterestedness and Greatness of Soul" (229), "romantic Generosity" (254), "Valour . . . Generosity . . . and Fidelity" (328), "Virtue, Courage, Generosity" (328)—of a traditional romantic heroine, which suggests that the novel rehabilitates (rather than ridicules) the romance tradition Arabella reads so devotedly, offering "a fictional world," as James Lynch says, "in which the qualities of love and fidelity" find "a more realistic, though no less ideal, mode of expression."[38]

I have argued elsewhere that the novel spends considerable energy insulating Arabella and her virtues from the charge of coquetry and, more broadly, from the damaging charge of self-interest often leveled at romance-reading women. The novel needs to portray its heroine as deluded because for her to be "in her head" would provoke the questions about motive and self-interest that texts such as *Harriot Stuart* raised.[39] The novel produces a *space*—of delusion or of quixotism—within which we can safely credit her romancing as nonstrategic, within which Arabella's embodiment of the romance disinterestedness and generosity cannot be debunked or misread as strategically selfish.[40] *The Female Quixote* paradoxically narrates a romance by depicting a woman deluded by romance: Arabella's practice of quixotism establishes her, as perhaps only quixotism could, as a romance heroine. Her quixotism establishes this, however, not by showing that Arabella has learned these virtues from reading romance, a claim the novel never makes. (These virtues seem inherent parts of her character, which some, such as Glanville, recognize *despite* the quixotism that threatens to obscure them.) Quixotism preserves Arabella as a romance heroine because it allows readers to trust that her generosity and disinterestedness are not strategic or dissimulated. Her quixotism, then, by guaranteeing that Arabella is *not* a coquet (she does not use romance cunningly or strategically), also ensures that she is a worthy "object" for Glanville to marry. The very phenomenon that for recent critics constitutes the source of Arabella's transgressive tendencies, that is, actually functions in this novel to establish her worth or desirability as an object within the dominant sex-gender system. As the novel's main means of securing her worth as a marriagable object, Arabella's quixotism reaffirms rather than subverts prevailing gender ideologies.

But this quixotism is also the "mist" that "clouds" or obscures the "real" Arabella, to borrow the Enlightenment language I have discussed in the Introduction and in chapter 1. It obscures her virtues from most of the novel's characters, who disdain or dismiss her, and, most crucially, it obscures her true nature from herself. "Discover me to myself" (370), she begs, as we have seen, near the novel's close. It is the mistaken account of herself, produced by her imagination's misconstruction of her own "Powers," that the novel needs to cure before Arabella is fit to marry Glanville. This process of cure, then, involves the elimination—not the celebration—of Arabella's imagination so that she can see herself as the object she has always been to others. Dissolved in this cure are any contributions her imagination has made to her image of who she is; what is left is an object, Arabella, "in itself," stripped of illusions and misperceptions. The text never suggests that Arabella's self needs reformation (her quixotism, as I have said, deflects any suspicions of her character). It does insist, however, that her imagination—the source of the representations that improperly mediate between her mind and the world it should passively register—requires serious reform. Arabella's tendency to offer an alternate account of "reality" or of herself gains no credit in the novel. If her practice of quixotism enables her to avoid marriage and to control her suitors (this is not, I have argued, her *deliberate* project), then the novel views this as a problem with Arabella rather than with the society that demands that she marry. To the extent that her romancing delivers to her a world that diverges from the world experienced by those around her—to the extent that it leads her to perceive differently than they do—it endangers her and must be eliminated.

The novel, then, does not regret curing her. The text on the Oxford paperback's back cover—Lennox "had to find an ending, happy or sad, and the one she chose underlines the bitterness which was in part the spur to writing *The Female Quixote*"—positions the ending as an unexpected conclusion that betrays the sympathies evident throughout the novel. Haggerty, too, suggests that, while Lennox's conclusion "pay[s] lip service" to the "marriage plot," her real sympathies lie in the "fantasy of female power" that this plot requires Arabella to abandon. But although, as Kate Levin contends, most critics read *The Female Quixote* as "Lennox's rebellion against eighteenth-century patriarchal structures" and thus find a "conflict" between "Arabella's use of romances to escape the patriarchal system and her 'cure' by the learned Doctor," Arabella's cure is not "an aberration in an otherwise subversive novel."[41] Indeed, Levin argues that Lennox offered *The Female Quixote* as a public testimony that she conformed to prevailing notions of proper womanhood. Lennox "purif[ied]" or "refashion[ed] her image as a writer" after literary culture "branded" her as "a dangerous example for female readers" when her first novel featured a heroine who "enjoys her power over men." By presenting a romance-reading woman "cured" into accepting a role as a "proper domestic woman" and "the perfect wife," *The Female Quixote* "dramatize[d] and advertise[d]" Lennox's "own literary reform."[42] Levin insists that Arabella's cure does not violate a narrative that otherwise celebrates women's subversive behavior or imaginative creativity: the novel shows Arabella violating "social consensus" precisely to justify her "cure" that brings her back into the fold. Catherine Gallagher's claim that Lennox's novel teaches Arabella about the (emergent) concept of fiction itself—she must stop thinking that fictions refer to "real people" and acknowledge instead the "fictionality of fiction," its portrayal of "nobodies" rather than "somebodies"—insists as well that the novel contains no "hidden code revealing female subversion of the male order." Indeed Gallagher suggests provocatively that "the acknowledgment of fiction," the goal of "the Quixote's cure," "helped women conform their emotional lives to the exigencies of property exchange" that encouraged young women to speculate " '*Could* you love Mr.—?' " Gallagher suggests, above all, that the very notion of "fictionality" embraced by Lennox's novel adjusted young women to a dominant social order that required them to be "marriageable."[43]

My account here confirms these descriptions of *The Female Quixote* as a conservative text that positions alternate perspectives as dangerously aberrant and thus justifies a cure that returns the quixote to common sense. This claim does not, of course, deny that the novel represents Arabella's "absolutism" or her "will to power." The text represents these phenomena, however, in order to focus on them as problems. Doody celebrates Arabella for "succeed[ing] amazingly in making her male kinsmen pay attention to her wishes" and for refusing to remain "under their control" (xxv), but *The Female Quixote* does not condone Arabella's use of romance to control others: it displays these phenomena to show the dangerous consequences for young women of novel-reading and the delusions that stem from it. Arabella surely occupies the text's center, but only some of the numerous men and women who circle around her gaze at her in homage; others use her, and still others simply cannot look away from a freak-show.[44] While everything may develop as she orders, the text consistently offers alternative explanations to the phenomena she imagines controlling. (She cannot, the text shows, control her lovers' health.) We run the risk of anachronism—or, more relevant to this study, of practicing quixotism—when we celebrate Arabella's exaggerated sense of what she calls "My Power" (182), or, at least, we run such a risk when we contend that the text itself celebrates these qualities. The mere presence of a particular figure—a young woman who controls the men around her—cannot establish a text's sympathy (perhaps necessarily covert). After all, both a text aiming secretly (or openly) to celebrate such a figure and a text aiming openly (or secretly) to marginalize such a figure need to represent this figure, even to give her voice, within its pages.

The text's need to depict the very things it aims to reject leaves it potentially open, however, to alternate constructions. No text can determine absolutely how readers respond to or understand its representations. It "scandalizes literary criticism," as Alan Sinfield has argued, to admit that "formal textual analysis cannot determine whether a text is subversive or contained" since "the historical conditions in which it is being deployed are decisive": readers "do not have to respect closures; they are at liberty to credit and dwell upon the adventurous middle part of a text, as against a tidy conclusion."[45] Patricia Meyer Spacks's most recent account of *The Female Quixote*, adopting a similar position, emphasizes "readers' unruliness" and "the fact that writers cannot dictate responses in those willing to commit themselves to textual perusal." Spacks notes that *The Female Quixote* "leaves room for a twenty-first-century reader, and for many twentieth-century critics . . . to suspect a subversive undertone" in it, but "what eighteenth-century female readers thought about the matter we can only surmise." The "most prominent male readers," she adds, "found Lennox's book a triumph of orthodoxy, warning young women against excessive indulgence in the reading of romances."[46] Catherine

Craft argues, too, that male and female readers may have read Lennox's novel differently: while the *Female Quixote*'s "overt story" satisifies "conservative reader[s]" with its "explicit rendering of female error and subsequent submission," Craft contends, "beneath the surface is a woman's tale of one woman's power." Some eighteenth-century readers, like more recent ones, certainly may have celebrated Arabella for creatively using romance to avoid the patriarchal system that struggles to manage her. But this recognition of readerly "unruliness" must allow for reading "against the grain" in both directions. Even if, as Haggerty says, *The Female Quixote* "covertly" embraces Arabella's powerful claims of self-assertion, readers might have missed such clues or, unsympathetic to such representations, may have received her as a dangerous lunatic. My argument here, in part, is that—absent the sorts of formal structures that forestall such assumptions (I explore these in later chapters)—readers were "prepossessed" to read quixote narratives in the orthodox mode.

It was not just eighteenth-century "male readers" who found Lennox's *Female Quixote* orthodox: Maria Edgeworth's *Angelina*, which aims to teach, as we have seen, that "it is possible for a young lady of sixteen to cure herself of the affectation of sensibility, and the folly of romance" (10: 302), also considers Lennox's *Female Quixote* to be a useful tool in this project.[47] (Barrett's *Heroine* is confident that Cervantes's *Don Quixote* can accomplish the same end [349].) The aristocratic Lady Frances, the agent of Angelina's cure, promises Angelina that "To morrow, as you like romances, we'll read Arabella; or, the Female Quixote; and you shall tell me which, of all your acquaintance, the heroine resembles most" (10: 296). This scheme aims to reverse the earlier moment when Angelina, "blind" to her "failings," cannot recognize "her own . . . striking resemblance to the female Quixote" (10: 287). Unlike most recent writing on *The Female Quixote*, which treats Arabella as a vehicle through whom readers might discover (and resist) the patriarchal oppressions under which they live, Lady Frances believes that Lennox's text asks readers not to heroize Arabella but to reject her practice of quixotism. She expects Arabella's negative example to be powerful and obvious enough to convince a woman "not in her right understanding" (105) to "clearly understand" that she has "been a simpleton" and, most importantly, that her reading has left her without "any knowledge of realities" (102). I have been arguing here, similarly, that Lennox's novel positions female imagination as a faculty that distorts reality by "misinterpreting the simplest things" and "magnifying commonplaces into something noble and rare."[48] Like its imitators fifty years later, Lennox's *Female Quixote* reaffirms "common sense" and insists that "reality" can be known only by "subtracting the contribution of the human mind."[49] For most of *The Female Quixote*, Arabella does not encounter reality at all; she experiences a world of her own making. No matter how sympathetically we may understand the oppressions that could have led Arabella to embrace romance as a solution, the text severely chastises her imaginative distortions of reality, treating her remaking of the world not as a creative response but as an illegitimate one, and it demands her cure.

CHAPTER 3

Suspicion and Experience in Sarah Fielding's *David Simple*

I. CREDIT AND CREDIBILITY

Sarah Fielding's *The Adventures of David Simple* (1744) and its sequel, *The Adventures of David Simple: Volume the Last, in which his History is Concluded* (1753), seem to conform to the orthodox quixote narratives I have described in the previous chapters. While both novels display sympathy with the content of David Simple's quixotism—his idealistic quest for a "true friend"—and use this idealism to critique the sordid world that surrounds him, neither seems willing to tolerate the practice of quixotism. These texts, that is, reject the practice of viewing the world through presuppositions and demand that one see, as the authorized alternative to this rejected activity, only what is really before one's eyes. In particular, these novels demonize "suspicion" by showing that suspicious individuals project their own ill-temper on others and thus "make" plots and dangers where none exist. Against such individuals, who allow their imaginations to shape what they see or how they interpret others, *David Simple* and *Volume the Last* marshal the quixote trope, implying that knowledge or understanding is possible only if we can shed our prejudices or hypotheses in order to see others as they really are. But this effort, I argue here, encounters severe problems in the novels, which imply, quite to the contrary, not only that we cannot help but view the world through presuppositions but also that we are better off when we do so. Far from dispelling suspicion as an improper practice of quixotism, *David Simple* seems, in effect, to educate readers into it.

Recent criticism has neglected this aspect of *David Simple*, perhaps, because of our own critical interests that have focused on the production of credit—on how disciplines produce belief in those matters that come to be accepted as objectively true—rather than on the production of disbelief or suspicion.[1] Increasingly convinced that both truth and facts are "produced" rather than "discovered," scholars in the humanities and social sciences have attempted to describe the practices by which different disciplines establish "matters of fact." Focusing on early modern scientific investigation, Steven Shapin's *Social History of Truth* (1994) describes in exhaustive detail the "early modern system of cultural practices by which credibility was accomplished"—by which, in effect, early modern England allowed itself to believe certain claims as fact or as credible truths about the external world. Shapin shows that these claims gained credibility not because practitioners abandoned reliance on previous authorities in favor of a new commitment to direct observation, although traditional histories of the scientific revolution offer this narrative. Instead, Shapin contends, a variety of social practices, their efficacy and persuasiveness dependent on *who* engaged in them, were developed in order to establish "matters of fact."[2] These studies challenge any discipline's claims to objectivity by showing the "technologies" necessary to establish creditable or "objective" matters of fact, which never merely speak for themselves.

Science, the discipline most committed to claims of objectivity, itself has been the focus of most of this work. But scholars have explored as well how other disciplines generate what Simon Schaffer calls "credit-making technolog[ies]." Schaffer himself shows that Daniel Defoe "used the literary techniques" of "Restoration experimental philosophy" to make his "reportage . . . creditable."[3] Detailing the "early modern system of cultural practices by which credibility was accomplished" and recovering the strategies used to "manage . . . apparently discrepant testimony" that could expose the tenuousness of the achieved consensus, these studies insist both how necessary and how difficult it is for cultures to create belief.[4] My account elsewhere of the complex strategies that eighteenth-century discourses deployed to reestablish "credit" in disinterestedness participates in this project.[5] Typically studies focus on how truths get produced in order to show the consequences of such communally endorsed "matters of fact" that serve some interests more than others: the "natural facts" of gender difference, for instance, were used to "prescribe appropriate behaviors" or to establish hierarchies that reify women's subordination and dimunition.[6] This focus on the production of "credit" and its cultural consequences, however, has left only half the story told: we have ignored the possibility that the cultural problem lay less in the difficulty of producing belief than in producing suspicion. Belief, for some, seemed to be all too promiscuously offered. It was suspicion, I shall argue, for which these writers saw a need.

In the early modern period, prudence or restraint came to dominate most discourses, which discouraged an economy of liberality increasingly construed as aristocratic. Scholars have traced though numerous early modern discourses the transformation of aristocratic extravagance into bourgeois prudence: an aristocratic practice of extravagance displayed in the "conspicuous consumption" and "promiscuity," sexual and monetary, of the Restoration rake loses in competition with the protestant "work ethic"[7]; the "excessive" and "spectacular" displays of sovereign power are superceded by an unobtrusive "minute web of panoptic techniques" that constitute disciplinary power[8]; the "gaping mouth, the protuberant belly and buttocks, the feet and the genitals" of the grotesque body give way to the "closed" classical body, manifesting the bourgeois values of " 'parsimony' of explanation and 'economy' of utterance"; the unruly tavern finds itself replaced by the coffee house, where "sobriety and profit hang together"[9]; the "Great Male Renunciation" marks the moment when male fashion ceases to privilege excessive show and conspicuous personal display (which, once marking power and status, come to be seen as foolish, effeminate, and vulgar)[10]; the "subdued, moderate, and calculated" public self, "in whom social taboos are built much more deeply into the fabric of instinctual life as self-restraints," yields its right to "vent" "emotions . . . more freely, more directly, more openly."[11] An ethos of restraint, in each of these accounts, triumphs over an ethos of extravagant display.

Sentimental fiction, however, testifies to how hesitantly *moral* discourse conforms to this larger movement. The eighteenth century's recuperation of Don Quixote from satiric butt to sentimental hero, through such characters as Henry Fielding's Abraham Adams or Sarah Fielding's David Simple, demonstrates the continued attraction of figures whose "deep unprudential goodness" leads them to trust and spend unwisely.[12] Typically in the sentimental tradition, the morally generous are economically liberal as well. As Janet Todd has argued, the "fictional sentimentalist is ardently anti-capitalist, despising those who hoard and increase money and dispensing his own wealth liberally and with speed."[13] This economic liberality, moreover, is matched by what I would call an equally liberal imaginative prodigality. Sentimental heroes extend credit to others' narratives as readily and immediately as they dispense money.

I argue here that Sarah Fielding's novels function, quite differently, to educate readers into suspicion. Many critics have argued that the novels of Sarah's brother aim to produce a similar practice, although critical tradition has followed Henry Fielding's usage and called that practice "prudence," a synonym for "suspicion" that lacks the latter's negative connotations.[14] In *The History and Adventures of Joseph Andrews* (1742), for instance, Abraham Adams, "entirely ignorant of the Ways of this World, as an Infant just entered into it could possibly be," cannot detect hypocrisy: "As he had never any Intention to deceive, so he never suspected such a Design in others."[15] George Sherburn naturalizes this phenomenon as if it were unproblematic: "The Good Man," Sherburn states, "cannot . . . be suspicious, since he is innocent of any knowledge of evil; and thus such persons" are "somewhat too easily duped." But Wolfgang Iser, noting that the "list of virtues that Fielding unfolds [in Adams] contains nearly all the qualities that would make up the perfect man," insists on the significance of this paradox: "it is his very possession of all these qualities that makes Adams totally incapable of dealing with this world," Iser notes. "The very character who is possessed of the highest degree of integrity is devoid of the faculty emphasized in Fielding's preface as the intention of the novel: seeing through hypocrisy." Iser resolves this paradox by arguing that the requisite level of "prudence," although present in none of Fielding's characters, can be produced in readers, who develop precisely the judgment that the characters lack. The text's meaning, for Iser, "is not to be illustrated by the characters, but is to take place within the reader"; the novel "serve[s] as training for the reader's sense of discernment."[16]

These claims about the novel's aim to encourage prudence have been strongly disputed, in part because *The History of Tom Jones: A Foundling* (1749) uses the word "prudence" "unfavorably three times to every one time" it uses it favorably[17]; its villainous characters consistently display prudence, matching the selfish villains described in Sarah Fielding's *David Simple* as "Men of Prudence."[18] What Battestin, Hutchens, and others treat as an ironic paradox—that "part of the task of the hero is to acquire one of the chief traits of the villain"[19]—seems to some to prove that prudence cannot be *Tom Jones*'s highest value. Mark Kinkead-Weekes, for instance, insists that Tom's defects are not "mainly of the head: of the rational faculty of prudence, cautionary memory, intelligent circumspection and foresight. His real failure is in the heart. He has failed to love *enough*." By the end of Book VI, Kinkead-Weekes claims, "it is clear" that "the novel is not about Prudence, but about the need to acquire wisdom through loving *more* and *better*." Claude Rawson concurs, noting that Fielding may recommend prudence as a "secondary virtue," but "there is a good deal of evidence that, as a form of self-interest, it has for Fielding a certain unattractiveness." A certain amount of "guileless imprudence is an occupational hazard of being generous and honest," Rawson notes, and the fact that this trait requires the addition of "necessary watchfulness" is a "regrettable fact," since "that very watchfulness risks becoming unattractive."[20]

This debate between recent critics reproduces one *within* the novels, which sustain both sides of this debate, as I will argue below, because they simultaneously aim to produce suspicion and feel deeply uncomfortable with that action. This discomfort is most evident in the presence in Fielding's novels of the quixote figure, whose unthinking goodness seems utterly incompatible with the reasoned choice and deliberation on which, as Battestin notes, practicing prudence depends: quixote figures, like their close cousin the man (or woman) of feeling, stand for nothing if not the unshakable resolve to avoid accommodating themselves to the prudential world. Sarah Fielding's David Simple embodies both these figures, likened in the novel to Quixote, identified by critics as the first sentimental "man of feeling."[21] David Simple does, on the one hand, embody the "man of feeling" described by G. A. Starr. Starr argues that in sentimental novels "the onset of adulthood, the goal of the *Bildungsroman*, is obstructed, evaded, or undone." "The power of time to transform boys into men and sons into husbands," Starr contends, "is the very thing that the sentimental novel seeks to elude or deny." The sentimental hero, says Starr, has a "child's eye view of the world" and, "far from learning or growing through his experiences," remains "essentially infantile"; he "does not mature or degenerate . . . because process itself is a sentimental *bête noire*." While the "man of feeling" may display an "openness to experience," this "openness does not extend to the point of allowing the hero to be changed by his experience . . . He can scarcely grow wiser."[22] Most critics have agreed that David Simple, one of these heroes, "does not basically change or develop but remains the same David we originally meet."[23]

But *David Simple* is more complicated than this: the novel *does* try to educate its hero, although because the subject about which David is educated is not "virtue" (about this he, like Arabella in Lennox's *Female Quixote, or The Adventures of Arabella* [1752], needs no education) his learning curve has fallen beneath the radar of most critics. David learns *to suspect*. He resembles, in this sense, the hero of Aphra Behn's *Oroonoko, or the Royal Slave* (1688), who "was too generous, not to give Credit to . . . Words" before encountering Europeans but soon learns that "for his own Security" he must "never . . . credit one word they spoke."[24] But even this formulation, that David Simple learns suspicion, is too categorical, for Fielding's novel also displays discomfort with the activity of suspicion and struggles to police its proper occurrence from improper ones. This policing occurs, in part, because the novel's determination to endow its quixotic hero with some prudence must keep him distinct from the negative prudential figures that populate it. The ground for this boundary-drawing exercise is, in Fielding's novel, the category of "Experience" itself. The novel tries to license suspicion only, it seems, *after* accurate observation reveals something awry. Yet the possibility of an unmediated encounter with reality or with "Experience" itself—the capacity to "*see things as they are*" (82)—is challenged by *David Simple*'s fascination with the quixote figure, whose pervasive presence in this novel hints that we never experience reality except through the mediation of an internalized lens or genre. Having undermined confidence that we can ever have unconstructed experience, the novel leaves readers to draw a very different conclusion: always suspect those around you.

II. Producing Suspicion

Sarah Fielding's novel initially describes David Simple, much as *Joseph Andrews* describes Parson Adams, as incapable of imagining in others what he lacks in himself: hypocrisy. When the novel opens, David is "too young to have had much Experience" and as he "never had any ill Designs on others, never thought of their having any upon him" (8). (Later the novel applies the same description to a clergyman "who had no Deceit in himself, nor was he apt to suspect others of it" [143–44].) David's brother Daniel, who "was what the World calls a much sharper Boy," stands in contrast: he "had more Cunning, and consequently being more suspicious, would often keep his Brother from being imposed on" (7–8). David wonders at his older brother's capacity to read other people. David found "that whenever [Daniel] marked out a Boy as one that would behave ill, it always proved so in the end. He was sometimes indeed quite amazed how *Daniel* came by so much Knowledge; but then his great Love and Partiality to him easily made him impute it to his uncommon Sagacity." Fielding's gentle ridicule suggests that David's "Love and Partiality" leads him *mistakenly* to believe that his brother is possessed of "Sagacity," an implication confirmed in the subsequent chapter where we learn that Daniel's "Wisdom" arose from a simple principle: "he could easily find out an ill-disposed Mind in another, by comparing it with what passed in his own Bosom" (9). The behaviors that seemed to mark

Daniel's virtue, to prove that he possesses "Sagacity" or "Wisdom," turn out to mark his vice. But if this exposure disputes the source of Daniel's interpretations, it cannot disrupt the fact that Daniel's suspicion—disreputable, generated by the "Baseness of his Heart" (9)— more accurately "find[s] out" the truth than David's trusting disposition does.

David Simple's opening chapters offer alternative accounts of the genesis of dispositions, trusting or suspicious. On the one hand, as we have seen, David's "Generosity" (8, 21), the trait that defines him throughout the novel, is linked to his lack of "Experience." But this is, on the other, immediately supplemented with an explanation—as he "never had any ill Designs on others, [he] never thought of their having any upon him"—that suggests that his lack of "Experience" is not the cause of his lack of suspicion. Instead of lack of "Experience," David's credulity seems temperamental, as the novel confirms each time it notes that David "was not at all suspicious in his Nature" (103). The text clearly marks the origins of Daniel Simple's contrasting suspicion as temperamental, the narrator asserting that he is "more suspicious" as a "consequen[ce]" of having "more Cunning." We learn in the next chapter that Daniel Simple was "one of those Wretches, whose only Happiness centers in themselves; and that his Conversation with his Companions had never any other View, but in some shape or other to promote his own Interest" (8). Rather than lack of experience, then, the novel suggests that different people are differently constituted, and that these different constitutions control what individuals see, what they overlook, and how they translate signifiers into signifieds, visual signs into meanings.

David's discovery that his brother is "so very different from what he had always thought him . . . capable of what he esteemed the greatest Villainy" (14) seems to do the trick of endowing this quixote with the necessary prudence. By chapter 3 David reflects on "how hard it would be for him ever to believe any one sincere, having been so much deceived" (20). Immediately after this reflection, however, David visits the New Exchange and is solicited by a stockjobber who "advise[s] him] as a Friend"—David's hobby horse—to purchase a particular stock. David declines to buy but gives the jobber "a great many thanks for his kindness," which he believes to have been genuine. Even when, a mere half-hour later, the stock falls precipitously, David still trusts the jobber's honesty. Only after another man tells David that "that very Man [sold] off as much of *that* Stock as he could, just before you spoke to him; but he having a great deal, wanted to draw you in," does David stand "amazed at such Treachery." He then begins "to suspect every thing about him, of some ill Design" (22)—precisely the lesson that, in the earlier chapter, he had supposedly internalized. David learns and relearns this lesson. Much later the narrator notes that "one of the Curses which attend the having ever been disappointed in our Opinion of a Person we have esteemed" is that the traces of this experience act as "an Alloy to all our future Pleasures;—we cannot help remembering, while we are indulging ourselves in any new Engagement.—that once we thought as well of another,—who, with the same seeming Innocence deceived us; and we dread the same thing may happen to us again" (215–16). But this statement, which testifies to the shaping power of previous experience on future expectations, seems questioned by the novel as a whole, which shows at least in David, whose past experience rarely shapes his present, just the opposite. Indeed these lines refer to David's disillusioning experience with Nancy Johnson, a woman who had jilted David for a wealthier lover, rather than to his earlier disillusioning experience with his brother—an experience whose traces disappear as soon as David reflects on it. It seems that learning suspicion is a difficult process.

David has seemed to have learned prudence by the middle of the second book. Although he remains, we are assured, "not at all suspicious in his Nature," he deliberately refrains from crediting as true what he believes about Camilla: he "lived in continual Fear, lest she might not turn out as he wished her." The narrator notes that "as he had been so often deceived, he was afraid of providing for himself those Sorrows he had already felt by too forward a Credulity" (103). But David is capable of keeping to this resolution for the rest of *David Simple*'s first two volumes only because the novel refrains from subjecting him to subsequent tests in the world whose signs, so difficult to read, have provoked the interpretative problems—when to trust? and when to suspect?—at which he consistently fails. Having shown David to have gained some suspicion, the text is wary of testing this faculty too strenuously lest David be positioned for readers as a standard prudential figure. The rest of *David Simple* consists of a series of narratives to which David listens (and sympathizes). The teller of each story assumes the role abandoned by David, who is safely outside the space that might test his credulity. And each of these stories focuses on the suspicion of one character for another.

Camilla's story, for instance, traces the process by which she and her brother, Valentine, became aware of the "Guile and Cunning" of their stepmother Livia. Livia successfully dupes Camilla and Valentine's father and, for the most part, succeeds in doing so with the children as well. Livia successfully interpellates into the ethics of suspicion Camilla and Valentine's father, who becomes, "like her, suspicious of every thing around him" (115), yet paradoxically the one person about whom he will harbor no doubt is his deceptive wife. When the two siblings "attempt to open [their father's] Eyes on her Faults," they fail to "give him any Suspicion of her" (124). When Camilla does finally realize that she has been repeatedly duped by the sinister Livia, she insists that she "shall never be ashamed to own, it was with great difficulty my Eyes were opened enough to see her in the true Light: for I shall always look on young People, who are apt to be suspicious, especially of their Friends, as Persons that can have no real Goodness in them." Such people may "boast their Judgment," but she imputes this suspicion "more to the Badness of their Hearts, than the Goodness of their Heads." (This sentiment, echoing the earlier account of Daniel Simple, recurs a third time when Cynthia asserts that too many people "fancy they prove their *Judgments* by being *suspicious*" [201–202].) But even after her awakening, Camilla admits that "several time[s]" Livia was capable of "deceiv[ing]" her, and Camilla notes that "I began to think I fancied things, which had no Existence but in my own Brains" (113). By the end of the narration, however, both brother and sister, like David Simple himself, have successfully learned suspicion, as Valentine's reaction to David's unusual generosity toward him and his beautiful sister makes clear. "I am not naturally suspicious," Valentine assures Camilla, "but the Experience I have already had of Mankind, and the Beauty of your Form, with the Anxiety I am always in for your Welfare, inclines me to fear the worst" (121). Valentine carefully carves out a space for "proper" suspicion: protected by his prefatory self-description from any association with those who are "naturally suspicious," he can declare that in this case his "Experience" has licensed him to suspect David's motives. While we shall see below that this emphasis on "Experience" as a prompt to (and check on) suspicion, which is justified only when *subsequent to* "Experience," proves more complicated than Valentine's examples suggests, we can note here that Valentine's suspicions are totally unfounded. David has no designs on Camilla's welfare.

Isabelle's long story (over thirty pages in Sabor's edition) itself contains an inset narrative by her brother—the Marquis de Stainville, self-described as "naturally excessively passionate" (160)—a narrative that explores the consequences of *his* credulity. At school a "friend," LeNeuf, warned the Marquis of "the *Folly* of People's confiding too strongly in others, unless a long Experience had convinced them of their *Sincerity*" (160). Despite this advice about the wisdom of distrust, the Marquis trusts LeNeuf's account of the Chevalier Dumont, *the* "Friend to whom" the Marquis was most "sincerely attached" (159). LeNeuf strategizes to destroy this "warm Friendship," first telling the Marquis that, in private, his supposed friend Dumont treats him "with great Contempt" and "keep[s] up the appearance of Generosity" only so that the Marquis "should [not] suspect *him*," then staging a scene, using a boy "who had a Voice so like *Dumont*'s, that in another Room it was very difficult to distinguish them from each other," so that the Marquis can witness the truth of these charges himself (160). The Marquis, who never "had the least Suspicion of [LeNeuf's] Aim," too readily suspects his friend Dumont. His hot "Temper" leaves him "quite incapable of attending to any Considerations of Prudence" and he challenges Dumont to a duel (161). This situation resolves itself without incident after Dumont discovers and reveals LeNeuf's plot, and the story aims in general to warn against *hasty* suspicion: if the Marquis too easily trusted his enemy, he also too easily distrusted his friend. The fact that the "Villain" LeNeuf offers the advice to *dis*trust may suggest that the story itself advocates the aristocratic value of generosity. The Marquis concludes his story by showing that Dumont's forgiveness exemplifies "Generosity—this was being a true Friend—for the Man who will bear another's Frailties, in my Opinion, is the only Person who deserves that Name" (163), which of course confirms the principles David has maintained throughout the novel. But the story reveals as well the perils of such "Generosity" in ordinary social interaction. When, after the plot has been discovered, the Marquis and Dumont examine the boy, they find that "he really spoke so like" Dumont that they "could not distinguish one Voice from another"; this "Imposition . . . must have deceived all the World" (163). The unreliability of experience is evident again in Isabelle's own story—a series of mistaken beliefs and cunning plots that leads the Marquis, now married, to develop "a Suspicion of his Wife and *Dumont*" (188)—where the reverberating effects of suspicion lead to tragedy: this time the enraged Marquis buries his sword in the body of his (innocent) best friend. Once again, although the story explicitly warns against avoiding quick suspicion, it shows as well that the perils of reading "reality" make this simple maxim difficult to put into practice. Dumont, dying, assures the Marquis that "the Appearances of my Guilt were so very strong, that it was impossible for you to avoid this fatal Jealousy" (192). Only more suspicion, indeed suspicion of the most apparently innocent or reliable phenomena, could have prevented these events. Isabelle's "Resolutions of retiring from [the]

World" (195) seem to be the only safe way of dealing with such epistemological problems.

The original two volumes of *David Simple*, then, seem to educate David Simple and his friends into suspicion.[25] When David applauds Camilla's description of "young People, who are apt to be suspicious . . . as Persons that can have no real Goodness in them," the narrator comments that David himself "never suspected any body without the strongest Proofs" (110–11). This comment seems to suggest that David has arrived at the proper balance of trust and suspicion. But the novel never shows this theoretical balance working outside the safety of the "laboratory": the narrative as a whole fails to convince one that reality *ever* offers "Proofs" reliable enough to enable one to judge properly when to distrust and when to trust. The only solution to this problem seems to be withdrawal from the world; the two sets of marriages at *David Simple*'s end form, as Terri Nickel has shown, just such a "utopian community that has no place within the social."[26] This community is asocial precisely because within it the problem that has defined the social throughout *David Simple*—when should one trust?—disappears.

When *Volume the Last* returns David to the world, he immediately becomes a trusting quixote again. This volume's untrustworthy characters, Ratcliffe, Orgueil, and Mrs. Orgueil, deceive David at every turn. They are enabled to do so, the narrator notes, because David "was entangled in the Snare of his Love for others, and his Inclination blinded his Judgment, till he in a manner forced himself to fancy he believed that *Ratcliffe* and *Orgueil* would be his Friends, against that almost infallible proof to the contrary, that the true Words of Kindness never fell from their Lips." These lines insist that, quite literally, David does not see what is in front of him and indeed they suggest that he willingly blinds himself to a reality he easily could have seen. The configuration of agency here (David "forced himself to fancy he believed" the two men) suggests that David blinds himself, but the result of such blindness, even if initially self-generated, is a quixote-like incapacity to see the world properly. David's subsequent capacity to be "imposed on by the Appearance of friendly Colours" occurs despite the fact that "the most certain Knowledge, Experience itself, had given him great Reason to believe those Colours hid beneath them . . . Hardness of Heart" (277). This description, central to the events that unfold in *Volume the Last*, contradicts the narrator's earlier declaration that David "never suspected any body without the strongest Proofs"; here, it seems, even *with* "almost infallible proof" and "the most certain Knowledge," David blinds himself from suspecting anybody.

It may seem unfair to press too hard this change in David Simple's character, since the novel needs David, structurally, to be exceedingly trusting so that vicious people can take advantage of him and leave him suffering in distress—the site from which virtue, in eighteenth-century discourse, can most confidently be displayed and credited.[27] It is important that the narrator identifies David's vulnerability in this way: Ratcliffe and Orgueil "got an Ascendancy over the Mind of *David Simple*, that no Creature on Earth could ever have obtained, had SELF alone been his Consideration" (277). David's virtue—his "Love for others," his refusal to consider only "SELF"—is made apparent through the suffering that his quixotic imprudence subjects him to. The novel can allow David to display the proper "Degree of Suspicion" only when its structural need for his duping disappears, when other characters' experiences substitute for his experience (in the original volumes) or when he is close to death (in *Volume the Last*): "*David*, in the Warmth of his Heart, was going to comply, but suddenly recollecting, that, whilst he lived in this World, some Caution in his Dealings with his Fellow Creatures was absolutely necessary, he put a Stop to the gratifying of his own Inclinations, and dared not so far trust a Stranger" (314). Still good at heart, David has learned to temper its promptings. But what seems equally important at this moment is that David has not noted by means of skillful observation something in "reality itself" that justifies such "Caution," any more than Valentine did when he warned Camilla that David might be "plotting your Misery, instead of your Welfare" (121). Both men have, on the contrary, simply learned or recollected that "Caution" is "absolutely"—and *always*—"necessary." They have learned, it seems, to always suspect.

The nearness of this position to the type of "suspicion" that *David Simple* clearly tries to demonize (those who are "suspicious of every thing around" them) leads Fielding to begin *Volume the Last* with an attempt to distinguish "unjust Suspicion" from "proper Caution" (254)—from what Eliza Haywood calls in *The British Recluse, or the Secret History of Cleomira, Suppos'd Dead* (1722) a "*justly* suspecting Heart."[28] The narrator "depart[s] from the Brevity" she has "promised in this first part of our History" to explain why David was "liable . . . in the former part of his Life, to be imposed on and deceived" (253). Defending her hero, the narrator carefully distinguishes those who learn "after some Experience of the World" to "be guided by that Experience, to act consistently with it, and . . . thereby avoid those Evils to which his Inexperience rendered him liable" from others who suspect more promiscuously. There is an "essential

Difference," the narrator declares, between "the proper Caution built on Experience, and that unjust Suspicion of all Mankind, which often, if not always, arises from the Knowledge of harbouring in our own Bosoms a false and malignant Heart" (254). Published five years after the first volume of *David Simple, Tom Jones* engages in a similar effort to draw a sharp boundary between "prudence," a positive term, and "suspicion," a negative term. In a chapter that "Contain[s] a Hint or two concerning Virtue, and a few more concerning Suspicion," *Tom Jones* analyzes two distinct types of behavior. The first "sees what is not, and always more than really exists." This version "is that quicksighted Penetration, whose Hawk's Eyes no Symptom of Evil can escape; which observes not only upon the Actions, but upon the Words and Looks of men; and as it proceeds from the Heart of the Observer, so it dives into the Heart of the Observed, and there espies Evil, as it were, in the first Embryo." This rhetorical excess signals Fielding's sarcasm which erupts in the next sentence when the narrator wryly observes that this would be "an admirable Faculty, if it were infallible." As it is fallible, however, he judges this faculty harshly: "I cannot help therefore regarding this vast Quicksightedness into Evil, as a vicious Excess, and as a very pernicious Evil in itself." There is, he adds, a different "Degree of Suspicion" that is "no other than the Faculty of seeing what is before your Eyes, and of drawing Conclusions from what you see." He describes this process as if it were simple: "The former of these is unavoidable by those who have any Eyes, and the latter is perhaps no less certain and necessary a Consequence of our having any Brains."[29] John Preston describes this distinction as "a rather mechanical formula," but this formula is less "mechanical" than, as we have seen above, difficult (if not impossible) to enact in practice.[30] These novels demand that readers discriminate between prudence and suspicion but they offer (to borrow words Patricia Meyer Spacks applies to Frances Burney's *Camilla, or A Picture of Youth* [1796]) "no principles for making such a discrimination, except by labeling one a vice, the other a virtue."[31]

The sharp distinction both Fieldings draw in an attempt to define when "suspicion" is justified depends on the confidence that the world can be accurately decoded if we only look carefully enough at it. Henry's confident separation of the tendency to "[see] what is not, and always more than really exists" from "the Faculty of seeing what is before your Eyes, and of drawing Conclusions from what you see" relies on the possibility of accurate observation. This same confidence appears in his "Essay on the Knowledge of the Characters of Men" (1743), which asserts that "however cunning the Disguise be which a

Masquerader wears: however foreign to his Age, Degree or Circumstance, yet if closely attended to, he very rarely escapes the Discovery of an accurate Observer; for Nature, which unwillingly submits to the Imposture, is ever endeavouring to peep forth and shew herself." Yet this essay, here confident of the legibility of nature's signs, also admits that "we almost universally mistake the Symptoms which Nature kindly holds forth to us"—only to recover its optimism again when it adds that these mistakes are "owing chiefly to want of Skill in the Observer."[32] Sarah repeatedly deploys the same metaphor of sight: Camilla has her "Eyes . . . opened," for instance, so that she could "see [Livia] in the true Light." The language used by both Fieldings implies that suspicion must never precede an accurate reading of one's experience; suspicion must be produced by such experience. When Henry Fielding's narrator insists that one must cultivate "the Faculty of seeing what is before your Eyes, and of drawing Conclusions from what you see," he limits proper suspicion to a secondary activity licensed, in the sense of both allowed and controlled, only when it follows an accurate perception of deceit or dissimulation. Sarah Fielding's consistent redescription of justified suspicion as "Judgment" implies similarly that the difficulty arises only in assessing, in judging, what one has already observed clearly. Suspicion is justified, for both Fieldings, only when it follows an accurate "penetration" of reality.

The effect of licensing suspicion only when generated by a prior accurate perception of reality is to exclude the possibility that theory, interpretation, or what seventeenth- and eighteenth-century writers often called "system," shapes perception itself. From early modern natural philosophers such as Boyle or Newton to writers such as Jonathan Swift, as we saw briefly in chapter 1, the attack on those whose "compleat Systems" (in Boyle's phrase) impose order on a recalcitrantly varied or chaotic nature insists that such activity reveals more about the "systematizers"—who, like Camilla, tend to "fanc[y] things, which had no Existence but in [their] own Brains"—than the objects they supposedly observe.[33] The alternative proposed to "false systematizing" is the empiricist ideal of "experimental inquiry" that involves the "observation of specific forms,"[34] an alternative that depends on the capacity to see objectively. *David Simple*'s elevation of "Experience" conforms to this empiricist credo that rejected "ancient authority" and embraced "the direct experience" gained during an "individual's sensory confrontation with the world" as the most reliable source for knowledge. Recent studies have shown that early modern scientific writing itself was far less dependent on the notion of "direct experience" than we have thought: Shapin shows, as we have seen, that early modern science depended in practice on structures of "trust" every bit as nonempirical as those the empiricist supposedly abandoned. If the "factuality" of early modern knowledge depended less on ancient authority, it depended more on the investigator's status as gentleman, positioned uniquely as "free" and "disinterested." *Who* reported a factual truth constrained its reliability. As Shapin argues, "knowledge of people was constitutively used to make and unmake knowledge of things . . . schemes of plausibility are built up through prior decisions about who, and in what connections, counts as a trustworthy source." Indeed Shapin shows that early modern discourse *dismissed* the "experience" of many potential knowers. Whole "categories of people," especially "women and the vulgar," whose "faculties were poorly developed" or had eroded, might be "constitutionally prone to undisciplined and inaccurate perceptions," and thus many common people in early modern England were "treated as perceptually unreliable when compared with gentlemen." "In one mood," Shapin summarizes, "early modern commentators vigorously endorsed direct sensory experience over preconception and theoretical prepossession, while in another . . . they were quite able to identify the fallibility of uninstructed sense."[35]

If early modern discourse had resources available to dismiss the category of "Experience," however, Sarah Fielding's *David Simple* obscures those resources to deploy that category as the anchor, the limit, on suspicion itself: suspicion is justified only if "Experience" itself, inspected by an "accurate Observer" (in Henry's phrase), reveals something to be suspicious about. The tautological cast to such a statement reveals its weakness; but even more problematically, these novels undermine the usefulness of the privileged category of "Experience," as we have seen above, by repeatedly showing that when characters encounter and interpret what they think to be "Experience" itself, these experiences are actually shaped by presuppositions or self-delusion. The novel shows that while experiencing, none of these characters recognize the preconstructed nature of their experiences. Indeed the figure of the quixote, central to both Fieldings' novels, challenges the capacity for clear sight on which the entire project of marking the boundary between just and unjust suspicion depends.

III. The Figure of Quixote

At one level *David Simple* and its boundary-drawing exercises aim to mark the suspicious character as the quixotic figure whose mind shapes (or mis-shapes) reality. We have already seen that the opening pages of *Volume the Last* insist that an "unjust Suspicion of all Mankind . . . often, if not always, arises from the Knowledge of harbouring in our own Bosoms a false and malignant Heart" (254); this matches the comments at the start of *David Simple* that Daniel Simple "could easily find out an ill-disposed Mind in another, by comparing it with what passed in his own Bosom" (9). Both these comments hint that suspicious persons project onto reality what they find within themselves, but curiously they stop short of asserting that this activity misrepresents reality. Daniel Simple's case, in fact, seems to suggest that his suspicions of people's motives match reality ("it always proved so in the end" [8]). Later, however, the novel does claim that the suspicious person sees what is *not* there: "The suspicious Man," the narrator declares, "may often thank his Inclination for Discoveries, which he chuses to place to the Account of his sagacious Penetration; and to the same Inclination also he may frequently return Thanks, for many fancied Discoveries, whose Objects have no Existence, but in his own Brain" (276). It is the "suspicious Man" who "fancie[s]" what is not there, who sees "Objects" that "have no Existence, but in his own Brain"—precisely as Quixote himself sees armies and giants instead of sheep and windmills. This language, as we have seen, reproduces Camilla's worry that her "fanc[y]" was minting "things, which had no Existence but in my own Brains" (113).

Sarah Fielding revisits this formulation in *The Cry: A New Dramatic Fable* (1754), a complex narrative that offers simultaneously a romance tale, narrated by Portia, and a skeptical commentary upon it by a chorus of meanspirited voices called "The Cry," who persistently misconstrue Portia's story in the worst possible light: "Why, O ye *Cry*," Portia complains at one point, "do you by leaving out my words, and putting in your own, entirely change my meaning? I said not anything like what you have represented."[36] The text opens with a debate about the propriety of "suspicion": the Cry thinks that Portia's trusting nature leaves her vulnerable to be "duped" by others' schemes, while Portia considers the Cry's maxim that "*mistrust is the mother of security*" to be needlessly suspicious. Suspicion, in Portia's analysis, resembles quixotism: she shows that presupposition—for instance, that "true and disinterestedness friendship" is "only the chimaera of a warm imagination" (1: 44) and so everybody always acts cunningly to take advantage of others—leads suspicious subjects to "find" danger where it does not actually exist. People who constantly "fear their friends and acquaintance" have "lai[d] some traps to deceive and gull them," who "are filling their brains with continual suspicions and stratagems about nothing," are, Portia contends, "*voluntary* seekers of objects of fear" (1: 37): they create and then find such objects where they do not exist. Such people "*voluntarily* mov[e] in continual chains, for fear of they know not what, they know not whom" (1: 39). Portia's emphasis on "voluntary" insists (like Sarah Fyge Egerton's "The Liberty," discussed in chapter 1) that these "chains" that bind are imaginary, formed by a distorted "imagination," but since they feel real to those who create them, such suspicious subjects "spend [their] li[ves] continually haunted with ghosts, form'd by [their] own capricious imagination" (2: 38).[37] Rather than allowing our presuppositions to create imaginary objects, *The Cry* implies, we must observe carefully what is really there: as Portia says later, it is as simple as "having eyes and opening them in order to discern the objects which are placed before us" (2: 1–2). As in *David Simple*, then, *The Cry* defines suspicion as an improper remaking of reality, such that individuals encounter as real the "objects" they have themselves created.

But this quixotic tendency to see "Objects" that "have no Existence" is hardly limited to the "suspicious Man." More typically, *David Simple* shows how often we are *all* self-deceived, an emphasis that undermines the confidence that we can simply see what is "before [our] Eyes" or "*see things clearly as they are*" (82). Indeed even without the presence of the quixote figure, which I will discuss shortly, *David Simple* consistently demonstrates the difficulty of accurate "penetration." One of the novel's chapters sports the title "Containing some small Hints, that Mens Characters in the World are not always suited to their merit, notwithstanding the great Penetration and Candour of Mankind" (199), and the novel as a whole, as we have seen, shows that the disguises individuals fashion for themselves can mimic "reality" perfectly. Dumont assures the Marquis that it would have been "impossible" for him to discern real from simulation; such mimicry "must have deceived all the World." This problem is serious enough for any theory that relies as heavily as Sarah and Henry Fielding's does on unproblematic "Experience" perceived by a skilled observer. I will focus here, however, on what seems an even more devastating problem that *David Simple* exposes: self-deception may play a larger role in perception than such "essential Differences" (as Sarah Fielding calls them) allow. The figure of the quixote suggests that vision is less simple than implied by the Fieldings' confident boundary-drawing project.

David Simple, rather than the "suspicious Man," is the novel's real quixote, an identification Henry Fielding made explicit in his revisions to Sarah's novel.[38] Adding a passage to characterize David's desire to "meet with a Friend that he could live with, who could throw off all separate Interests" (20), Henry wrote:

> This was the Fantom, the Idol of his Soul's Admiration. In the Worship of which he at length grew such an Enthusiast, that he was in this Point only as mad as *Quixotte* himself could be with Knight Errantry; and after much amusing himself with the deepest Ruminations on this Subject, in which a fertile Imagination raised a thousand pleasing Images to itself, he at length took the oddest, most unaccountable Resolution that ever was heard of, *viz.* To travel through the whole World, rather than not meet with a real Friend.[39]

We should wonder how the presence this early in *David Simple* of a passage that explicitly identifies David as a quixote changes a reader's experience of the novel, since this language of delusion ("Fantom," "Idol," "mad") and religious possession ("Worship," "Enthusiast") undermines the validity and sense of David's project. And while we should be careful in ascribing this ridicule of David's project entirely to Henry's revision (this passage's final words, describing David's plan as "the oddest, most unaccountable Resolution that ever was heard of," are from the first edition), Sarah Fielding uses the quixote figure very differently. *David Simple*'s narrator does note that the "Man of Goodness and Virtue was, to [David], what *Dulcinea* was to Don *Quixote*; and to hear it was thought impossible for any such thing to be found, had an equal effect on him as what *Sancho* had on the Knight, when he told him 'His great Princess was winnowing of Wheat, and sifting Corn'" (76)—which is to say, it had no effect whatsoever. But if this passage, like the one Henry Fielding added, likens David Simple to Don Quixote, it is important to note that the narrator's words here lack the ridicule present in Henry's addition. The lines immediately preceding these place a sentiment almost identical to Henry's in the mouth of Spatter, a character typified by his ridicule of others. Spatter "believed [David] was mad; for no Person, in his Senses, could ever have enter'd into such a Scheme as that of hunting after a *real Friend*; which was just the same thing as little Children do, when they cry for the Moon" (76). If both the narrator and Spatter, then, liken David to a Quixote, it is only this latter sentiment, clearly marked as a reprehensible character's utterance, that uses this simile to ridicule David. The novel as a whole does not seem to consider the search for a "*real Friend*" who "could throw off all separate Interests" (20), to be "mad," senseless, or childish, and in rewarding David at its conclusion with three such friends, the novel testifies that such people do exist and heroizes those who search after them. We can see in this juxtaposition, identical in content (*David is like Quixote*) but so different in evaluation, the competing accounts of Quixote available as resources in mid-eighteenth-century Britain: Quixote as admirable dreamer and Quixote as satiric butt. David Simple is protected from the scorn or satire still cathected to the quixote character by having his fantasies confirmed, rather than cured, at the novel's end. His search for a "*real Friend*" discovers the object in pursuit of which he seemed to be questing quixotically.

Part of David's quasi-admirable quixotism, of course, is his unreliability or, more accurately, the unreliability of his reports of "reality." While we cannot say altogether that David sees "Objects" that "have no Existence," since his quest establishes *as real* the very "Object" (a "real Friend") others (including Henry?) considered to be just a "Fantom," his lack of suspicion does lead him to misread and reshape the experiences he has. He does eventually find a "real Friend," but he also, over the course of the novel's first books, sees what he takes to be "real Friend[s]" where there are none. We have seen that at the start of *Volume the Last*, the narrator describes David, far more deeply, as a quixote whose romantic tendencies blind him (or he blinds himself) from seeing what is directly "before [his] Eyes." And *David Simple* suggests how pervasive this tendency to deceive oneself, to project oneself onto the phenomena one encounters, may be. Indeed *David Simple* suggests that everybody sees through individualized lenses; if this is clearest in the case of the reprehensible characters (the "suspicious Man" sees evil everywhere because he has evil within his own heart), it applies to the admirable ones as well. When, for instance, David and his friends wonder why a woman of Isabelle's "Quality" would be "leading a Life so unsuitable to the Station Fortune had placed her in,"

> *Camilla* could not forbear enquiring of *Cynthia*, if this *young Lady had not a Father alive*, and *whether it was not probably his marrying a second Wife might be the cause of her Misfortunes*. But before there was time for an Answer, *David* said, "*I think, Madam, you mentioned her Brother; he possibly may have treated her in such a manner, as to make her hate her own Country, and endeavour to change the Scene, in hopes to abate her Misery.*" (152)

As each interprets Isabelle's situation through his or her own experience, *David Simple*'s characters suddenly resemble those in Sterne's *The Life and Opinions of Tristram Shandy, Gentleman* (1759–1767), in which, as Max Byrd argues, "[c]ompeting consciousnesses offer competing interpretations of reality," no one of which is more authorized than the other. Since "[n]o correct interpretation buffers their collisions," Byrd notes, "each consciousness rebounds and rolls free again, loose cannons on the deck of Tristram's narration."[40] In Book Two Mr. Orgueil, after narrating the story of a dissolute but attractive young man, warns David that even those who have heard of the young man's dissolute past "are so inclined to love him, that while they are with him, they can believe nothing against him: No wonder he could impose on a young unexperienced Creature, when I have known him impose on Men of the best Sense." David cannot believe that "any body's Wits and Parts should have power enough to make the World forget they were Villains" (49), but this is precisely what occurs to David throughout *Volume the Last*. Although David resolves early on to "no longer give Faith to such cruel Promises of Friendship" (280) as those supposedly tendered by Orgueil and his wife, each act of friendship that Orgueil simulates (he offers, for instance, to bury David's father-in-law when David cannot afford it) "renewed *David*'s former Blindness, again enslaved his Mind to *Orgueil*, and fixed his Chain as strong as ever" (284). The text may describe David as "blind," since indeed he does not see what he should see, but he is blinded from seeing these phenomena because, like a quixote, he sees reality by means of a particular lens that reshapes whatever he encounters into what he wants to see: proofs of generosity.

David's trusting quixotism is familiar from many early prose texts, from *Oroonoko* to *Joseph Andrews*. Few texts explore this phenomenon as explicitly as Eliza Haywood's *British Recluse*, which warns at its start that nothing is of "more dangerous Consequence, than too easily giving Credit to what we hear." Haywood's "we," while often tricky to parse, here refers explicitly to women. Women, Haywood insists, need to guard not merely against cunning men but against idealistic self-deceptions. The passion of love inspires such a "good Opinion . . . of the darling Object," Haywood contends, that it is "almost an Impossibility to suspect his Honour and Sincerity, and the Pleasure which arises from a Self-assurance of the Truth of what we so eagerly desire is too great for a young Heart . . . to repel." She promises that her tale will offer a "sad Example of what Miseries may attend a Woman, who has no other Foundation for Belief in what her Lovers says to her than the good Opinion her Passion has made her conceive of him," a complicated formulation that hints that women's "Passion" leads them to "conceive" of an object that has little "Foundation" in reality itself. Repeatedly showing that "the seeming Sincerity" of men's language elicits the "easy Faith" of young women, *The British Recluse* naturalizes such self-deceptions as the inevitable structure of a young woman's imagination.[41] This account enables the text to offer a solution to the problem that does not rely on altering men's behavior: young women must temper their quixotic imaginations that tend to find what they desire. But it also displaces attention (and blame) from deceptive men to self-deceiving women. Toni Bowers argues that amatory fiction "almost always include[s] complicating factors that mitigate the helplessness of victims (i.e., women), making them complicit in their own undoings,"[42] and while Bowers does not include "self-deception" among these "complicating factors," self-deception structures amatory fiction's representation of the female imagination. Even Haywood's *Fantomina, or Love in a Maze* (1722), which seems to universalize self-interest and pleasure-seeking by featuring a female protagonist who, like a male rake, crafts one disguise after another to pursue her desire, uses its protean trickster to prove the prevalence of female misperceptions: " 'tis thus our silly, fond, believing Sex are served when they put Faith in Man," Fantomina asserts: "So had I been deceived and cheated, had I like the rest believed." Fantomina's strategic disguises gain her an almost "scientific" knowledge of a truth (of men's inconstancy) typically hidden from "the rest," but it is hidden, the tale implies, because women's "Expectations" and "Hopes" blind them to a reality from which each must "wake at last."[43] These tales consistently naturalize the female "Sex" as "believing": women's desires lead them routinely to misperceive their surroundings.[44]

Haywood wishes that women "could bring ourselves to depend on nothing but what we had Proof for," but her tales, like *David Simple*, consistently expose the "Impossibility" of discerning in one's experience such "Proof" as this hope requires. Words, documents, and actions all admit the misconstructions fueled by one's preconceptions and desires. In *The British Recluse*, one man's "Words expressed so real a Tenderness, so perfect a Sincerity, and so pure a Zeal that even" those "too sadly skilled in the vile Arts of false deceiving Man, must have believed and trusted him."[45] Even extensive experience (here described as a "skill"), then, cannot insulate a woman from extending "trust" to men's "seeming Sincerity." Mary Davys's *Reform'd Coquet: Or Memoirs of Amoranda* (1724) features a heroine who eventually learns this lesson. Her mentor, Formator, struggles to convince the witty Amoranda that her independence leaves her vulnerable, "prey to every designing Rascal," but it takes a series of incidents that put her "in jeopardy" to lead Amoranda to become "afraid of every body, and durst do nothing without *Formator*."[46] This growing fear and dependence may seem like a backward development in our eyes, but the tale celebrates this burgeoning timidity. The problem is that, as in the case of David and his friends, learning suspicion is more difficult than it seems: Amoranda continues to trust those around her. Indeed her continued credulity enables one of her friends, about whom Formator harbors "suspicions" (53), to smuggle into Amoranda's presence a suitor dressed as a woman, who abducts and threatens to rape Amoranda. That this terrifying event teaches Amoranda an important lesson is evident when a "fine young Lady" whose servant has broken his leg asks for Amoranda's help: "the late Attempts which had been made on her, made [Amoranda] afraid to desire her to come in" (69). Though "pleased with her Caution," Formator continues to "try her a little farther." Amoranda's safety, it seems, *does* depend on her remaining "afraid of everybody." The lesson seems clear for women: trust no one.

There are, of course, too-trusting men in early fiction (Oroonoko and Abraham Adams come immediately to mind), but Haywood's texts help us see the gendering of trust and suspicion in eighteenth-century thought. Men, it seems, do not need to be educated into suspicion: their participation in the commercial, prudential world shapes them into necessarily suspicious subjects (or, as they imagine themselves, agents). Most men occupy the position represented by the "doubting *Captain*" in Behn's *Oroonoko*, who "could not resolve to trust" and would "not . . . Credit" others' words,[47] or by *David Simple*'s Mr. Nichols, a steward who will extend credit only "provided he had proper Security" (289). This assumption is famously naturalized in the opening pages of Adam Smith's *An Inquiry into the Nature and Causes of the Wealth of Nations* (1776), which asserts that "it is not from the benevolence of the butcher, the brewer, or the baker, that we expect our dinner, but from their regard to their own self interest."[48] A quixote's delusion separates him or her from the self-possession and rationality that, for better or worse, enables the masculine world of self-interest constructed by political, ethical, and economic writers. Women's imaginations, as Haywood's text implies, detach them from the "real" itself and deposit them in a fantasy world that refuses to recognize such simple facts.

It is this quixotic detachment from reality that complicates the gendering of David Simple. Critics have considered men of feeling such as David as gendered female, tending to ground these arguments on David's social "predicament" or on his odd sexlessness: Janet Todd insists that "Fielding makes her protagonist a man although his predicament remains quintessentially female" (David "is forced like a woman into the cruel stasis of family and dependent friends"), and Carolyn Woodward similarly describes "the narrative of David's life" as a "woman's story," depicting David as one "whose central beliefs are feminist, and who, finally, is unable to effect his dreams because he is femininely 'virtuous' to an extreme." Felicity Nussbaum has argued that David Simple "is less effeminate than feminized," an unmasculine man whom the text celebrates rather than critiques; Alexander Pettit explores David's lack of "phallic energy" and describes him as "unmotivated by phallic desire."[49] Another mark of David's femininity, however, is his need for a "suspecting Heart" that could protect him from the dangerous consequences of his quixotism, of his idealistic perceptions of reality. It is David's lack of suspicion that marks him as feminized. David's problems, that is, arise not so much because aggressive men target him as a dupe, although of course this is true, but more significantly, he is vulnerable to such plots because his quixotism leads him to actively misconstrue those with whom he interacts as friends who think as he does. It is David's imagination that causes his problems (or so the text suggests). David Simple, in this sense, resembles a female quixote—in that his imprudent self-deception leaves him vulnerable to, even unaware of, the many around him who are, in Valentine's phrases, "plotting [his] Misery." If men *know* not to trust, women must be repeatedly reminded.

David's encounter in *Volume the Last* with Mr. Nichols reveals the dependence of David's feminization on his quixotic trust. In the "uncommon Dialogue" David conducts with Nichols, "neither Party could well comprehend the other"—largely because David, speaking from a position within the economy of generosity, promiscuously extends trust and credit, while Nichols, speaking from a position firmly within the economy of suspicion, understands only prudent distrust. At one point David, realizing the problem, says to Nichols, "You don't talk our Language, Sir," to which Nichols responds (after he "*sneers*"), "I think I talk plain *English*; and only want to know what Security I should have, should I advance any Monies?" (290). Nichols speaks the language of economics, his speech peppered by words such as "prudent," "Security," "Obligation," insisting that "no one can accuse me of Imprudence" (290–91). Always suspicious, Nichols is "fully satisfied" only "that *Valentine*'s Friendship was mere Pretence, and had been hitherto counterfeited, in order to make an Advantage of *David*'s Credulity" (291); that is, he imagines that Valentine has acted toward David precisely as he is about to act. He too projects onto the world his own partial beliefs. Nichols cannot even register sense in the words David uses. "The Trust and Confidence *David* expressed in *Valentine*'s Friendship, sounded as nonsensical in [Nichols's] Ears, as if he had affirmed he could safely trust a Fox with the Care of his Poultry," and "Expressions" such as "the Pleasure of serving Friends" sound to Nichols like "unintelligible Gibberish" (291). When Nichols imagines himself as a "Fisherman" having the "Knowledge of the proper Baits to catch the several Sorts of Fish" (292)—one sort of which is David Simple—he strips David of the rational agency and self-control crucial to eighteenth-century constructions of masculinity. It is significant that Nichols's loan of £5 leads David to retreat into his "little Garden," where he raises both vegetables to "support his beloved Family" and "little Flowers too, such as Roses, Honeysuckle, and Jessamin" (292–94)—a circumscribed, domestic, feminized space into which David contentedly confines himself. This sequence makes clear that David's way of seeing, here directly opposed to a language of self-interest and distrust, deposits him in a feminized space. Only learning to suspect could qualify David's release from such space. But of course learning to suspect would transform David into something perilously close to Nichols.

If David's imagination is the problem, one might argue that *David Simple* advocates "curing" David of his imaginative distortions so he can—as Henry Fielding might say—join the rest of us, who are, ostensibly, "accurate Observer[s]" with the capacity to "see what is before [our] Eyes." Then David could accurately collect the "proofs" of perfidy that, the quixote trope implies, are there to be seen if one were to only look carefully. But *David Simple* reveals that the demand that suspicion wait upon "proof" is too rigorous and risky a requirement, since the capacity to read the "real" accurately seems foreclosed by the tale's many example of the impossibility of accurate reading, and the consequences for waiting are, these stories show, devastating. Both because we reshape the world according to our desires, and because others in the world make it a treacherous place, we cannot encounter "experience" first and then "interpret" it, skillfully, afterward: our experience *is* already an interpretation. If *David Simple* tries to elevate "Experience" as an unproblematic guide to interpretation, that is, it also shows how distant our "Experience" may be from "reality" because of the expectations, desires, and presuppositions that shape our experience and irremediably separate us from reality. The only prudent course, so to speak, is to practice quixotism, to adopt a "way of seeing" or a means of experiencing reality that anticipates dangers that cannot, strictly, be simply registered by the senses.

One response to this problem offered by this "moral romance," a mid-century form that explicitly differentiates itself from the amatory tradition, seems to be to suggest that vulnerable women should withdraw from the public altogether.[50] In this sense, *David Simple* affirms the domestic ideology endorsed by a short poem by Mary Wortley Montagu: "Let this sure Maxim be my Virtue's Guide, / In part to blame she is, who has been try'd; / Too near he has approach'd, who is deny'd."[51] But *David Simple* offers another suggestion as well: trust no one. David's failure to learn this lesson registers, I have argued, the novel's worry that any heart depicted as "justly suspecting" tends to be read as self-interested: the novel cannot let the generous David become the selfish Daniel Simple. But the novel prevents David's education into suspicion, too, because suspicious subjects too closely resemble quixotes, "overreading" evidence so that it always proves the same thing. The novel's effort to avoid such quixotism, however, leaves it no where to go: it has so dismantled what we might call the "nonquixotic" position (accurate observer)—to believe one can see clearly only leaves one still vulnerable—that *David Simple* ends up showing that the only thing that could protect David from his quixotism (trust) would be an alternate quixotism (suspicion) that anticipates, rather than dutifully follows, experience or evidence. Like the many heroines of amatory fiction, David *needs* to be more suspicious "for his own security." Despite this risk—despite the possibility of appearing self-interested—the novel seems likely to produce suspicious subjects, even if to suspect is to engage in the practice of quixotism.

CHAPTER 4

Mary Wortley Montagu and the Quixotic Dream of Objectivity

Early in the morning of October 14, 1721 an armed footman named Arthur Gray entered Griselda Murray's bedroom and, according to evidence that led to his conviction, attempted to rape the twenty-nine year old woman. At the time of the incident Murray was part of a close circle of friends including Lady Mary Wortley Montagu and her younger sister, Lady Mar. The traces of the intimacy between the three women remain visible in 1728, when Montagu and Murray fought in court for custody of Lady Mar, who had been declared of unsound mind; two years earlier, in 1726, they had practiced for this custody battle by fighting at an auction over Lady Mar's portrait. In 1721, however, the three women still appear to have been close friends. John Gay's "Mr Popes Welcome from Greece" (1720) testifies to this friendship, depicting the "Sweet Tongu'd *Murray* . . . attend[ing]" at Montagu's "Side."[1] In the months before and after the attempted rape of Griselda Murray, Montagu frequently mentioned Murray in correspondence, identifying her to Lady Mar as the person through whom she should communicate sensitive information. Indeed the incident with the footman—which caused public scandal when Gray claimed he had entered her bedroom to see if the married (but separated) Murray was in bed with a lover—seems initially to have intensified Montagu's sympathy for Murray. During the fall of 1721 Montagu herself was menaced with public humiliation when a man with whom she had corresponded promised to publish her letters to him. In a letter to her sister, Montagu recognizes the pathos of Murray's situation: "I have just receiv'd a threatening Letter to print I know not what Stuff against me. I am too well acquainted with the world (of which poor Mrs Murray's affair is a fatal instance) not to know that the most groundless Accusation is allways of ill Consequence to a Woman."[2]

It is "odd" (as Isobel Grundy notes), then, that Montagu's "Epistle from Arthur G[ra]y to Mrs M[urra]y" (1721) portrays the attempted rapist, rather than her "poor" victimized friend, in an admirable light.[3] One would expect Murray, not Gray, to have drawn Montagu's sympathy. The "Epistle" is also odd because it deploys as its principle poetic device the sort of first-person sentimental narrative Montagu would disparage in the novels she read. Montagu's "Epistle" casts the footman-cum-rapist as a "romantic Ovidian suitor"[4] whose delicate sentiments testify that his value is far higher than his position as "servile Slave" would indicate:

> But when I saw! (Oh had I never seen
> That sounding softness, that engaging Mien!)
> The mist of wretched Education flys,
> Shame, Fear, Desire, Despair, and Love arise,
> The new Creation of those Bounteous Eyes.
> But yet that Love persu'd no Guilty Aim,
> Deep in my Heart I hid the secret flame;
> I never hop'd my fond Desire to tell,
> And all my Wishes were to serve you well.[5]

Gray's noble words, which position him as a lover elevated by the sight of his mistress, match his noble actions: he hides his love, he wants only to serve his mistress. Both behaviors follow precisely the practices endorsed by countless English and French romances. Montagu's poem obscures the moment of male violence itself precisely in the manner earlier romances had, not just by omitting events (as Robert Halsband notes, Montagu "leave[s] entirely unmentioned his entry into the bedroom and the ensuing struggle"[6]), but also by locating the stimulus for the action in the woman:

> I saw the languid softness of your Eyes,
> I saw the dear Disorder of your bed,
> Your Cheek all glowing with a tempting red,
> Your Nightclothes tumbled with resistless Grace,
> Your flowing Hair plaid careless round your Face
> . . .
> I fix'd my Eyes upon that heaving Breast
> And hardly, hardly, I forbore the rest. (75–83).

It is Griselda Murray herself, this poem suggests, who provokes the incident. Her "heaving Breast" and "glowing" cheek signal the hidden passion that "tempt[s]" the delicate footman.

A reader desiring to recuperate Lady Mary's literary production as feminist practice might argue that this poem asks the reader to see through this sentimental language, to *both* recognize its solicitation for sympathy *and* to reject it—much as, in Stanley Fish's account, Milton endows Satan with powerful language first to elicit readers' admiration and then to rebuke them for it.[7] But it is precisely the difficulty of resisting such generic language (for Milton's Satan, the heroic; for Montagu's Gray, the pathetic) that Montagu recognizes elsewhere. Montagu worried, as Cynthia Lowenthal shows, that first-person sentimental narratives disabled readers' judgments: while she was "drawn to declarations of individual identity and feels the power of their emotional sway," Montagu considered these narratives dangerous because they prevented readers from "judg[ing] characters according to what they *do* rather than the quality of their sentiments."[8] Lowenthal's words perfectly describe, however, what occurs in Montagu's "Epistle from Arthur G[ra]y to Mrs M[urra]y," which leaves readers judging Gray according to the quality of his sentiments rather than according to his actions. Whatever its motives, Montagu's "Epistle" shows that casting events in particular genres shapes their meaning. Her "Epistle" leads one to suspect that genres can produce effects no matter what events are fed into them, proving, in effect, the power of literary genre over events themselves: the heroic epistle can transform a rapist into a noble suitor and convert a victimized woman, assaulted by a man whose sentiments testify to his nobility (as Gray's do), into a heroine who should grant her love.

Montagu recognized, from her own experience, genre's power. Lowenthal has shown that while Montagu's early correspondence features a number of literary styles (natural philosopher, witty Restoration heroine, romantic heroine), Montagu became painfully aware that "epistolary style and social codes of behavior are perceived as equivalents. Thus she finds herself trapped by the very forms she chooses": she learns to "moderate her witty Restoration heroine's discourse" when she understands that for Edward Wortley, her suitor, "wit indicates insincerity."[9] Lowenthal's example reveals that Montagu recognizes that Wortley reads her generically. He sees her through a lens produced by his reading; the many "witty heroines" in Restoration drama have shaped his expectations and his perceptions of Montagu herself. Montagu's discomfort with this situation, her anguish at being, quite literally, misread, may well have led her to recognize not only the power of genre but its omnipresence: can we ever escape being seen, or seeing, through some genre? Like many of her contemporaries, Montagu comes close to suggesting that we all see through some delusion or another. These delusions may not correspond to established genres as closely as, for instance, Don Quixote's fantasies correspond to the chivalric romance, but the tendency to perceive the world through our imaginations places us, Montagu seems to suspect, at one remove from reality. Writing to her Italian lover in 1739, Montagu likened herself to Cervantes's hero: "I commend myself to you in all perils like Don Quixote to his Dulcinea, and I have an imagination no less heated than his. Nothing frightens me, nothing diverts me a moment; absorbed in my own thoughts, neither the fatigues of the road nor the pleasures offered me in the towns have distracted me for an instant from the sweet contemplation in which I am immersed." Montagu gestures toward the landscape through which she passes, the "road" and the "towns," but insists that she is too "absorbed in [her] own thoughts," too "immersed" in her "contemplation," to see them as she presumes they are: pleasant, tiring, and frightening. And she was capable of generalizing this tendency from individual to national psychology. In 1757 she described to her daughter her "Impatience" with a sort of "English Heroism" that leads the nation to "[throw] away so many Millions without any prospect of advantage to them selves, purely to succour a Distress'd Princess." Montagu argues that recent events teach that England, like all nations, should "endeavour to extend our Commerce rather than the Quixote Reputation of redressing wrongs and placing Diadems on Heads that should be equally indifferent to us." England has wandered from its proper course because, like Quixote, it sees itself as playing a role from heroic romance. We need, Montagu insists, to "open our Eyes."[10]

Montagu's suggestion that we need to "open our Eyes" implies not only that we are often blinded by our imaginations, which shape our perceptions of ourselves and of the world itself; it also implies that we can shed these delusions. Her letter imagines a place outside of genre or "beyond quixotism" from which we can see clearly, a place typically implied, as we have seen, when one invokes Quixote, who is cured of his delusion. As E. C. Riley notes, while Cervantes's novel depends on his hero's mad belief that "a kind of literary fiction is historical fact," we readers "are required to see through the pretense." We must "admire and enjoy the illusionism, but not be taken in by it." Cervantes's "novel leaves no doubt as to where the truth lies," Christopher Braider shows: "What makes his madness funny is its transparence: our cogent laughter presupposes a self-evident order of things."[11] But if *Don Quixote*'s reader exists comfortably in the "reality" to which Quixote eventually returns, Montagu's poetic production enables us to consider, more unsettlingly, that we may never know whether or not we are outside of genre. Her "Epistle" shows how natural it can seem to think by means of the heroic romance: seeing through that genre does not seem like "delusion," yet it shapes how we perceive an attempted rape. The rest of this chapter focuses on a poem quite different from the pathetic "Epistle": Montagu's *Reasons that Induced Dr S[wift] to write a Poem call'd the Lady's Dressing room* (1732) appears to be a satiric response to Jonathan Swift's grotesque satire, "The Lady's Dressing Room" (1730). Indeed critics have consistently represented this poem as (merely) out-Swifting Swift. I show here, however, that this poem exposes a more radical doubt about the possibility of ever seeing "clearly." Montagu's *Reasons* undermines Swift's antifeminist satire by resituating it in a minor Restoration genre that narrates a man's loss of sexual capacity, a strategy that manages to unsettle eighteenth-century satire's most basic claim to expose the "real" that lies hidden beneath superficial appearances.

I. Satiric Objectivity

Swift's "Lady's Dressing Room" narrates a deceptively simple story. An idealistic man, Strephon, sneaks into his lover's dressing room only to discover that his "Goddess" depends on an ugly material reality: a "dirty Smock," a "forehead Cloth with Oyl upon't," towels "Begumm'd, bematter'd, and beslim'd," "Stockings ... Stain'd with the Marks of stinking Toes," and, finally, a chamber pot filled with Celia's shit.[12] This last discovery leads the "disgusted" Strephon to "sl[i]nk" away, and the experience permanently reconfigures his "Imagination" to associate "All Women" with "Stinks" (116, 121–22). The narrator, whose presence until this point the poem has downplayed, spends the last stanzas of the poem denouncing this association of ideas or what it calls a mechanical "coupl[ing]" (when "unsav'ry Odours fly," Strephon immediately "Conceives a Lady standing by"). Strephon's experience, the narrator insists, need not deform his relations with women (123–27). "When *Celia* in her Glory shows," Strephon should learn to "stop his Nose" and, like the narrator, to "bless his ravisht Eyes to see / Such Order from Confusion sprung, / Such gaudy Tulips rais'd from Dung." The narrator, distanced and differentiated from Strephon, argues that the "Rogue" has responded improperly to the facts he discovers. One can know what Strephon knows and not end up, like Strephon, "blind / To all the Charms of Woman Kind" (129–44).

The presence of this narrator, whose voice ("*I* pity," "should *I* the Queen of Love refuse," "he soon would learn to think like *me*" [129, 131, 141]) emerges so strongly at the poem's end, distinguishes "The Lady's Dressing Room" from the other "grotesque" poems with which it is often linked. Neither "A Description of the Morning" (1709) nor "A Beautiful Young Nymph Going to Bed" (1731), for instance, features a narrator who invokes his own experience as a standard against which his character's experience should be judged. In effect, the narrator, seeing precisely the same things as Strephon, privileges *his* way of making sense of or dealing with the observed reality. The presence of this narrator positions Strephon himself as a quixote who, as Ronald Paulson writes, "has read the poets who refer to their beloved as a goddess, and instead of accepting this as a poetic convention, [he] acts upon it."[13] By offering in the narrator a way of seeing that competes with Strephon's, the poem deploys the quixote trope—rejecting one set of perceptions as distorted to establish another set (the narrator's) as objective. One mark of this strategy's success is that critical tradition, repeatedly affirming Strephon's blindness, has endorsed and claimed for itself the narrator's position of distanced and objective observer.

More important than the content of the narrator's philosophy, however, is this structural position of outside observer. Since Strephon, the poem's first observer, is himself observed by the narrator, the narrator occupies a privileged epistemological position: his observation effectively makes Strephon's behavior as much the poem's subject as the grotesque "reality" that Strephon discovers. Indeed this observing narrator's presence has enabled critics to detach Swift himself from the "misanthropy and incipient madness"[14] that critics once saw the poem itself manifesting. The accounts that establish a moral or Christian purpose to Swift's poem argue that, far from endorsing misanthropy or misogyny, the poem explores and exposes the pride and delusions that lead individuals to behave like Strephon; the narrator's presence models a distanced position from which we can see misogyny as an object. For Donald Greene, Swift's "poem pillories" Strephon's "madness" and "obsession" that first "demanded for his inflated ego a superhuman partner" and later, "when his fantasy world collapses, [makes] him see in every woman *only* her excretory functions." Despite disagreements with Greene, memorialized in an exchange in *PMLA*'s Forum pages, Thomas Gilmore agrees that the "Lady's Dressing Room" ridicules Strephon's "idealization" that makes him vulnerable to "drop . . . into misogyny." Gilmore's account shows, furthermore, the structure on which this ridicule depends: "There is a burlesque resemblance between [Strephon's] search and the traditional, self-appointed mission of the satirist. But training laughter on this mission is one of Swift's saving graces and his most distinctive characteristic as a satirist. Strephon totally lacks this ability."[15] The distinction Gilmore asserts between the poem's different figures is crucial: Swift becomes a "satirist" by shattering the "resemblance" between Strephon and himself and, once distanced from his object, by observing Strephon's behavior as if through the sight of a telescope or gun (he "train[s]" his laughter on it).

Some recent critics have challenged this sharp separation of narrator from object, knower from known, on which the poem's production of knowledge seems to depend. William Freedman shows that at times the narrator urges Strephon on: both men are both "magnetized voyeur" and "repelled observer."[16] Freedman argues that the "distinction between the prying Strephon and the recording narrator . . . barely outlasts the lines that define it." The two figures represent competing aspects of Swift's personality (who is "drawn to the revolting excrescences as powerfully as he is repelled by them"), and the poem traces Swift's doomed "effort to separate himself from the prying Strephon." Freedman's account of Swift's poem enacts (and anticipates) the impressive description of satiric rhetoric in general offered by Fredric Bogel, who contends that critics have too often accepted "one half of the structure of satiric rhetoric . . . for the entire structure": Augustan satire both displays a stark opposition between "satirist" and "satiric object" and reveals the "threatening proximity" or resemblance of the two. Satire functions by "convert[ing] an initially ambiguous relation of identification and division . . . into one of pure division," thus making or "establish[ing] the distance that it pretends is already there waiting to be registered." Although readers of satire have "conspired with satirists to ignore that ambiguous state and treat satirist and satiric object as simply opposed," this opposition is actually "produced rather than merely registered" by the satiric text itself that functions, in effect, as a "textual machine" or "literary mechanism for the production of differences in the face of anxiety and replication, identity, sameness, and undifferentiation."[17] Bogel's account insists, that is, that satires themselves unmake the sharp separation between satirist and satiric object, knower and known, on which they seem to rely. Swift's "Meditations upon a Broom-stick" (1703), likening the satirist to the broomstick, which "raiseth a mighty Dust where there was none before; sharing deeply all the while in the very same

Pollution he pretends to sweep away," captures this resemblance between satirist and satiric object.[18]

But readers typically fail to perform the unmaking on which Bogel focuses. The rhetoric of differentiation not only works (Bogel's persistent critiques of previous readers of satire confirm this) but is often also what the satire itself aims to achieve, as Bogel himself admits when he notes the "alacrity with which readers have *conspired with satirists* to ignore that ambiguous state and treat satirist and satiric object as simply opposed." This formulation, along with the description of satires as "machines" for producing difference, implies that when satire "works," it convinces readers that the differences are not made but found. (This does not invalidate Bogel's readings; it merely suggests that satiric rhetoric aims to obscure the deconstructive move he views as "essential" to "the satiric structure itself."[19]) The tendency of readers to embrace the sharp difference between satirist and satiric object is evident in Freedman's reading, whose contention that earlier critical accounts too easily differentiate knower (narrator) from known (Strephon), observer from observed, ends up reaffirming these rigid distinctions. Freeman simply fills each category with a different figure: Swift-the-author occupies the position of observer, both Strephon and the narrator ("both are Swift") that of the observed. A "perplexed inquiry into the relative virtues of denial and exposure whose ambivalence, articulated through the dynamic interplay of character and speaker, is the principle subject and the focus of informed attention": Swift-the-author, then, differentiated from both "character and speaker," remains sufficiently distanced from these objects to "inquire" into or "focus" his "informed attention" on them. Even if the narrator himself turns out to be an unreliable knower, then, he exhibits a *way to know* that, in making sense of this poem, critics have adopted. Freedman's subtle reading, reproducing the structure within the poem, exemplifies most readings of the poem, readings that struggle to install some figure with enough distance from the poem's subject to understand it.[20] Whether the narrator observes Strephon, Swift-the-author observes himself (split into narrator/Strephon), or the reader observes Swift-the-author and each of his creations, the poem or its critics separate out a knower authorized precisely by his distance from that which he sees and knows.[21]

Swift's poem thus models a fundamental assumption of Western epistemology that, as Katherine Hayles has put it, "we know the world because we are separated from it." Evelyn Fox Keller has described more fully this "scientific ideology" that first "divide[s] the world into two parts," "the knower (mind) and the knowable (nature)," and then "prescribes a very specific relation between the two": "The relation specified between knower and known is one of distance and separation . . . The scientific mind is set apart from what is to be known, that is, from nature, and its autonomy—and hence the reciprocal autonomy of the object—is guaranteed." Keller summarizes that the very "definition of objectivity we have inherited from classical science" is "rooted in the premise that the subject can and should be totally removed from our description of the object."[22] Hayles and Keller join a large group of feminist writers who interrogate the effects of this dominant epistemology that in privileging the strict separation of subject from object seems to reify a masculine developmental trajectory; Keller, Susan Bordo, and Carolyn Merchant argue that the early modern scientific separation of known from knower reproduces a psychological separation from the mother primarily required of male children.[23] Above all this extensive feminist critical intervention into the discourse of Western epistemology has exposed how thoroughly science and philosophy depend for their knowledge claims on a strict separation of knower from known to both sustain the objectivity of the knower, whose "subjectivity" is "controlled by rigid adherence to neutral procedures designed to produce identical measurements of the real properties of objects," and to preserve "the existence of the world independent of the human knower."[24]

While this rigid separation guarantees both the objectivity of the knower and the truth of the known, most attention has focused on one side of this binary opposition: the status of the observer. The emergence of Western science marks the highpoint of cultural confidence in the "objective" observer, enabled in large part by the development of a "scientific method" and of scientific instruments. Both developments promised to erase the observer's agency in producing that which he saw. "In the traditional view," Helen Longino notes, "the natural sciences are characterized by a methodology that purifies scientific knowledge of distortions produced by scientists' social and personal allegiances." The "paradigmatic knower in Western epistemology," she adds, is "an individual who" has "free[d] himself from the distortions in understanding and perception that result from attachment."[25] Part of the struggle to control the "subjectivity of the observer," as Mary Hawkesworth shows, occurs by enforcing "rigid adherence to neutral procedures designed to produce identical measurements of the real properties of objects": the scientific method itself.[26] Contributing to this confidence were new scientific instruments, such as microscopes, increasingly available in the 1660s. It may seem that these instruments' capacity to expose the presence of another "visible world," spectacularly displayed by texts such as Robert Hooke's *Micrographia, or, Some Physiological Descriptions of Minute Bodies Made by Magnifying Glasses with Observations and Inquiries Thereupon* (1665), beneath what our senses see as the "real" would have unsettled individuals' confidence that they could accurately apprehend the world.[27] But if, as Steven Shapin and Simon Schaffer have noted, these discoveries "warn[ed] that the senses were inherently fallible" and "inadequate to constitute proper knowledge," science compensated for its denigration of the senses with confidence in machines and in method. The new "optics," Joseph Roach reminds us, "appeared to advance a science of what was really there to see."[28] Science promised that if only our visual instruments were sensitive enough, we could see what things *really* look like—precisely satire's claim, from Dryden (who promised that satire would expose "those Persons, who wou'd appear to the World, what they are not in themselves") to Byron (who promised that satire could "show things really as they are").[29]

Some thanked God for allowing us *only* to see surfaces. In Francesco Algarotti's vision of the Newtonian world, translated by Elizabeth Carter as *Sir Isaac Newton's Philosophy Explain'd* (1739), a countess who has seen her skin under a microscope exclaims that "Nature has done us a great favour in not making our senses too refined"; Richard Bentley's *Confutation of Atheism from the Structure and Origin of Human Bodies* (1692), anticipating *Gulliver's Travels* (1726), remarked similarly that "If the eye were so acute as to rival the finest microscopes and to discern the smallest hair upon the leg of a gnat, it would be a curse and not a blessing to us: the most finely polished crystal would be uneven and rough; the sight of our selves would affright us; the smoothest skin would be beset all over with ragged scales and bristly hairs."[30] These comments all concur, however, that the microscope had uncovered not just an invisible world but the visible world's "real" structure. That this "reality" had, until recently, gone unnoticed seemed proof that it preexisted any observer's gaze.

Such ideology contends that while regular sight cannot perceive "reality itself," certain carefully constructed vision *can*. Augustan satirists, like scientists, could claim a special capacity to see reality as long as they grounded their knowledge in this epistemological assumption that separates knowers from the objects they claimed to know. Indeed the truth claims of eighteenth-century satire depend largely on their participation in emergent scientific structures, not only in its tendency to figure truth as hidden beneath deceptive surfaces (the satiric urge to "unmask, to anatomize, to expose the unpalatable truth" borrows language from science) but also, and equally to our purpose here, in the satirist's *structural* position: Alexander Pope's claim to be "Un-plac'd, unpension'd, no Man's Heir, or Slave" asserts just such structural independence.[31] If, as Dustin Griffin notes, eighteenth-century satirists "needed to preserve the idea (was it only a fiction?) that their pens or their silence had not been bought," this need arose because the reliability of their diagnoses depended on their separateness, their independence, from the things about which they wrote. Unlike recent critics, who, as we have seen, rightly debunk this claim of disinterestedness or objectivity as a useful fantasy rather than an accomplished goal, earlier critics articulated precisely the satirist's own self-image: "The satirist," Ricardo Quintana declares, "is himself not involved: he is . . . an observer . . . outside all the fuss and nonsense"; the "satirist," Louis Bredvold concurs, "is perforce a judge."[32] The opening couplets of Samuel Johnson's *Vanity of Human Wishes: The Tenth Satire of Juvenal Imitated* (1749) link such distance to omniscient vision: "Let observation with extensive view, / Survey mankind, from China to Peru; / Remark each anxious toil, each eager strife, / And watch the busy scenes of crowded life."[33] In this account, distance and separation are not disabling but enabling.

This distance or lack of involvement does not (in practice) prevent satirists from displaying anger or bitterness, but these displays (in theory) *result from* their objective analysis of their culture. Satirists see as they do not because they are disturbed; they become disturbed because of what they clearly see.[34] According to convention, as Bogel notes, the "original moment of satire" occurs when the satirist "perce[ives] . . . an object that exists anterior to the satiric attack," which constitutes a "response to a pre-existent" reality: the satirist is "a figure in touch with the external world rather than someone generating fantasy-objects to attack" and "satire begins when a repellent object obtrudes itself on a justifiably outraged sensibility."[35] While we need, as Bogel insists, to recognize the conventionality of these positions and to resist granting them the reality they claim, we must recognize that satires typically ask readers to accept these conventions as the "real": satire works, as I argued above, when these differences that satire *makes* appear to the reader as simply *found*. Such satires aim to represent the satirist (again in theory) as a mechanical observer, who exposes what Rawson has referred to as the "ugly facts" ignored by fools out of stupidity and by knaves out of interest.[36] This erasure of the satirist's personality constructs an objectivity similar to that which later would be installed in scientific writing by the "passive voice" ("It has been observed that"), which "abdicates responsibility" by positioning scientists as "passive observers, victims of the truth" and "implies that the observation did not originate in the head of a human observer . . . but out there in the world."[37]

Although writers mostly focus on the knower's side of things, the dichotomy between knower and known affirms the objectivity or givenness of the opposite pole. Establishing the objectivity of the knower preserves, in Lorraine Cole's words, "objects of knowledge . . . separate from knowers and investigators" and insists that these "objects" remain "separate and unchanged throughout investigative, information-gathering, and knowledge-construction processes."[38] The dichotomy between knower and known enables, above all, the production of *pure facts*, which, as we saw in chapter 1, was a category first privileged by seventeenth-century empiricist ideology: preserving facts as things discovered, rather than invented, required the elimination of the scientist's subjectivity or agency in creating them. Early modern science's claim to provide knowledge about a reality that preexisted—and remained untouched by—observers and their theories depended on this figure of the distanced and detached observer.

It is unsurprising, then, that eighteenth-century satire, which claims to deploy the distanced observer privileged by early modern science to discover matters of fact, produces as strong a reality effect as any literary form, even the realist novel itself. Crammed full of things, the eighteenth-century satires that describe familiar social spaces (a city street, a lady's dressing room) convey above all the sense of a world of objects, each occupying its own space. The trope often associated with this form—the catalog—perfectly embodies this principle. Pope's famous description in *The Rape of the Lock: An Heroi-Comical Poem* (1714) of Belinda's dressing table ("Here Files of Pins extend their shining Rows, / Puffs, Powders, Patches, Bibles, Billet-doux"[39]) reveals, as critics have noted, the sort of mind that treats these incommensurable objects as the same,[40] but above all it confronts the reader with a series of objects unrelated in any way other than that they are all present. The end of Swift's "Description of a City Shower" (1710), placing all its objects in motion, displays the promiscuous mingling of things whose separate existences emerges clearly through their juxtaposition in a common space: "NOW from all Parts the swelling Kennels flow, / . . . / Sweepings from Butchers Stalls, Dung, Guts, and Blood, / Drown'd Puppies, stinking Sprats, all drench'd in Mud, / Dead Cats and Turnip-Tops come tumbling down the Flood" (53, 61–63). It is precisely that these objects are so unlike ("Dead Cats and Turnip-Tops") that keeps their boundaries so clear. While few critics would now say, as Basil Willey did, that these satires present each object "as in itself it really is,"[41] these objects that tumble down, flow through, jam up, clutter, or simply occupy space in eighteenth-century satire do testify to what Roland Barthes called "referential plenitude" or "the incessant need to authenticate the 'real' ": they signify that "*we are the real.*"[42] Resisting as much as possible even grammatical relations, these items in satiric catalogs seem to exist outside of or anterior to any discourse about them.[43]

This project of presenting objects ("Dead Cats and Turnip-Tops") outside of any human construct, theoretical or interpretive, reaches its apex in seventeenth- and eighteenth-century satires that simply itemize "objects." The antifeminist *Mundus Muliebris, Or, The Ladies Dressing-Room Unlock'd and her Toilette Spread* (1690), for instance, contends that women need "Short under Petticoats pure fine, / Some of *Japan* Stuff, some of *Chine,* / With Knee-high Galoon bottomed, / Another quilted White and Red, / With a broad *Flanders* Lace below: / Four pair of *Bas de soy* shot through / With Silver, Diamond Buckles too, / For Garters, and as Rich for Shoo." This description, which perseveres for more than 250 lines, simply lists the objects associated with women. Its absence of syntax—the poem, overflowing with substantives, offers no help in putting these objects together into any meaningful sentence—draws notice from subsequent poems: *Mundus Foppiensis, or the Fop Displayed* (1691) remarks that the previous satire "looks much more like an Inventory than a Poem."[44] But it is precisely the deployment of this kind of "Inventory," with its lack of any filtering consciousness, that implies that these objects speak for themselves. As Barry Barnes puts it, such accounts assume that individuals "intrude minimally between reality and representation: they apprehend reality *passively*, and, as it were, let it speak for itself."[45] Indeed *Mundus Foppiensus*'s attempt to refute the antifeminist *Mundus Muliebris*—its "Preface" announces that "Men ... are ten times worse in all respects"—confirms the power of such inventories: *Mundus Foppiensus* merely itemizes the objects on which men, too, rely ("Now let us then the *Beau* survey," it begins).[46] Both these satires testify to the givenness of the "real" objects that surround us, enacting what Bogel calls an "important convention of satire itself: the implicit assumption that there exists a historical world, 'out there,' elements of which are both solidly specifiable and distinct from the other of discourse in which they are specified."[47]

Swift's "Lady's Dressing Room," like these poems, generates a strong "reality effect," one which has remained invisible, however, to a critical tradition that has largely accepted the objects Strephon sees in Celia's room as the "real" itself. The critical disputes this poem has generated, as we have seen, typically focus on the poem's conclusion and assess the validity of the narrator's "admonition" that "urge[s]" Strephon, in Melinda Rabb's words, to "reconsider the disgusting vision of the dressing room."[48] Should one blind oneself entirely to "the disgusting vision"? Can one integrate such knowledge into a healthy vision? Should one never have been in a position, created because of quixotic idealizations, to be shocked by "the disgusting vision"? These multiple interpretations, each using Strephon's "discovery" to make a different point, serve above all to establish the "ugly facts" of this dressing room as existing prior to the moment when an observer's gaze intrudes. The critical focus on the many potential responses to the "disgusting vision" has overlooked that the poem never disputes the "fact" that bodies (and rooms) *are* disgusting. The poem's success, indeed, has been to place this "ugly truth" itself beyond analysis. The many recent suggestions that the poem directs its ridicule at Strephon's "assumption about womankind, his conclusion that women and stink are one" reifies ("making something more real than it is," in Robert Proctor's gloss[49]) what he discovers and problematizes only this discovery's meaning. Harry T. Solomon argues that Swift "wishes to expose Strephon's preconceptions about women to the light of reality." Louise K. Barnett speaks for most critics when she suggests that Strephon comes into "contact with reality": "Strephon has seen what he has seen rather than only imagining it." "All that Swift . . . ask[s] . . . of any of us," declares John Aden, is that "we see things for what they are."[50]

Barbara Johnson has taught us to ask what is "at stake" in critical disputes whose exclusive focus on particular questions (in this case, assessing various responses, each of which can be "equally supported by textual evidence," to Strephon's discovery) reproduces structures present in the primary texts themselves.[51] What seems at stake in the critical response to Swift's "Lady's Dressing Room" is the "real" itself, or, more accurately, establishing as "real" Strephon's and the narrator's common vision of the dressing room. The critical debate about proper response to Strephon's discovery has blinded us from seeing that all our responses assume that Strephon sees accurately. To borrow Michel Pêcheux's terms, critics have consistently separated "*thought*" from the "*object of thought*" and assumed that "the latter preexist[s]" the former: the objects Strephon "discovers" are the "real" that exists independent of any observer's gaze.[52] What remains debatable is only the proper *reaction* to what he sees. Our critical tradition, devoted to assessing the proper response to Strephon's discovery, merely reproduces the poetic structure I have discussed earlier, which, by featuring the multiplication of viewers, introduces a clear distinction between subject and object, between the knower and known. In effect the poem's diagetic pattern, in which a narrator/subject observes a character/object, has generated as many duplications of itself as critics need until some subject—the narrator himself, Swift-the-author, perhaps the reader—stands outside the things observed. (When Thomas Gilmore, for instance, argues that the "persona" of the narrator can with a "metaphorical glass" "scrutinize the truth carefully and without distortion,"[53] he demotes Strephon and promotes the narrator to preserve some figure who possesses the necessary scientific distance to arrive at an undistorted truth—capable, that is, of preserving what gets seen as a preexisting "reality" that must be understood.) The critical disputes about what response Swift's poem advocates to the "fact" of the ugliness of bodily reality, I am arguing, reproduces the "dichotomy" crucial to the "empiricist project" between " 'facts' and 'values' " or between "observation" and "theory": the supposed objectivity of science (or satire) ostensibly enables the "abstract accumulation of knowledge" whose "content" is "value neutral; values only enter the picture when the knowledge is applied or used in certain ways."[54] While critics dispute about how to "use" the knowledge Strephon discovers, its validity itself has entirely escaped comment.

"The Lady's Dressing Room," then, despite (or because of) the continuing dispute surrounding the proper attitude toward the reality Strephon discovers, has performed precisely the work seventeenth-century science attempted: separating theory from observation, thought from object of thought, it has guaranteed the status of the latter as the "real" that preexists any observer's presence or commentary. When Strephon takes "a strict Survey" of Celia's room, he sees a bewildering variety of objects—"Whereof, to make the Matter clear," the poem notes, "An Inventory follows here." Making the "Matter clear" is Swift's pun: his poem claims to expose the brute "Matter" underpinning Celia's existence. Strephon cannot stop thinking about these matters of fact; the narrator claims the ability simultaneously to see and *not* see them; Swift himself may understand something different. But neither Swift's poem nor critical tradition ever doubts that "ugly facts" lurk beneath palatable exteriors, that "To him that looks behind the Scene, / *Satira*'s but some pocky Quean." The poem "treat[s] reality," to borrow Pêcheux's phrases again, "as if it were the set of 'things,' each being designated by its *proper name*" and as if "objects" preexist any "thought" about them.[55]

II. Quixotic Standpoints

Mary Wortley Montagu's response to Swift, her *Reasons that Induced Dr S[wift] to write a Poem call'd the Lady's Dressing room*, narrates a visit by a "Dean" to a prostitute named "Betty."[56] Initially the Dean expects Betty to respond to his carefully constructed public persona of elegant dress ("With care his Di'mond Ring displays") and sparkling wit (he "Try'd all his Galantry and Wit"), but when he learns from her maid the stark truth that "For twice two pound you enter here, / My Lady vows without that Summ / It is in vain you write or come," he quickly offers her "Gold" (3, 10, 18–25). He then attempts a "warm Embrace" only to discover himself incapable of doing much more: "The Reverend Lover with surprize / Peeps in her Bubbys, and her Eyes, / And kisses both, and trys—and trys" (30, 63–65). Frustrated by his impotence, the Dean then lashes out at the prostitute: "The Evening in this Hellish Play, / Beside his Guineas thrown away, / Provok'd the Priest to that degree / He swore, the Fault is not [in] me. / Your damn'd Close stool so near my Nose, / Your Dirty Smock, and Stinking Toes / Would make a Hercules as tame / As any Beau that you can name" (66–73). Montagu's poem refuses, however, to end with the disappointed man's invective. Betty contradicts the Dean, contending that the "blame lyes all in Sixty odd," and utters the poem's closing insult: "She answered short, I'm glad you'l write, / You'l furnish paper when I shite" (75, 88–89).

Most critics who have addressed Montagu's *Reasons* represent it as simply out-Swifting Swift, a satire of the satirist. Donna Landry suggests that Montagu's poem "turn[s] the Swiftian rhythms and deflatingly comic rhymes back on their creator" or shows "the prostitute as able to defend herself in true Swiftian style."[57] The poem certainly does both these things. But Landry's account limits Montagu's *Reasons* to simply repeating Swift's practice: Montagu's defense remains according to Landry in the same discourse or "style"—satirically exposing the "ugly facts" beneath deceptive surfaces—that she assaults. This account treats Montagu's poem as if it deployed identical strategies as the other responses to Swift's poem, such as Miss W—'s "The Gentleman's Study, In Answer to [Swift's] The Lady's Dressing Room," which argues that men are dirtier than women. The closing lines of "The Gentleman's Study" reinscribe the trope, characteristic of Swift's work, of piercing beneath surfaces to reach reality: "though [men] dress in silk and gold, / Could you their insides but behold, / There you fraud, lies, deceit would see, / And pride, and base impiety. / So let them dress the best they can, / They still are fulsome, wretched Man." Another anonymous poet, having read the whole series of poems, sums them up: "I find all the Knowledge we have by what's writ / Is, that both, Male and Female, sweat, stink, fart, and sh-t."[58] This remark seems to dismiss this "Knowledge" as insignificant, but it never doubts its validity or that knowledge is gained by looking beneath deceptive surfaces.

Montagu's poem offers a more elaborate and clever critique, however, than merely deploying satire against the satirist, a strategy that would accept as given the ugly facts exposed in Swift's poem (and add ugly facts about men) and, more generally, would credit satire's capacity to "show things as they really are." Montagu's poem performs its critique of the "ugly facts" exposed by Swift's satire through its use of genre. No critic has before enrolled Montagu's poem in the genre of the Restoration "imperfect enjoyment" or "disappointment" poem, which, as Warren Chernaik describes, "portray[s] the embarrassment . . . of a sudden, catastrophic failure by the male to perform adequately in a sexual encounter,"[59] but Montagu's poem of failed sexual consummation slyly alludes to these generic antecedents when it describes its impotent man as "the disapointed Dean" (85). The disappointment poem flourished in Restoration England: Etherege, Behn, Wycherley, and Rochester (whose "Imperfect Enjoyment" was titled "The Disappointment" in Edmund Curll's 1714 edition of his *Works*) each wrote one of the fifteen or so surviving examples.[60] These poems depict a libertine's movement from confidence to collapse, from pride to despair. *The Reasons*'s Dean fancies himself just such a libertine, as prideful as any in the Restoration disappointment poems. Overconfident of his seductive charm, he issues out into the streets armed visually and linguistically for battle. He visibly carries a "Golden Snuff box" and sports a "Di'mond Ring" which he "displays / and Artfull shews its various Rays" (2–4). The Dean's deployment of romance discourse—he tells stories from "days of yore," asks for entrance to Betty's "Bower," thinks of his "Gold" as a "Destin'd Offering," makes a "low Bow" to his lady (8, 12, 21, 23)—may mark another of his strategies, though the Dean (like Strephon) may believe in the idealized image of women this language implies. It is clear that the poem considers the Dean's self-image, whether of masterful libertine or romance lover, as delusory: its "small digression," whose thirty-one lines, ignored by critics, occupy a full third of the poem, uses the Dean to prove that everybody acts out delusions. Described as "with Learning Mad" and "with wisdom blind," all "Humankind" are fundamentally unfit to the world in which they live. Those who stutter imagine they are skilled speakers; those who can "Rhime" imagine they are philosophers; none know "their proper merit." In "all Heads," the poem summarizes, there's "a touch of Fool" (31–62).[61] Much as during her travels in 1739 Montagu described herself as so "absorbed" that reality itself could not "distract" her "imagination" from its own "thoughts," so too here the Dean occupies what the narrator calls a "paradise of thought" (22).

Most critics have contended that the Dean's disappointing experience dissolves this "paradise of thought" and restores his "contact with reality." They thus treat the poem (as, we have seen, critics treat Swift's poem) as a conventional quixote narrative: when the Dean finally "open[s his] Eyes," he encounters reality itself in the "damn'd Close stool," the "Dirty Smock," and the "Stinking Toes." But the poem actually leaves uncertain the relation of this "paradise of thought" or the Dean's subsequent vision to "reality," and this ambiguity allows *The Reasons* to offer a pervasive critique of the earlier poem's "reality effect" and the satiric project of objectivity that upholds it. We might begin understanding how the poem undermines this "reality effect" by considering that it describes the state that *follows* the Dean's "paradise of thought" as a "Hellish Play": imprisoned in a disappointment poem, which always propel men from pride ("paradise") to despair ("Hell"), the Dean's satiric observations merely enact this generic logic that compels the male speaker to find some way to displace blame from himself. Lysander in Behn's "Disappointment" "curs'd his Birth, his Fate, his Stars; / But more the *Shepherdess*'s Charms," while the lover in Etherege's "Imperfect Enjoyment" tells his mistress to "condemn yourself, not me"[62]; Rochester's speaker blames not his mistress but his penis, imagined as an "independent force, following its own priorities and ignoring its nominal master," perhaps even as "another being, separate from himself, his enemy."[63] Protagonists in disappointment poems, then, *must* fantasize (or "make") a potent antagonist to blind themselves to their embarrassing failure, and the Dean's vision of Betty's "damn'd Close stool so near my Nose, [Her] Dirty Smock, and Stinking Toes" enacts this necessary excuse-mongering of the disappointment poem's impotent speaker. Bogel's description of Swift's "Satiric Elegy on the Death of a Late Famous General" applies here as well: "the swerve away from conventional registers of discourse . . . produces an intensely conventional utterance."[64] In envisioning this room *as* ugly, the Dean experiences precisely what is demanded by the genre that he acts out: the biggest joke on the Dean is that he is written by a genre, trapped like an allegorical figure in a rigid definition.

This claim differs from accusing the Dean of deliberately falsifying what he sees, although his final words ("I'll so describe your dressing room / The very Irish shall not come") may justify suspicion that his impotence provokes him not to reveal the dressing room's squalor but to invent it: his adverbial "so" hints that he would generate any description disgusting enough to punish Betty by ruining her trade. It differs, too, from the claim that *The Reasons* exposes the "male interests," in Jill Campbell's words, that "determine [Swift's] fixation" on this ugly reality, the "scandalous image of a decaying female body."[65] As Mary Lefkowitz has reminded us, while the exposure of "personal animosities" may make "motive . . . more important than facts," it stops short of challenging the "reality" of the "facts" themselves. "Knowledge is no less objective (that is, true or reliable)," Robert Proctor explains "for being in the service of interests": geologists may "know more about oil-bearing shales than about many other rocks, but the knowledge is thereby no less reliable."[66] To expose the "motive" or "interests" that lead Swift's poem to focus on the "ugly facts" of women's bodies, that is, may preserve the validity of that knowledge itself. Any account that contends only that *The Reasons* exposes the causes for Swift's fixation on "a decaying female body" runs the risk of reinscribing these "ugly facts" themselves.

Montagu's use of genre to explain how the Dean comes to see the objects described in "The Lady's Dressing Room," however, disrupts the "reality effect" that authorizes the "ugly facts" exposed by the previous poem. If Swift's "Lady's Dressing Room" implies that an ugly reality *preexists* any observer's gaze, Montagu's *Reasons* suggests that the observer's gaze *shapes what he takes to be* reality. Montagu's poem suggests that these objects look—*must* look—grotesque to the Dean because he is in a particular genre. If the poem's opening labels the Dean's romantic vision as quixotic, the poem's end too marks his satiric vision as quixotic. At the poem's end, the Dean's eyes are no more "open," if this means he has shed all illusions to see at long last reality itself, than they were at its start. He has not landed in reality (as critics seem to assume); he remains in a genre.

Rose Zimbardo has recently described Rochester's satires as debunking idealizations without ever arriving at "the *real*": Rochester's satires features "armies of literary conventions . . . in dubious battle on a darkling plain." Zimbardo argues that in his poems one genre that "exists *nowhere but in our minds*" (such as pastoral) gives way to an "*equally fictional* realm" (such as libertine erotica). Zimbardo finds that these satires depict "no nature . . . at all," "simply the clash of literary stereotypes," the "violent collisions among images, genres, linguistic constructs" that "engage in senseless, chaotic battle," a "continuous game that has neither beginning nor ending," "a continuous process that exists for the sole end of undoing itself."[67] *The Reasons* may similarly convince readers, as I have argued, that they see through literary "constructs," but far from depicting the rivalry between genres as a "senseless, chaotic battle," Montagu's poem shows that the worlds produced by different ways of seeing have consequences: the genre of satire that *The Reasons* disputes underpins a particularly noxious view of women. Pierre Bourdieu rejects the linguistic theories (on which Zimbardo's account relies) that proceed as "if words always assumed all their meanings at once," as if "discourse" were "an endless play on words." Only the "academic mind," Bourdieu argues, that "treats language as an object of contemplation rather than as an instrument of action and power": the "all-purpose word in the dictionary" is "in practice" always "immersed in situations."[68] Montagu's poem foregrounds the "situation" that drives people to enact the particular fiction or genre of antifeminist satire. It tethers the satiric vision itself, a vision that claims objectivity and disinterestedness, to particular, situated interests: the Dean may think he simply observes and exposes certain "ugly facts," but we find that he sees through this genre because he needs to sell—largely to himself— the "ugly facts" of the lady's dressing room. The poem, then, not only exposes the "motives" or "interests" that would lead somebody to appropriate such language: more crucially for my argument here, Montagu's *Reasons* reveals the vision that such language produces.

The Dean's satiric vision, the poem shows, is not "the view from no where"; he sees only what the world looks like from inside a disappointment poem.[69] Embedding the Dean's description of the "damn'd Close stool," the "Dirty Smock," and the "Stinking Toes" (satire) in a larger structure (disappointment poem) qualifies the status of these "facts"—assumed in the satire for which they metonymically stand—as "reality itself." His satiric barbs that demean women, which have served critics as evidence that he arrives in "reality itself," merely fulfill a disappointment poem's conventional logic. The poem makes clear, indeed, that satire is the Dean's third attempt to reassert the mastery he has lost: first the Dean blames Betty, then he commands her ("Give back the Money" [80]), and then, after these strategies fail, he threatens to deploy satire to "be reveng'd" on Betty (84). This final effort implies that he will reverse his "disappointment" by generating "The Lady's Dressing Room" itself, which, like many antifeminist satires, simultaneously inverts the Petrarchan *blazon* and shares its tactic of mastering women's bodies by poetically dismembering them. As Peter Stallybrass and Ann Jones argue, the Petrarchan poet believes that he "controls . . . experience insofar as he articulates it," and recent studies of disappointment poems detect a similar structure in which the male speaker's "verbal wit mak[es] up for his physical failure, his poetic performance compensating for his sexual inadequacy": "narrative authority" offsets the "loss of physical vigor."[70] At the end of *The Reasons*, the Dean tries to control Betty by writing her: thinking, even at the poem's end, that he can deploy satire's "narrative authority" to regain mastery after his embarrassing situation, Montagu's "disapointed Dean" never sheds his self-image of satirist. The poem consistently undermines these pretensions to mastery, however, most obviously by diverging from generic conventions (which rarely focus on the woman's response to the male speaker's "disappointment"[71]) so that Betty utters both the poem's sharpest barb and its last line: "Perhaps you have no better Luck in / The Knack of Rhyming than of—."[72] But *The Reasons* undermines the Dean's mastery not only by allowing the woman to speak back: it does so more completely by also confining him, as I have described above, in a genre of which he is unaware. The poem subordinates his self-conception (satirist) within a larger structure (the disappointment poem) that explodes that image and its pretensions to accurate and unprejudiced vision.

Montagu's depiction of the Dean's barbs as generic implies, of course, that they are not transparent transcriptions of reality but rather formulaic: the Dean's vision reproduces the antifeminist representations in countless other contemporary texts. Ten years after Montagu's poem, Sarah Fielding's *Adventures of David Simple* (1744), the subject of the previous chapter, makes a similar point, mocking its quixotic hero, David Simple, for his response to his "discovery" (wrong, it turns out) that his "Mistress" has been unfaithful:

> [David] walked about, and raved like a Madman; repeated all the Satires he could remember on Women, all suitable to his present Thoughts, (which is no great wonder, as most probably they were writ by Men, in circumstances not very different from his.) In short, the first Sallies of his Passions, his Behaviour and Thoughts were so much like what is common on such Occasions, that to dwell long upon them, would be only a Repetition of what has been said a thousand times.[73]

These "Satires . . . on Women" are "suitable" to or match David's "Thoughts" only because they were "writ by Men" in identical "circumstances": explicitly undermining the claim that such "Satires" correspond to reality itself, Fielding's text shows that David's misogynist "rav[ings]" are fantasies available for appropriation by "Madmen" in such situations. The "common"ness of such utterances may seem to testify to their accuracy, but we ought to ascribe such "remarkable uniformity," as Mary Hawkesworth argues, to "the social dimensions of inner consciousness" or to the "social constitution of subjectivity"[74]: men in certain "circumstances" are taught—by a satiric tradition that depends on the "Repetition of what has been said a thousand times"—to blind themselves to their failures by seeing the cause elsewhere. David is not deceptive; he is self-deceived, he himself is his only audience. These utterances seem true to him because they "fit" how his traumatized mind sees things. Montagu's Dean similarly appropriates available modes of antifeminist thinking to deal with his uncomfortable situation. I have been arguing that Montagu's *Reasons* gestures toward a similar insight by identifying the Dean's discourse as generic: the Dean sees what he sees because of where he stands. Perception and knowledge is mediated through a complex interplay between "circumstance" and the culturally available genres, Montagu's poem suggests, despite the attempts of one genre, satire, to position itself outside of genre, as providing a "view from no where" in particular. It is crucial, then, that *The Reasons* deposits the Dean in, and links his vision to, a genre. Although critics have for the most part treated the exchange between Montagu and Swift as a contest between individuals, Montagu's poem provokes wide-ranging questions about the function of satire, the possibility of objectivity, and the omnipresence of genre.[75] The poem's play with genre, that is, expands its target from a particular pretentious man to a genre with pretensions to objectivity.

This is a crucial move because, on the one hand, Montagu's "Reasons," a rare instance of a woman-authored satire,[76] seems to embrace the satiric urge to unmask. The speaker's effort to expose a hidden "truth" about the Dean and about satire itself, that is, seems to constitute a claim to stand on objective ground. The poem's ostensible genre seems to encourage us to adopt the privilege of distanced, satiric objectivity, to accept the speaker's account instead of the discredited Dean's. *The Reasons*'s long digression invokes this ideal of objectivity in suggesting that if those of us who are "Mad" or "blind" would just "open our Eyes" then we would encounter "reality itself." In this account, *The Reasons* is a conventional quixote narrative that deploys what I have called the quixote trope with its deference to objective reality.

But *The Reasons* undermines its ability to claim this objective ground, which satire typically claims to occupy, because within the poem it has exploded satire's pretensions to objectivity. Montagu's poem has redescribed satiric vision—which claims to expose objectively the ugly facts that others, due to hypocrisy or prejudice, cannot or refuse to see—as the view produced by a particular standpoint. When it embeds "satire" within a "disappointment" poem, that is, *The Reasons* shows not only that the Dean's savage vision is in no way the result of his return to reality (he remains within a genre): this challenge to the objectivity of satiric unmasking spreads also to the outer frame, where Montagu's speaker is positioned. The objective position typically occupied by a satiric speaker such as Montagu's, who aims to tell a truth unavailable to the Dean himself, has been construed by the poem as contested ground.

Other features of Montagu's poem may forestall the possibility that the reader will claim confidently this possibility of objective sight. Montagu's *Reasons* refrains from offering the "real" facts about this lady's dressing room, a depiction that might compensate for the way its challenge to Swift's satiric standing affects its own satiric pretensions. It might, that is, replace Swift's "ugly facts," their authority now diminished, with the "true" picture. But Montagu's poem never makes this move. The poem depicts the dressing room itself only through the words of the "disapointed Dean", carefully avoiding any other account of the space in which the Dean and Betty meet. We never see the dressing room as a "matter of fact," separated from human agency. This restraint ensures that the lady's dressing room never occupies a space more "real" than the verbal utterances of this unreliable Dean. By refusing to anchor the Dean's description in an authorized "reality," the poem's structure leaves readers unable to tell whether the Dean's embarrassed anger leads him (1) to accurately expose "reality itself," (2) to deliberately invent a false "reality" for revenge, or (3) to report faithfully what he sees, although his vision matches "reality itself" no more than Quixote's vision of giants match the windmills that they "really" are. *The Reasons* embeds "facts" within a frame that unsettles their status, unmoors them from immediate correspondence to "reality itself," but it also avoids exploding them altogether as unreal by installing a "more true" account. If *The Reasons* were to deny explicitly the accuracy of the Dean's "ugly facts" or to volunteer an authorized depiction of the dressing room, the poem would replace Swift's reality (marked as invalid) with another (marked as valid) and thus reaffirm the standard of objective truth. But this poem stops short of offering what satire typically provides, what Sandra Harding calls a "powerful transcendental, Archimedean standpoint from which nature and social life fall into what we think is their proper perspective."[77] Disabled from knowing how the "real" objects in the room appear, readers know only that they appear grotesque to a man who needs them to appear that way to excuse himself (as the genre in which he exists demands) from blame.

Of course, at the same time that the poem suspects that genre always shapes our vision, it insists that we must "open our Eyes," a tension that leaves Montagu's poem fractured by an ambiguity that anticipates much recent writing that both challenges claims to objectivity while also recognizing their power. In simultaneously undermining satire's claims to objectivity itself and, in the process of dislodging Swift's vision, using satire to substitute one vision of reality for another, the poem seems caught in the sort of bind experienced by much recent theoretical writing that tries often both to offer a more valid account of reality than other theories and to establish all knowledge claims as culturally constructed. As Donna Haraway has argued, one problem for feminist practice that tries to "insist on a better account of the world" is "how to have *simultaneously* an account of radical historical contingency for all knowledge claims and knowing subjects . . . *and* a no-nonsense commitment to faithful accounts of a 'real' world."[78] I discuss these recent explorations more fully in my Epilogue; here I mean to note that Montagu's satire has similarly complicated relations to claims of objectivity. While its trope of unmasking seems to deploy the quixote trope and thus invoke objectivity for its own purposes, its interest in genre, in the prepossessions that structure minds and produce visions, gestures in a different direction that undermines satiric objectivity and may lead us to apply the equation of satire and delusion to our own stance. *The Reasons* may expose precisely what critics of Swift's "Lady's Dressing Room" have placed beyond discussion: that we can never tell when "a touch of Fool" has reshaped the objects we believe to preexist our observation.

CHAPTER 5

Quixotic Perception in Sophia Lee's *The Recess*

I. Haunted by Genre

Resurgent interest in the gothic has brought renewed attention to Sophia Lee's rich and bizarre *The Recess, or a Tale of Other Times* (1783–1785), the "secret history" of Matilda and Ellinor, two twin daughters of Mary, Queen of Scots, whose lives conventional histories have failed to record. But while *The Recess* features the "landscape of imprisoning spaces" that, according to Kate Ellis, characterizes Gothic fiction, it lacks the supernatural figures, the unearthly music, the mysterious groans, and the buried secret we expect from gothic texts.[1] The daughters themselves, who narrate the story and who gain full knowledge of their identity in the novel's opening sequence, hardly constitute a buried secret whose existence and consequences the novel's plot gradually uncovers. The story would look more gothic if narrated from the perspective of Queen Elizabeth, for whom the twins do embody hidden crimes—she has executed their mother and persecuted them—that cry out for redress. Indeed what we might think of as "Elizabeth's gothic" surfaces when Ellinor, whom Elizabeth believes is dead, wanders into her presence and raves madly about her murdered lover Essex; the guilty queen mistakes her for a ghost and faints. But *The Recess* is not Elizabeth's gothic, and this novel of many voices hardly pauses to hear hers.

It is characteristic of Lee's text to embed familiar generic conventions—here the hauntings that Horace Walpole's *Castle of Otranto: A Story* (1764) made popular—in a narrative that leads readers to look at, rather than through (or by means of), them. These gothic terrors seem to Elizabeth immediate experiences, but readers recognize that "preknowledges," to use Barry Barnes's term, ensure that Elizabeth reads Ellinor as a ghost.[2] Rather than contend that no ghost—only the mad Ellinor—haunts *The Recess*, however, I will suggest that Lee's novel does reveal a force from the past that persistently haunts its characters: the ghosts of narratives past. That the characters lack awareness of this force may seem to undermine the analogy with conventional gothic specters, of which characters are all too aware. *The Recess* shows, however, that genres, like ghosts, persist from the past into the present and, although invisible, exert palpable effects on thoughts and actions. Terry Castle has argued that Radcliffe's *Mysteries of Udolpho: A Romance* (1794) leaves the supernatural not so much "explained" as "displaced," "diverted," or "rerouted . . . into the realm of the everyday," a "supernaturalization of everyday life" in which "spectral images of those one loves," rather than "old-fashioned ghosts," occupy one's mind.[3] Extending Castle's model, one might say that *The Recess*'s characters are possessed by genre.

Those critics who have devoted attention to *The Recess* (most general surveys of the period's fiction ignore Lee's text entirely) have recognized the text's interest in genre. Generally critics have contended that *The Recess* depicts, in David Richter's words, "history . . . turned into romance, or even a soap opera." "For Lee," he continues, "history is 100 percent personal: it is made in the bedroom, the nursery, the court banquet, rather than in the study, on the battlefield, or in the countinghouse." In *The Recess*, J. M. S. Tompkins contends, "private loves and vengeances replace political motives, and love . . . accounts in Miss Lee's eyes for Essex' behaviour in Ireland and Sidney's death at Zutphen"; Kate Ellis, too, believes that "Lee . . . unabashedly recasts history in such a way as to make passion its motivating force."[4] The "history" to which these critics (and, they believe, Lee) oppose "romance" seems equated with a narrative of events, focused on public action and invoking interest and ambition as primary motivations, that has systematically ignored women. Erased from recorded history and denied the recognition by powerful men such as James I, the twins figure the suppression of women by the interest-narratives characteristic of conventional historical writing. "By turning history into romance," Jane Spencer suggests, Lee aims to "reinstate women in a properly prominent place in history"; Jayne Lewis concurs that Lee exposes "women's exclusion from recorded history and the suppression of female lines, both literary and political."[5] Others, including Lewis, maintain that *The Recess* tilts not only at the content of "history" (its exclusion of women) but at its form, at the "unified, linear, and didactic systems of representation" deployed by the "coherent narratives of Enlightenment historiography" that suppress "the multiple, the particular, the indeterminate." Lee's *Recess* reverses this suppression by "render[ing] the private and feminine side of national history."[6] Depicting Lee's text as a feminist attempt to replace the interest-narratives of traditional "history" with a subversive "romance," then, critical consensus positions *The Recess* as an important document in a feminist tradition.[7]

It is far from clear, however, that *The Recess* does turn history into romance as these recent critics have contended. Its narrators certainly do: Essex fails in Ireland, Ellinor believes, because he "sacrifice[s] every consideration to the recovery of one adored individual," herself.[8] But the text hints that these narrators are quixotes who systematically filter their experience through a genre of which they are unaware. *The Recess* as a whole never authorizes these coherent and persuasive narratives of Elizabethan and Jacobean history that invoke not interest or ambition but love to explain events: each time a narrator replaces history with romance, a subsequent voice exposes her blindness. Characters within the novel, that is, anticipate the opposition between romance and history but reverse the recent critical current, rejecting romance as something that blinds individuals to the "real." The twins' quixotism suggests that Lee's text critiques those who (mis)construe experience according to romance conventions for living an illusion rather than recognizing the " 'real world' of power" that determines "history."[9] This reading, while differing from accounts that consider romance itself an oppositional strategy, need not compromise the feminism of Lee's text. Indeed, many eighteenth-century texts, including Wollstonecraft's *Vindication of the Rights of Woman* (1792), warned of the dangers of romantic expectations and advocated a system of education that would credit, and nurture, women's "improveable reason."[10]

Viewed in this light, *The Recess* seems a conventional quixote-cured narrative that opposes romance and history only to privilege the latter: most quixote tales aim to dissolve the genres that have shaped perception so the quixote can see reality plain. Quixote tales often use retrospective narration to trace the process by which a narrator recognizes past perceptions as delusion and comes to recover clear sight. In Wollstonecraft's *The Wrongs of Women: or Maria. A Fragment* (1798), Maria understands in retrospect that romantic prepossessions, what she calls the "romantic turn of my thoughts," shaped what she thought to be unmediated experience itself. She realizes too late that her romantic "imagination" produced the "colouring of [her] picture" of Venables, that she was "in love with the disinterestedness, fortitude, generosity, dignity, and humanity, *with which I had invested the hero I dubbed*": "I gave a meaning" to his actions, she admits.[11] Even texts in which a narrator fails to shed his or her quixotic perceptions typically allow readers to see what these unreliable narrators cannot. Wendy Motooka has argued that quixotism in eighteenth-century writing exposes "the difficulty of distinguishing between rational and irrational rules" or demonstrates that "reason and quixotism" are "indistinguishable,"[12] but this claim ignores the ease with which individuals *avoid* pondering the quixotism of their own perceptions. *The Recess* exposes that individuals establish and maintain the confidence that their own perceptions are rational precisely by deploying what I have called the quixote trope: dismissing others' perceptions as deluded, distorted, or partial to claim clarity or objectivity for one's own. When one identifies a quixote, that is, one implies the presence of an alternative space (in which one positions oneself) that possesses unmediated, undistorted vision.

The Recess, then, may encourage readers to believe that they, unlike the text's quixotes, possess unmediated vision. After all, Lee's text does both question its narrators' perceptiveness (indeed, their very perceptions) and tease readers to assemble from the text's hints an alternative narrative that seems to capture the "real" that their quixotic romancing obscures. This process may only further readers' sense of superiority: as Dorrit Cohn and Margaret Doody have argued, in narratives that "plant sufficient clues" to provoke readers to engage in "the intellectual business of noticing gaps where all appears to be unified," the reader is "tacitly complimented on his own wit and judgment in being able to see the difference between the character's and the author's views."[13] The chance that *The Recess*'s readers would glimpse an interest-narrative through the "gaps" of its narrators' romances is increased if, as is likely, Lee's readers were familiar with (or prepossessed by) the eighteenth-century histories of Elizabeth's reign that depict "history" as a series of intrigues fueled by actors' ambitions and interests: William Robertson's *History of Scotland During the Reigns of Queen Mary and of King James VI* (1759), the Tudor volumes of David Hume's *History of England* (1759), Oliver Goldsmith's *History of England from the Earliest Times to the Death of George II* (1771). *The Recess* might function, then, as a conventional quixote narrative that allows its readers to claim clear sight once they reject the romancing to which its characters are quixotically devoted.

I believe, however, that *The Recess*'s structure forestalls such positioning and disables the text from generating the space beyond genre that is typically proffered by quixote stories. Avoiding the comfortable clarity of both retrospective narration (in which a "cured" narrator recognizes past perceptions as delusory) and overtly ridiculous quixote figures (which enable readers easily to distinguish real from fantasy), *The Recess* deploys "stealth" quixotes: its structure confines readers in a series of potentially deluded consciousness as securely as the heroines themselves are confined in a series of prisons. Depositing readers in lengthy first-person narratives without allowing a view from outside to disrupt the trust they elicit, *The Recess* encourages readers to experience a quixote's filter. Matilda's romance-redescription of Elizabethan politics, which extends for the text's first four hundred pages, seems a credible "secret history" until another character unexpectedly reveals its blindness and misconstructions.[14] These subsequent narrators, moreover, are as unreliable as those whose tales they critique as quixotic. No narrative stands outside, above, or beyond the potential charge of quixotism. *The Recess* imbeds all its narratives within a three-volume-long letter written by Matilda, who is accused of blindness both by her sister and by her daughter. It is difficult to understand why one critic contends that in *The Recess* "the tendency of the narrative voice to make confident generalizations about human behaviour has a . . . stabilizing effect" because readers feel they are "in the hands of a thoughtful and wise director, whose moral values resemble [their] own," since *The Recess* refrains from authorizing one of its competing narratives as valid and labeling others as quixotic or fantastic.[15] Each narrator who earns trust by critiquing what has gone before as quixotic—and thus, it seems, uncovering the "real" masked by quixotism—is herself eventually revealed to be subject to similar prepossessions.

Yet these romance narratives are compelling, coherent, and satisfying (so satisfying that critics have overlooked the possibility that they *are* quixotic). They do not seem ridiculous or absurd, terms commonly used to abuse the romances of female quixotes, and it would be a mistake to substitute *interest* for *romance* as the truth that *The Recess* aims to convey. Lee's text is unusually willing to leave readers hesitating between unresolved alternatives, repeatedly staging the conflict between interpretive modes, pitting one productive "filter" against another. Indeed, *The Recess* skillfully weaves its narrative within the fabric of traditional history so that (as its "Advertisement" says) "the characters interwoven in this story agree, in the outline, with history" (5), and this procedure ensures that both romance-narratives and traditional interest-narratives offer coherent and satisfying accounts of Elizabeth's and James's reign. The sisters' challenge to official history lies less in the scandalous news of their existence than in the way in which they have "recounted and reworked" familiar events "from the point of view of the female heroines."[16] Matilda and Ellinor offer few new facts. Instead they offer redescriptions that posit love rather than ambition as the cause of well-known events (Leicester's sudden return to England, Essex's failure in Ireland, Sidney's flight to his death at Zutphen). This structure guarantees that key events remain *permanently* subject to alternative readings; competing and contradictory voices, each possessed by a genre that produces what it sees and what it overlooks, what it registers and what it ignores, mediate the "real."[17] The romance narratives that mediate the twins' experience are no different than the traditional interest-narratives that claim to see only what's there. Lee's novel implies the identity, rather than the difference, between the romance and history that critics still oppose. Lee's text may resist altogether the opposition between history and romance (used, typically, to privilege one side of the opposition for its capacity to deliver "true" narratives), showing instead that no narrative of events can occur outside some genre.[18]

I am suggesting, then, that *The Recess* is less concerned with telling a new story that redresses women's exclusion from recorded history. Its concern is to explore storytelling itself: Lee's text, as Tilottama Rajan says about other texts, "shift[s] attention from what happens to how people narrate what happens." In particular, it explores the role of genres, internalized but invisible to the subject, in mediating what seems like immediate experience, an exploration of what today we call the discursive or constructed nature of experience. If Wollstonecraft's *Vindication of the Rights of Woman* traces the way words and ideas "slid[e] from essays into novels, and from novels into familiar letters and conversation," Lee's *The Recess* is equally aware of the residue one's reading deposits in one's mind and demonstrates the presence of these ghosts of narratives past not just in the minds of "frivolous" women (to borrow Wollstonecraft's term) but in those who seem rational and clear sighted.[19] Although the term "prepossessed" is often glossed as "prejudiced" (Johnson's *Dictionary of the English Language* [1755]) and used pejoratively, *The Recess* implies that every narrator is prepossessed. When in *The Recess* Matilda's daughter suggests that the earl of Somerset's "distant homage confirmed the prepossession I had already conceived," she reveals that Somerset's actions—"distant homage"—conform to the genre of romance that had already helped her construe him as a "humble lover" (316–17). A chapter in Frances Burney's *Camilla, or A Picture of Youth* (1796) called "The Power of Prepossession" shows that prepossession produces both blindness and insight: "the magic of prejudice" both blinds individuals from registering things ("prepossession only,"

Mrs. Arlbery tells Camilla, "can blind you to his merit") and produces what they do see (Eugenia's "prepossession," the narrator notes wryly, "could alone give any charm to [the] sight" of Melmond). One's prepossessions shape the world one perceives and to which one responds, as Nelson Goodman argues: "Habit, context, explicit instruction, interests, and suggestions of all kinds can blind or activate our perception, conceal or reveal a mountain or a molehill. Far from merely recording what is before us, perception participates in making what we perceive; and for perception there are processes and stages of preparation."[20]

The Recess makes its readers aware of the genres that "prepare" or haunt perception, and in so doing it provides readers with precisely what neither the quixote nor the ostensibly rational subject possesses. We have seen that a quixote, as Motooka says, is "one who attempts to universalize his or her own peculiar way of thinking," which seems to the quixote as self-evident and reasonable as ostensibly rational subjects' perceptions seem to them.[21] Both the quixote and the rational subject are confident that their perceptions reproduce an unmediated reality. The peculiar structure of *The Recess*, however, disables its readers from settling into this position of perceptual confidence. Instead, it leaves them suspended between crediting an interpretation shaped by the ghost of romance narratives and crediting an alternative, largely assembled themselves, whose structural similarity to quixotic narratives undermines its validity. Keeping both these possibilities in play, *The Recess* denies its readers (like its characters) the capacity to know the "truth" about events and leaves them "wonder[ing]," as Anne Stevens says, "where the truth of the novel resides."[22]

The fact that readers' epistemological difficulties reproduce those of the characters themselves may suggest that Lee's text is primarily not about *historical* understanding at all, despite claims that "Lee dramatizes the inevitable partialities of point of view in the perception and construction of historical character" or that *The Recess* demonstrates that "modes of mediation like fiction and fantasy" are "crucial" to the "reproduction of the past."[23] *The Recess* shows that "fiction and fantasy" are involved not merely in the "reproduction of the past" but in the production of each individual's present: the genre that haunts Matilda and Emily, after all, shapes their present experience. Fredric Jameson has suggested that those attempting to understand the past are "haunted by the nagging suspicion that we have all the while remained locked in our own present . . . that we have never really left home at all, that our feeling of *Verstehen* is little better than mere psychological projection."[24] *The Recess* suggests that such suspicions, too often visible only when we try to understand "Other Times" (in the words of Lee's subtitle), ought to haunt our understanding of everyday experience.

II. Quixotic Sisters

It may be that critics have overlooked the quixotism of Matilda and Ellinor, which, as I demonstrate in this section, the novel carefully constructs, because *The Recess* obscures the convention with which, as we have seen, so many eighteenth-century quixote tales begin: a description of the solitary childhood of a young heroine kept company only by her books. Lennox's *The Female Quixote, or The Adventures of Arabella* (1752), in which Arabella's "Fondness for Reading" the "great Store of Romances" in her father's library leaves her "supposing [that] Romances," from which "she drew all her Notions and Expectations," "were real Pictures of Life," famously begins this way. But Arabella's quixotism is only more evident than other characters', from the protagonist of Frances Sheridan's *Memoirs of Miss Sidney Bidulph, Extracted from Her Own Journal* (1761) who "formed [her] notions" of the world "only from romances" to the heroine of Mary Hays's *Memoirs of Emma Courtney* (1796) who "sigh[s] for a romance that would never end" after reading "the Arabian Nights, Turkish Tales, and other works of like marvellous import." Jane Austen's *Northanger Abbey* (1818) "show[s] a character," as Claudia Johnson says, "in the grips of self-delusion," which has resulted from consuming too many gothic novels.[25] *The Recess*'s heroines, raised in isolation, alone with their books, resemble these heroines. "Young hearts," Matilda notes, "teem with unformed ideas, and are but too susceptible of elevated and enthusiastic impressions" (8). Their nurse empties her "memory . . . overcharged with those marvellous tales children always delight in" into the sisters' ears, and books were another "customary resource" for amusement. The tales they tell each other about their confinement reveals the type of book they read: "Ellinor, whose lively imagination readily imbibed the extravagant, conjectured we were in the power of some giant; nay, such was her disgust to Father Anthony, that she sometimes apprehended he was a magician, and would one day or other devour us. I had a very different idea; and fancied our retreat a hallowed circle to seclude us from the wicked, while Father Anthony was our guardian genius" (9). Eugenia DeLamotte notes that the sisters' two "opposing theories" portray domestic space as either "nightmare or hallowed retreat," but this opposition masks the girls' shared practice of explaining their experience by filtering it through romance discourse.[26] Matilda excuses these fancies by declaring that a "young heart is frequently engrossed by a favorite idea . . . nor is it then wonderful ours were thus possessed" (10), but Lee's novel suggests that having once "possessed" these sisters, romance discourse continues to shape their perceptions throughout their lives.

The Recess begins, however, by *not* stressing its heroines' quixotism. On the contrary, it encourages readers to credit their stories. The text's first long narrative (16–35), in which the twins' governess, Mrs. Marlow, "reveal[s]" to them the "secret" that they are the Queen of Scots' daughters (16), seems to establish *The Recess* as a "secret history." Such tales, familiar from Delarivier Manley's *Secret History of Queen Zarah and the Zarazians* (1704) and her *Secret Memoirs and Manners of Several Persons of Quality of Both Sexes. From the New Atalantis, an Island in the Mediterranean* (1709), assume that while "official" accounts "tell false stories . . . secret histories tell true ones."[27] Matilda notes that their governess delivered this "history of our parents" with "an ardor that evinced the sincerity of her words," and Mrs. Marlow's story is authenticated by a "casket, which contained the papers she mentioned, and divers attestations, signed by herself, and the late Lady Scroope" (36).[28] When, only pages after Mrs. Marlow's history ends, Matilda begins her own, her narrative seems to continue the secret history that Mrs. Marlow's had begun. When the fugitive Earl of Leicester arrives at the Recess, he and Matilda fall in love, marry, and necessarily hide their marriage from a queen known (as Robertson's *History* shows) for being "naturally jealous."[29] Leicester installs the sisters, disguised as musicians, in his estate, and at Kenilworth and London they meet Elizabeth herself and Philip Sidney (who falls in love with Matilda). Elizabeth's jealousy repeatedly threatens their happiness, however, as she summons Leicester to court and decides to marry him. Leicester flees with Matilda, eventually reaching France where he is assassinated. Little encourages readers to doubt Matilda's secret history, in large part because she narrates it herself: we cannot see how others see Matilda.

It is Ellinor's narrative, beginning late in the second volume, that suddenly repositions Matilda as a quixote. Revealing that she "judge[d]" Leicester's character "in so different a light" than her sister, Ellinor contends that Leicester's "passion" was only "apparent" although it "had to [Matilda] the charms of reality" (155–56). Ellinor insists that Matilda's "delusions of love" enabled her to endure a "situation . . . so obscure and abject" and to ignore Leicester's "ambition, pride, and vanity." Leicester "amuse[d] himself" with Matilda only because her lineage established her as a contender for Elizabeth's throne. "Uniting thus in your own person the strongest powers of charming, with such as were peculiarly congenial to the heart you wished to win," Ellinor tells Matilda, "it laid itself at your feet" (156–57). Ellinor's suggestion that Leicester has pursued Matilda as a means to gain power and prestige had been proposed earlier by Father Anthony, the sisters' second guardian. Anthony initially suspects that Leicester, "the favourite of Elizabeth," has an "interest" in "deliver[ing] them up to exalt himself by the total silent ruin of the Stuarts" (61–62), but he soon suspects that Leicester plans not to betray but rather to ally himself to the twins. Anthony predicts to Matilda that when Leicester "demands your hand, you will indulge a thousand romantic sallies, and see in his request a love as blind as your own," and he warns her that Leicester "recollects that your mother is the next in succession to the crown of England—that she may die in prison, and that the aversion the English ever entertain to a foreign sway, may prevail over the prior claim of your brother James, and his [Leicester's] ambition may be gratified by a preference given to you" (62–63). Anthony is right that Leicester "recollects" this political situation. Leicester himself reminds Matilda that "Elizabeth is now declining" and the "compassion of the people has been kept alive for Mary these seventeen years; should we lose Elizabeth, [Mary's] very imprisonment would turn to her advantage, by keeping her in the midst of a kingdom to which she is the lawful heir" (70). More crucial than the presence of these remarks is the way in which Matilda's romance narrative renders their significance nearly invisible: only when Ellinor introduces suspicions by insisting that romantic prepossessions have "blind[ed]" or "delu[ded]" Matilda from seeing Leicester's political "ambition[s]" do Anthony's and Leciester's words attain the status of clues to a truth that Matilda herself cannot perceive.

Matilda's narrative delivers to the reader (as romance delivers her experience to her) a world shaped by the romance narratives she has read. Lee's text leads readers first, that is, to see *by means of*—only later to *look at*—the romance prepossessions that shape Matilda's account. The text initially leads us "not to see" romance "at all" (to paraphrase Hans Kellner), but instead to experience the "knowledge of reality" romance produces.[30] Matilda's initial encounter with Leicester, for instance, rehearses the moment in Shakespeare's *Tempest* when Miranda first glimpses Ferdinand's "brave form"—an association Matilda herself acknowledges when she admits that she spoke "in the language of Miranda" and quotes from *The Tempest* itself (63). Leicester is the first man, other than her priestly uncle, that

Matilda has ever seen, and, like Miranda, she falls hard. Before she even sees Leicester his "voice ... sunk at once from my ear to my heart" and, despite her desire for safety, her "eyes longed to claim acquaintance with the features to which that voice belonged." Prospero warns Miranda to be wary of immediate attraction: "Thou think'st there is no more such shapes as he, / Having seen but him and Caliban," Prospero notes: "foolish wench! / To th' most of men this is a Caliban, / And they to him are angels."[31] But Matilda has no Prospero to advise her or, for that matter, to train the man to whom from first sight she seems bound. The filter of romance through which, as her reference to *The Tempest* signals, Matilda's experiences pass continues to shape her narrative. She "blushes ... when the stranger took [her] hand" (39), "tears [steal] from under their lids" when with "anguish" she and Leicester part, and she believes they communicate instantaneously through glances ("Oh, how much passed in the silence of that moment!"). Her enthusiastic assertions of their love—"No, he will never forget me, sighed I to myself, in whatever remote solitude I am again lost to him; this dreary Recess, the daughters of Mary, in their rustic garb and lowly manner, will eclipse all the glories of a court, all the gifts of Elizabeth" (60–61)—confidently depict ideal romance lovers.

Yet after Ellinor drops her bombshell (and perhaps to suspicious readers earlier), this mutual love seems more a product of the romance prepossessions that filter Matilda's experience than an accurate reading of Leicester's feelings. Her testimony that between her and Leicester "the intercourse of the eyes and heart took place of that of the tongue"—because the "serene delight" that "animated us alike" could not "be conveyed by language"—shows how the romance convention that lovers communicate by glances can explain away to one lover the other's silence. Matilda's admission that "nothing was more remote from our thoughts than what we conversed about" implies that the two exchange no love banter. Her romance filter, that is, consistently enables Matilda to not see Leicester's lack of concern or, more accurately, to see it as "proof ... of a matchless affection" (65). When Leicester "delay[s] our meeting for some little time, lest his immediately retiring from court should lead the curious to search into the cause," she enthuses that with such "proofs of his attention" all her "doubts" about his affection can "vanish" (65). His equal attention to Ellinor requires all Matilda's quixotic powers, but she manages to interpret Leicester's decision to place both sisters equally in charge of Kenilworth during his absence (he "directed that I should preside one month, and my sister the next") as a sign of his concern that nobody be able "to fix on his favourite" (69). When she notes that "a thousand times he assured Ellinor of his esteem and affection: to me he said nothing, but pressing the hand he still held, its trembling confessed it knew all the distinction," Matilda makes Leicester's hand "confess" a secret that his lips refuse ("to me he said nothing"). Matilda's ability to squeeze confessions of devotion from even the most unlikely events reveals the power of prepossession to make certain things signify (his trembling hands) and others disappear (his silence).

It is easy in retrospect, prompted by Ellinor, to see that Matilda's romance prepossessions prevent her from seeing Leicester as a skilled politician. Matilda sees "his fondness" everywhere (64), but for Leicester these "daughters of Mary" never "eclipse all the glories of a court, all the gifts of Elizabeth," and he never ceases to favor Elizabeth over Matilda. Immediately after their wedding, Leicester abandons Matilda for court, a "peculiarity" she registers and that prompts her resigned sigh that she was "born for obedience" (63). Leicester rejects Matilda's plea that he work to release Mary from prison by insisting that he owes his "perfect duty" to Elizabeth, and he threatens Matilda not to encourage him to violate this duty lest he "remember, with regret, the fatal advice which had misled me." Matilda calls these remarks "reasoning so just," but they fall short of the ideal response of a romance lover caught between love and duty (70). That Leicester's initial words to the two sisters, which promise to "claim the guardianship of the Royal Mary's beauteous children," invoke political rather than romantic interests may reflect his permanent priorities. Matilda believes that love for her motivates his political ambition, but the text suggests that political ambition may have produced Matilda as a desirable object.

Ellinor's exposure of Matilda's quixotism is not, however, the last stop in the narrative's journey; had it been, we might properly describe *The Recess* as a conventional quixote-cured narrative. But quixotism runs deep in this family, and Ellinor, who sees Matilda's quixotism, is blind to her own—a common characteristic, as we have seen in chapter 2, of quixotes. Immediately after Ellinor punctures Matilda's romantic confidence that her "generous Leicester" acted from love, Lee's text shows that the same genre that possessed Matilda possesses Ellinor, who narrates her own history with the man she calls "the generous Essex." Although she redescribes her sister's experience as an interest-narrative, her own as she tells it enacts a romance: Ellinor blames Essex's failure to subjugate Ireland on his jealousy of Tyrone, the Irish rebel leader, who had taken her hostage. In particular, she "impute[s]" the "rash proposal of Essex to confer with Tyrone from the opposite banks of a rivulet," an event that had puzzled historians such as Hume,[32] to "the passionate desire a lover ever has to judge of the person and talents of the man who dares to rival him." Ellinor insists that despair over her capture transformed Essex from "a cool and prudent General" to "a mad and extravagant lover, ready to sacrifice every thing to the recovery of one adored individual." Subjected by "passion, to terror, to agony, to every torturing excess of overstrained sensibility . . . the generous Essex was gradually sacrificing the whole renown of a life hitherto so glorious." Ellinor dismisses the "misjudg[ments]" of the "busy world which sees only the surface of things," almost as if she had read different accounts of Essex's behavior and aimed to assert her own: "to timidity, to avarice, to indolence, to ambition, by turns, has been ascribed an incident, of which love had all the merit or the shame" (226–27).

It is Lady Pembroke who redirects the charge of quixotism that Ellinor leveled against Matilda at Ellinor herself. Immediately after Ellinor's account breaks off, Lady Pembroke describes her as a "fair visionary, who so easily adopts the romance of her lover" and who "had a very partial knowledge of his character, or information of his actions" (220, 256). She substantiates this charge by renarrating events of Essex's career such that Ellinor disappears as its central figure. Borrowing Robertson's depiction of Elizabeth's court as "divided . . . between two powerful factions, which contended for the supreme direction of affairs," one led by the "earl of Essex," the other by "sir Robert Cecil, the son of lord treasurer Burleigh,"[33] Lady Pembroke's account foregrounds the court politics in which "the Cecil family" acted as Essex's "inflexible enemies" (257). Lady Pembroke posits "dangerous and precarious projects" to seize the crown as Essex's ruling motivation (259). Essex himself, indeed, admits these political considerations, differentiating Leicester's "policy" to establish Matilda's claim from his own "project" to "establish [Ellinor's] rights" to the throne once "Elizabeth should expire" on the grounds that he is "more capable" than Leicester and "noble in many generations, and princely in some": both "circumstances and merit . . . entitle [him] to match with" Ellinor. Essex admits that the Crown has "long been the ultimate object of my life; every action and view has had a secret reference to it"; it was to further this project that he "continually ranged the seas, watched in camps, disciplined armies, and by every possible means studied to increase my military fame, knowledge, and popularity, as what must one day decide more than my own fate" (214–15). But these remarks never lead the "visionary" Ellinor to suspect "the romance of her lover." She "instantaneously adopt[s]" Essex's "aspiring project" (215–16) and construes his ambition as romantic generosity: "the generous Essex" has offered her a "throne" to "share . . . with the choice of my heart." Ellinor never suspects that it is her lineage—Essex calls her "born . . . for empire" and vows to employ "every art to procure . . . incontestable evidence of your birth"—that draws Essex to her so he can realize the "ultimate object of [his] life."

It is tempting to believe that these interest-narratives—which narrators use to explain others' experience but cannot apply to their own, and which my reading here has assembled—mark the "real" beneath quixotic delusion. But *The Recess* cannot insulate these interest-narratives, merely because they cohere around explanations of interest rather than of love, from the suspicion of quixotism. Assembling textual hints to make ambition *The Recess*'s "true" story, my reading has forced the sisters' narratives to confess what they do not want to; the similarity of this hermeneutical practice to theirs should be evident. If their romance narratives claim to discover the "real" obscured by official history, my attempt to expose their quixotism claims to discover the "real" obscured by romantic delusions. The quixote trope, whose deployment separates readers who believe they have "ferret[ed] out the truth behind appearances" from those deluded by them,[34] is both elicited and rebuked by *The Recess*, which refuses to allow readers to know whether in seeing an interest-narrative "behind appearances" they have completed the text's message or have merely enacted their own prepossessions.[35] Lee's novel disables readers from committing to either a romance- or interest-based narrative, producing instead an awareness of the symmetry of these accounts. To devote oneself unsuspiciously to either of them, *The Recess* suggests, is to be a quixote.

III. Escaping From Quixotism?

What is the effect of this awareness? Does it enable us to shed our prepossessions, to escape what Rajan calls the "prison-house of . . . particular social texts" and to "cleans[e] the doors of perception"?[36] We might pause to consider whether Mailtida's opportunity to read Ellinor's narrative, and thus to see her own blindness, cures her of quixotism. Here is Matilda's "meditation" on "the strange and unaccountable difference in my sister's opinion and my own, respecting Lord Leicester":

> as this difference became obvious only from the time we arrived in London, I could not help imputing her blindness to the same cause she

assigned for mine.—Certainly she imbibed the unreasonable prejudices of Lord Essex; whose ambition . . . always inclined him to dislike a Nobleman born to supersede him. I saw but too plainly from the irritation and vehemence to which her temper from that period became subject, how much a woman insensibly adopts of the disposition of him to whom she gives her heart. Lord Essex, I will frankly own, . . . was gifted like herself with every captivating advantage . . . One must have loved Lord Leicester to see Essex with indifference—one must have loved him to the excess I did perhaps, not to remark the attachment my sister avowed.—Innumerable instances of it now flashed on my memory, I was astonished could at the moment escape me. If *she* was indeed more clear sighted than myself—But why do I enter on so vain a discussion?—Alas, dear Ellinor! beloved Leicester! I have no right but to lament ye. (271)

This passage registers Matilda's effort to *avoid* confronting her own blindness: her first thoughts distinguish Ellinor's "blindness" from her own clear sight ("I saw but too plainly"). If Ellinor suffers from "unreasonable prejudices," "insensibly" adopting another's "disposition," Matilda's careful and measured rhetoric ("meditation," "yet," "I could not help imputing," "Certainly") testifies that *she* is not similarly prejudiced. But Matilda's confidence in her perceptions stumbles as she confronts her complete failure to "remark" her sister's attachment, and she acknowledges that the "excess" of her own love may have caused what she observed. Matilda's momentary admission of her own blindness leads her to wonder whether "*she* [Ellinor] was indeed more clear sighted than myself—" only to abandon the question in mid-sentence as "vain" since her sister is dead. Matilda's flight from this question marks, in effect, her effort to preserve the quixote trope that enables her to dismiss her sister's reliability and shore up her own. That she never pauses again indicates that the quixote trope has done its work.

Some critics have considered Ellinor "more clear sighted than Matilda,"[37] but the novel never assesses the sisters' discernment. Ellinor's critique of Matilda's narrative does not authorize her credentials as a reliable narrator, despite our readiness to credit narratives as "plausible or true" because they "point to an error" in a prior narrative. Narratives "enforc[e] belief in something real through a denunciation of the false," according to Michel de Certeau, implying that "what is not held to be false must be real." But *The Recess* thwarts this tendency to credit "as 'real' whatever is placed in opposition to the[se] errors" by revealing Ellinor's narrative as equally blind.[38] Lee's text positions these critical discourses—these deployments of the quixote trope—not as revelations of the "truth" but as compensatory or strategic: *The Recess* shows how stories enable the sisters to repair in fantasy the damage Elizabeth has inflicted on them. Rather than recover a "real" distorted by the twins' prepossessions, *The Recess* explores the "real" produced by their prepossessions. Spencer describes *The Recess* as "romance's revenge on recorded history," but it seems better to say that romance is the twins' attempt to revenge their situation. These two daughters of the Queen of Scots, legitimate heirs to the English throne, construe history so that they, rather than Elizabeth, are its major actors. That they can take few public actions to establish their identities and rights (the men whom they love act toward this end, perhaps largely for themselves) only exposes more visibly that they establish themselves by means of their own "way of seeing," their practice of quixotism. Passing experience through the filter of romance deposits them centrally in the stream of history.

The Recess's interest in the use, rather than the accuracy, of stories is evident in its final 150 pages, neglected by critics who nearly unanimously describe the novel as if it featured only the two sisters' competing narratives.[39] Anticipating Emily Bronte's *Wuthering Heights: A Novel* (1847), however, *The Recess* portrays a second generation's misfortunes. These final pages feature Matilda's account of the passionate, though necessarily secret, courtship between her daughter Mary and Prince Henry, son and heir of James I, which develops after he rescues mother and daughter from a coach accident. Before they can marry, however, Henry takes sick and dies, an event significant in that James learns, from Henry's ravings while ill, that rival claimants to his throne, Matilda and Mary, exist. Soon enough Matilda and Mary are abducted while traveling to meet James and imprisoned in a castle owned by the earl of Somerset, James's favorite whom Matilda dislikes. There the guards isolate daughter from mother (so Somerset can rape Mary, Matilda is sure) and their reunion, after Matilda bribes a guard, is short-lived, as Mary quickly dies in her mother's arms. Before she dies, however, Mary tells a story that reveals that *The Recess*, once again, has led readers to credit a narrative from an eyewitness who is later revealed to be a quixote. Contrary to Matilda's quixotic perceptions, Mary has loved Somerset, not Henry. This revelation is surprising because Matilda has confidently reported signs of Mary's devotion to Henry. She notes that Henry's presence in "in the adjacent palace . . . heightened the soft red of my daughter's cheek" (281), that Henry's actions "constantly regulated our motions, and employed my daughter's thoughts even more than my own" (282), that Mary avoids Henry because of a "delicacy from which I drew the most happy presages"

(281), that Mary's "soft reserve," "the deepening roses of her cheek, and the low accent of her harmonious voice," were "symptom[s]" of her "passion" (284). Only when Mary reveals her love for Somerset can readers suspect that the symptoms Matilda describes might signify quite different meanings. This is not to say that the phenomena Matilda mentions are more "apparent" than "real," as if she saw things that were not there. *The Recess* shows, rather, that Matilda's prepossessions control the significance of the signs she reads.

The Recess, that is, is interested less in establishing a truth than in exploring how and why perceptions get produced as "true" (or feel "true" to the perceiver). Lee's text shows that a narrative inside Matilda's head produces Henry as an object so desirable that all must adore him. Matilda expects her own story to follow a plot made familiar by Thomas Leland's *Longsword, Earl of Salisbury: A Historical Romance* (1762), Walpole's *Castle of Otranto*, and Clara Reeve's *The Champion of Virtue: A Gothic Story* (1777: retitled *The Old English Baron* a year later), all of which trace "the restoration of legitimate authority" after a usurpation.[40] Matilda adopts this sense of an ending for herself and assumes her daughter adopts it as well; Lee's novel may count on readers being prepossessed with the same expectation so that they will not register, until too late, Matilda's misconstructions. Matilda herself admits that in deciding to "hire a mansion" near Henry's estate, she was "perhaps ... influenced almost without knowing it, by a latent motive": "delighted to understand a Stuart was rising to redeem the glory of his declining race, I passionately longed to see, know, and be valued by the royal Henry" (281). Her longing includes not just a private acknowledgment of her legitimacy but also a public restoration: the "happy prospect" that Henry's marriage to Mary would "end the persecutions of my family, by thus blessedly uniting the last sprung branches of it" (287–88).

It is this restoration plot, which possess Matilda, that shapes Henry into an object of supreme interest. "In thy unblown youth, oh, royal Henry, was comprized every promise that could dilate or fill the heart," Matilda mourns after his death; "mine centred at once in thee, and my daughter: finding in the mere hope of so glorious a union, a total suspension from suffering and sorrow" (288). The reader encounters Henry as the "glorious" creature he appears to be for Matilda: "the admired Prince of Wales, the idol of the People, the heir of Empire, the endued of Heaven" (285). The extent of her fetishistic transformation is indicated by her curious tendency to position herself, rather than Mary, as Henry's beloved (this despite her tendency to stress her maternal relation to Henry and her pleasure when he calls her "Mother"). Their relationship seems to reenact the romance script she had performed with Leicester. Her narrative, which fails to record one moment in which Henry and Mary speak, admits that "it was through me alone he addressed himself to her" (284); it is Matilda who rhapsodizes over Henry's "superior soul, living irradiated in the bright orbs" of his eyes (283), whose "soul" greets Henry with a "secret transport" (284), and who notes admiringly that "virtue herself seemed to sublime every happy lineament" of his features (283). It is Matilda and Henry who exchange histories, she "resolv[ing] to confide" her story to him after he "deigned to repose" his "regrets and anxieties" (284) with her. And it is Matilda and Henry who part sorrowfully: "The Prince fixed his suffused eyes on mine, with a mysterious melancholy, almost amounting to despair; and touching with his lips those hands his trembling ones still grasped, rushed precipitously into the courtyard. The sound of his voice drew me to the window—the graceful youth made me a last obeisance, and galloped away; while my partial eye pursued him" (292).

The fact that Matilda projects these romantic sentiments onto her daughter is hidden from the reader, misled by Matilda's consistent use of "we" and "us" into believing that mother and daughter feel identically. "They were often so near, we fancied we heard the voice of Henry, when both mother and daughter would give way to the same impulse, and hastily retire. The summer might have elapsed in this manner had no chance been more favorable to our wishes than we could resolve to be" (282). Such sentences prevent suspicions that their "wishes" and "impulses" are not identical. Mary, we learn, is unaffected by the prospect of restoration, but Matilda cannot imagine that Henry's attractiveness depends on her having cast him in the role of savior in her restoration narrative, "invest[ing] the hero" (like Wollstonecraft's Maria) with qualities she mistakenly believes self-evident. Mary says that she tried not to "awaken" her mother's "suspicions" about her love for Somerset and her diffidence toward Henry, but Matilda has seen (and, at the same time, not seen) evidence that Mary's desires differed from her own. Prepossessed by a story about the restoration of legitimate authority, however, Matilda assimilates all her experience, even that which she later recognizes to be contradictory, into a coherent narrative that promises to end with union and happiness. We tend to "live by the pattern," Frank Kermode has proposed, "rather than the fact," a proposition that resembles the claim by Lionel Gossman that "evidence only counts as evidence and is only recognized as such in relation to a potential narrative, so that narrative can be said to determine the evidence as much as the evidence determines the narrative."[41] Matilda's prepossessions ensure that she perceives Mary's silence as evidence of modesty rather than diffidence.

The Recess never describes an interpretive struggle in which Matilda first observes evidence and then (mis)interprets it to dispel the suspicions that such evidence awakened. For Matilda and for readers who share her way of seeing, experience is not a two-step process in which first one sees and then one interprets. (Francis Bacon, as we saw in chapter 1, also critiqued such an account.) Yet this model continues to characterize the way critics talk about quixotes. We have seen that Motooka suggests that "the senses of English quixotes are always reliable. Their unusual views cannot be dismissed as the raving results of faulty perception. Rather, English quixotes are characterized by their uncommon ways of *interpreting* the findings of common sense." It is a "consistent fact," she repeats, "that eighteenth-century English quixotes . . . never err in their senses . . . they err only in their judgments about the empirical evidence before them." But *The Recess* problematizes Motooka's separation of "judgement" from perception, or of interpretation from "the findings of common sense," by refusing to distinguish "fact" from "interpretation" or to describe a process in which all perceive an object alike and then some interpret it wrongly. *The Recess*'s stealth quixotes effectively collapse these stages into each other. Matilda sees and interprets simultaneously, her pre-knowledges and prepossessions determining the significance of phenomena, placing them in a pattern that is known in advance. "We are *interpreting* in seeing, hearing, receiving," Gadamer has contended: "In seeing, we are looking *for* something; we are just not like photographs that reflect everything visible."[42]

Matilda's "fixed" and "unalterable" "prejudice" (319) against Somerset, whom Mary really loves, caters to her need to keep her restoration narrative intact. Casting Somerset as villain, mastermind of all her troubles, ensures that she will fail to register Mary's love for him and thus continue to believe that she and Henry will marry. Easily assembling abundant evidence of Somerset's villainy, she "conjecture[s] . . . that I did not err in supposing Somerset directed" their guards and ascribes to him a "refined artifice of offering to introduce me to the King, and even remaining at my side, while perhaps my ruin was effecting by his will" (308). Mary's revisionary narrative depicts Somerset not as persecutor but as savior: "it was to Somerset's interposition," Mary insists, that "we owed the prolongation of [our] lives" (319). But Mary's effort functions not to deliver the truth about Somerset's motivations but rather to reposition attention on Matilda's storytelling, her "artifice," itself. At this point in the novel, that is, Matilda's misconstruction is less striking than the clarity with which the text exposes her activity in crafting a coherent narrative:

> I recollected too late the singularity of [Somerset] being with Prince Henry when first we beheld that amiable youth;—the assiduous respect he had shewn in waiting on me at Richmond;—the affected offer of his interest with a tyrant whose will he so well knew how to make subservient to his own;—the combination of refined arts by which we had been led to throw ourselves into the prison selected for us;—and, finally, that the prison was probably a house of his own.—Through the whole of this, as well as the manner we were guarded, there was a policy too minute for a King to plan. (312)

Matilda expects this renarration, in which she herself seems merely to find the real (though hidden) connections between "facts," to clinch Somerset's guilt. But this passage turns out to expose not "facts" but Matilda's own interpretive prowess at producing "facts." More precisely, we see here the power of a narrative or generic lens—of the restoration of legitimate authority—to select, assimilate, and order experience. Like the historians analyzed by Hayden White, Matilda "makes [her] story by including some events and excluding others, by stressing some and subordinating others."[43] The narrative that to Matilda (and, initially, to her readers) seems self-evident once she "recollect[s]" all the pieces turns out to have been what Kaja Silverman calls a "compensatory drama" that functions to preserve the sense of an ending (union and restoration) she desperately desires.[44] Matilda's practice of selecting and assembling evidence is not anomalous or ridiculous. It anticipates, indeed, the very practice in which *The Recess* has provoked readers to engage by hinting at the interestedness of characters whom the narrators themselves think act out of love.

The earl of Somerset, the text's last and most enigmatic character, exemplifies *The Recess*'s commitment to multiple perspectives. Mary's deathbed narrative qualifies our contempt for Somerset, but Matilda maintains her "intuitive conviction" that he is an "artful, insidious traitor, who had alienated [Mary's] affections, and warped the rectitude of her mind" (320). Mary herself even suspects that she has "bestow[ed]" her heart "unworthily" and that her "eyes conceived" a "partiality" that her "reason could never erase" (316–17). She even wonders whether Somerset performs romance conventions—paying "distant homage," delivering secret romantic letters ("The whole world appears [a prison] to him who beholds with pleasure only the spot where you dwell" [3: 324]), falling at her feet—only for his own "profit." This picture of a cunning Somerset dissolves, however, when, as Matilda lies dying, Somerset's priest visits to "vindicat[e] the innocent" and presents her with a letter in which Somerset reasserts his romantic attachment to Mary, his "dear lost angel" who was as "precious" to him as to Matilda herself. He acknowledges his "grief, horror, [and] despair" (but *not* "guilt")—and testifies to his own "breaking heart"—over Mary's death: "the last words of an expiring saint are not more ardent, more sincere than those I now utter." Although earlier Ellinor's sentimental narrative failed to convert Matilda to her views, this sentimental narrative works as eighteenth-century convention promised: Matilda cannot "[refuse] credence to this letter" and "accus[es her]self of having hitherto perhaps wanted candour towards the author" (324). Belief in a rehabilitated Somerset, however, rests on shaky foundations. Its primary advocate has been Somerset's "household Chaplain," on whom Matilda bestows a trust so absolute—"The author of universal being," she declares, "seemed to speak to me through his Minister" (323)—that readers might question her confidence even if the narrative had not repeatedly exposed her unreliability. *The Recess* provides no guidelines for integrating or transcending these contradictory representations—cunning politician, evil mastermind, romance lover—of Somerset's character.

The text's failure to fix authoritatively Somerset's character reproduces in miniature its more general refusal to arbitrate between romance narratives and interest narratives. *The Recess*'s critics have considered this multiplicity as merely a stage in a journey toward coherence. Noting that the text's "central portion" is "taken up by two long letters, one by each sister, recounting their different perspectives of substantially the same events," David Punter contends that "Lee makes no attempt to resolve this conflict, and we are left with a text embodying attitudinal contradictions and allowing the reader more freedom of realisation, it is fair to say, than any other novel of the period." "Essentially," Punter concludes, "*The Recess* allows us to make up our own minds about history." Punter follows much theoretical writing that suggests that texts with contradictory accounts of the same events shift responsibility to the reader, who gains a perspective that is denied to any of the "partial" participants. "Multiplicity of narration," William Riggin writes, "often affords the reader more information and perspective with which to make his own evaluation of persons and events than is possible for any of the individual narrators in the work." Wolfgang Iser, too, contends that "conflicts" or "gaps" in the text "give the reader the motivation and the opportunity to bring the two poles meaningfully together for himself," a process he, like Punter, calls the "realization of the text." Rajan's study of political texts agrees that a "gap in the text . . . stimulates us" to "read beyond the ending," a process by which the text provokes us to imagine something it never represents: "the meaning of the text does not inhere anywhere in it but remains to be produced." In these "interactions between the text and its future reader," Rajan suggests, the text is able "to write beyond itself" on readers who are "invited" by "hermeneutical signal[s]" to "read beyond and between the lines." This "future reader," Rajan suggests, "who will complete the text by unfolding a truth it does not yet contain," is "essential to any political reading," since it is in this reader that "the truth of what really should happen rather than of what really did happen" forms.[45] Such readings posit the reader's mind as the site where a single and unified narrative, absent *in* the text but predicted *by* it, can cohere. But if these readings assume rightly that texts with gaps often "motivate" readers to perform such work, then their more questionable assumption is that the text has, as it were, already imagined the coherent narrative that these motivated readers produce.

No text can prevent readers from feeling that they have reconciled competing narratives; readers may believe that, although *The Recess*'s characters remain blind, they can attain what a rejected conclusion to William Godwin's *Things as They Are, or The Adventures of Caleb Williams* (1794) called an "unprepossessed" mind.[46] But such coherent narratives are precisely what *The Recess* depicts as quixotic. Lee's text seems capable *both* of provoking readers to assemble coherent narratives *and* of forcing them to look at themselves performing this work. *The Recess* may forestall the superiority readers typically earn when they assemble such hidden narratives by identifying as quixotes those characters *in* the novel who perform the identical act: Matilda's (mis)construction of events anticipates the very activity the text elicits from its readers. This implied equivalency of the reader's and the quixote's activity, along with the text's sequence of quixotic and contradictory narratives and its determination to trick and to retrick readers, suggests that *The Recess dis*ables us from "mak[ing] up our own minds"—indeed, and that "our minds" are not entirely our own, that they are made up, as it were, by genres that possess us. *The Recess*, that is, may dislodge rather than reaffirm readers' belief that their sight is unfettered by prepossession, may hint to readers that genres haunt not just *others'* but *their* perceptions, may prevent them from deploying the quixote trope in order to claim for themselves a position of clear sight that is denied to the text's characters.

Punter's suggestion that Lee "does not shirk the intractable nature of much of her material" is odd, since *The Recess* generates intractable material by ensuring that two equally coherent narratives can explain the events of Elizabethan history, by excluding an authorized narrator who could discriminate between contradictory explanations, by tricking readers into crediting narratives that are later revealed to be blind. The genre that possesses the quixote's mind, visibly absurd or ridiculous in typical deployments of the quixote trope, is so invisible that readers find prepossessed vision indistinguishable from the unprepossessed vision they imagine their own to be. *The Recess*'s determination to repetitively redeposit the reader in a quixote's mind—its refusal of a linear narrative that exposes and then cures a quixote—implies the resilience of the genres that occupy us. For its readers *The Recess* seems to produce what Tzvetan Todorov has called the "first condition of the fantastic": "*the reader's hesitation*," caused by his or her "ambiguous perception of the events narrated." Most texts, Todorov suggests, resolve the ambiguity that provokes this hesitation, but some texts "sustain their ambiguity to the very end, i.e., even beyond the narrative itself." *The Recess* seems to be just one such text, rejecting the familiar opposition between quixotic delusion and rational clear sight (two poles that, paradoxically, rely on perceptual confidence) in order to produce a reader riven inescapably by competing narratives. In *The Recess*, however, readers are forced to hesitate not between "the laws of nature" and "apparently supernatural event[s]" but rather between alternate constructions of reality.[47]

Recent critical practice has focused on Lee's text as an early gothic or historical novel, but *The Recess* reveals the ineluctable mystery not of marginal experiences—confrontations with the supernatural or with the past—but of routine, everyday experiences. Alliston suggests that the "dissonance of perspective on the historical figures encountered in the novel" forms an "epistemological critique of contemporary historiography" that "locate[d] so much of its claim to truth and probability in the stability of character," but *The Recess* problematizes not merely the "perception and construction of historical character"—as if it were the attempt to understand "Other Times," or the "chasms in the story" left by "the depredations of time" ("Advertisement," 5), that provokes "epistemological" uncertainty.[48] The dissonant perspectives on Somerset, for instance, suggest that the epistemological problems that we tend to confront only when we ponder our ability to know the past *The Recess* applies to everyday experience. William Godwin's unpublished essay "Of History and Romance" moves similarly from considering the possibilities of historical truth ("the reader will be miserably deluded if, while he reads history, he suffers himself to imagine that he is reading facts") to asserting a general epistemological difficulty of knowing others and even oneself:

> The conjectures of the historian must be built upon a knowledge of the characters of his personages. But we never know any man's character. My most intimate and sagacious friend continually misapprehends my motives. He is in most cases a little worse judge of them than myself and I am perpetually mistaken.[49]

The Recess's structure, its mischievous determination to lead readers repeatedly to credit narratives that it later undermines, seems more likely to shake our confidence that we can ever apprehend the "real" than to correct our vision so that we can apprehend a "real" denied to its characters. Lee's text suggests the resilience of generic narratives, the "others" that haunt us and that shape the phenomena we register and the meanings we "find" in them.

CHAPTER 6

Ann Radcliffe's *The Mysteries of Udolpho* and the Practice of Quixotism

I. Objects and their Auras

While sightseeing in the Lake District late in 1794, the celebrated author of *The Romance of the Forest* (1791) and *The Mysteries of Udolpho: A Romance* (1794) stopped with her husband at Hardwick, "once the residence, of the Earl of Shrewsbury, to whom Elizabeth deputed the custody of the unfortunate Mary," Queen of Scots.[1] The "real" that Ann Radcliffe believes she encounters at Hardwick—the authenticity of its objects—captivates her. Often, it is true, her *Journey Made in the Summer of 1794* (1795) embeds these objects in narratives that, as her prose acknowledges, aspire only to probability:

> The upper end of the room is distinguished by a lofty canopy of the same materials, and by steps which support two chairs; so that the earl and Countess of Shrewsbury *probably* enjoyed their own stateliness here, as well as assisted in the ceremonies practised before Mary. A carpeted table, in front of the canopy, was, *perhaps*, the desk of Commissioners, or Secretaries, who here recorded some of the proceedings concerning her . . . (my italics)

But more typically her account isolates objects themselves as kernels of "reality" that underpin these imaginative reconstructions. Radcliffe has been criticized for sloppiness about historical fact, but her *Journey* tries to set facts straight: in Mary's bedchamber, she notes with puzzlement, "the date 1599 is once or twice inscribed . . . for no reason, that could relate to Mary, who was removed hence in 1584, and fell, by the often-blooded hands of Elizabeth, in 1587." Radcliffe documents each authentic object that has survived since Mary's stay: in "the gallery of a small chapel" she observes that the "chairs and cushions, used by Mary, still remain"; on the "first story" only "one apartment bears memorials of her imprisonment, the bed, tapestry and chairs having been worked by herself"; on the "second floor," where "nearly all the apartments . . . were allotted to Mary," she sees much "furniture [that] is known by other proofs, than its appearance, to remain as she left it"; in her "own chamber," Radcliffe sees "bed and chairs . . . of black velvet, embroidered by herself." These rooms, Radcliffe writes, first strike by their "grandeur, before the veneration and tenderness arise, which its antiquities, and the plainly told tale of the sufferings they witnessed, excite." Radcliffe's account implies that these "antiquities" themselves, having "witnessed" Mary's suffering, "plainly" tell Mary's "tale," and she depicts her response to them—the "grandeur," "veneration" and "tenderness" she feels—as an inevitable response to the power that inheres in these relics themselves. She is passive before these objects that "strike" her and that "excite" responses, independent, as it were, of her will. "The scene of Mary's arrival and her feelings upon entering this solemn shade came involuntarily to the mind," Radcliffe says, as if these objects give off stories just as automatically as food emits odors or, in Edmund Burke's account, as massive mountains produce sublimity.[2]

Undoubtedly Radcliffe would have been disappointed had she learned that Mary never was imprisoned at Hardwick, a lesson that, it is likely, would have drained from these objects the sublimity and grandeur that had seemed their inalienable qualities. But Radcliffe's disappointment would likely have been mixed with fascination, since her novels, in particular *The Mysteries of Udolpho*, repetitively invest objects with and divest objects of charismatic power. The many objects that its heroine, Emily St. Aubert, misconstrues—the picture over which she observes her father weep, the wax figure she spies behind the screen, the flickering lights at Udolpho—have exemplified this process most memorably, and the novel's frequent exposure of the "real" object beneath Emily's mystifications (the technique of the "explained supernatural") seems to define "reality" as that which is left, so to speak, after subjects' illusory projections have been dispelled. The technique of the "explained supernatural" relentlessly exposes the reality hidden under Emily's delusions: after Emily hears "a rustling sound" and "perceive[s] something move," the "sudden terror of something supernatural" immobilizes her until she realizes she has been frightened by a dog.[3] This comical instance contains in miniature the novel's general practice of replacing objects or events that had seemed to possess one meaning ("something supernatural") with the mundane reality ("dog") that had always existed behind the delusion. The flexibility, but also the limits, of this project can be seen in the novel's willingness to value imagination only for enabling one to *perceive* (not to *shape*) the "real": as one critic writes, "imagination is, in [Radcliffe's] view, an instrument for experiencing reality, not for creating it."[4] This structure encourages readers to credit as objective the reality that is left after the subject's distortions, delusions, or projections have been dissolved. Legitimate or accurate perception, this model implies, occurs only when the subject contributes nothing: the object must control the process in which knowledge is produced on and for a subject configured as a passive responder. If, as we have seen in chapter 1, Locke's description of a mirror that receives impressions "whether [it] will or no" represents the ideal subject in the knowing process, then Emily's tendency to filter her experience through her superstitious belief disables her from gaining a legitimate purchase on the "real."[5] The critical commentary, in focusing for the most part on *Udolpho*'s mystery plot, tends to depict the novel as a conventional (if inconsistent) "quixote cured" narrative, in which Emily learns to differentiate the real from the projections of her own mind.

But Radcliffe's *Mysteries of Udolpho* registers as well, perhaps contradictorily, the competing uses of the quixote story that we have seen in earlier chapters. If on the one hand *Udolpho* aims to cure Emily St. Aubert of quixotic superstitions so that she sees only the "real" objects before her eyes, on the other it abandons quixote narratives' traditional task of policing representation when it shows that the Baconian epistemological two-step, explored in chapter 1—the mind must be a "receptive wax tablet" before it can legitimately be an " 'active' interpreter of what nature has there imprinted"[6]—misrepresents a process in which minds actively endow nature with the capacity to imprint them. Indeed on her visit to Hardwick, Ann Radcliffe herself seems to have been haunted less by the ghost of Mary than by the texts about Mary's imprisonment she had read. Elizabeth's imprisonment of Mary in Hardwick, for instance, prompts Radcliffe to recall (and misquote from memory) William Mason's *Elfrida; Written on the Model of the Ancient Greek Tragedy* (1752), a long poem in which a young Earl confines a beautiful young woman in the depths of Harewood forest.[7] Radcliffe had also read Sophia Lee's *The Recess; or, A Tale of Other Times* (1783–1785), the subject of the previous chapter, and, it is likely, *The History of the Life and Reign of Mary Queen of Scots, and Dowager of France* (1725), which was written by her great-uncle Samuel Jebb. Although Radcliffe's *Journey* privileges the "real" over the merely imagined, her prose reveals the traces of the narratives that shape what she sees.

The margins of *Udolpho*, similarly, model a process of perception that not only exposes but legitimizes the subject's contribution to the knowing process. These moments suggest that the "reality" typically considered as pre-given is actually produced by its interaction with a subject. This is not to say that objects such as trees or castles do not exist until subjects apprehend them. It is to say that *Udolpho* explores the possibility that the "reality" that subjects think they "find"—the discrete boundaries between things, the relations between things, the givenness of the reality they register—actually emerges as a product of their interactions with, experiments on, and hypotheses about a reality initially experienced as threatening, confusing, and ambiguous. *Udolpho* traces the process by which subjects select (in what should not be imagined to be conscious activity) from the stream of experience—varied, confusing, ambiguous, partial, and obscure—those objects and relations they register and that come to make up the world they take, or misrecognize, as given. The text shows, moreover, that subjects do not necessarily make the same "worlds," and what registers for one may fail to register for another. In *Udolpho* the "given" emerges from an interpretive situation: a genre, a representation, an interpretation, a filter, participates in producing those "givens" that exert real effects upon us. Most importantly, *Udolpho* explores this quixotism without attempting to cure it. The text hopes to produce, not to cure, quixotes.

II. Quixote Cured?

Treating Radcliffe's novel as if it belongs in the genre of "quixote cured," many of *Udolpho*'s critics have argued that Emily, its heroine, "learn[s] to separate reality from illusion" and finds that only "by paying close attention to actualities of the external world can [she] hope to check her fantasies." Such critics focus on *Udolpho*'s mystery plot in which Emily struggles to make sense of ambiguous signs: flickering lights, unidentifiable music, gliding human figures, sheets that rise unexpectedly off beds. By exposing the natural cause or mundane object beneath Emily's fantasies, the text routinely ridicules her tendency to use supernatural explanations to make sense of these objects or events. Assuming that the text attempts to purge Emily of delusions that disrupt her immediate encounter with the "real," critics frequently contend that Emily must learn "to distinguish the real from the imaginary, to see the truth behind the various ambiguous signals of nature and imagination," or that *Udolpho* aims to "bring readers and characters back to eighteenth-century conventions of realism, reason and morality" by rebuking their tendency to "credulity."[8] Eugenia DeLamotte speaks for many critics of *Udolpho* when she contends that "there is no doubt in Radcliffe's works that objective reality exists outside the mind"[9]—and that, in effect, *Udolpho* reifies this "objective reality" by repetitively deploying a technique that, quite theatrically, removes from objects or events the distortions or modifications added on by a perceiving subject. The object or event left after such an operation can be seen as it truly is.

The tendency to treat Emily as a female quixote is evident in the way that critics often consider Montoni himself, the novel's villain, as the product of Emily's imaginative distortions. Montoni's "sublime," according to Patricia Meyer Spacks, is largely Emily's projection, and by its conclusion the text strips him of the "add-ons" (his "phallic power") bestowed by Emily's imagination so he can be seen as he really is. Kim Ian Michasiw concurs that Emily compensates for "the inadequacy of her senses" by positing a force that controls the varied things that happen to her: "the name of her god is male power or, in Italian, Montoni." Emily "sees as if enchanted," Michasiw demonstrates, "and all her visions lead her towards Montoni," a "petty *condottieri* captain" who "becomes a figure imbued with supernal power, a transformation effected almost entirely by Emily and her aunt." Agreeing that "the illusion" of Montoni "is more potent than the reality," Kenneth Graham declares that the "potentially-explosive force of obscure purposes who smoulders in the shadows of his castle" is "almost wholly the creation of Emily," who "creates of [Montoni] a figure of Burkean sublimity that both attracts and repels her."[10] These accounts assimilate Emily to a conventional quixote, whose penchant for passing the "real" through a set of aesthetic representations transforms a petty bandit into a sublime god—much as Quixote's internalized romances turn windmills into giants. In these accounts, *Udolpho* seems a conventional quixote story in which a deluded and inexperienced young girl must learn to stop creating objects that do not exist.

Coral Ann Howells's exhaustive analysis of *Udolpho*'s prose implies that the novel deposits readers within the sort of quixotic imagination it aims to critique. Emily's "feelings have been presented in such detail and the reader's identification with those feelings so encouraged that we find we are accepting something as fact which is, or could be, merely a projection of the character's imagination."[11] Lee's *Recess*, as we have seen, could have modeled this technique for Radcliffe. Critics have long speculated that Radcliffe absorbed gothic conventions—the British setting of Radcliffe's early *Castles of Athlin and Dunbayne: A Highland Story* (1789), the focus of her *Sicilian Romance* (1791) on a pair of sisters—from Lee.[12] Only one, David Punter, has proposed that Radcliffe's "detailed and often poeticised depiction of states of mind," her interest in "those points of vision and obsession where the individual blurs into his own fantasies," "owes more than a little to Sophia Lee": "[a]s with the heroines of *The Recess*, it is never clear to what extent those circumstances are genuinely imposed on the characters by outside forces and to what extent they are projections of paranoia and vulnerability." But Punter's normative language, sharply distinguishing the "genuine" perceptions that experience "impose[s]" on (passive) characters from their "projections," equates anything that emanates from the subject with "distortion," an equation evident when he contrasts Emily's " 'imaginary terrors' " with her "real difficulties." Emily considers the "reality" of Udolpho as nightmare only because she reads "through the medium offered by her dislocated mind."[13] Howells, too, cannot see Emily's "projections" as anything but illegitimate: if *Udolpho* "encourag[es] our sympathetic identification with an intensely focussed though totally one-sided point of view,"[14] it does so to expose the dangers of "los[ing] all sense of how feeling may be distorting judgement" and to "condemn [such] emotional indulgence." This "learning programme," Howells summarizes, "places Mrs. Radcliffe squarely in the line of eighteenth-century moralists such as Richardson and Dr Johnson and leads straight on to Jane Austen."[15] These dismissals of Emily's activity— her perceptions are "merely . . . projection[s]," her feelings "may be distorting judgement"—positions *Udolpho* as a conventional quixote narrative that aims to discipline an excessive imagination that distorts the "real."

Udolpho, I argue below, seems far less concerned than its critics with policing this boundary between "fact" and "distortion": Lee's *Recess* (as the previous chapter shows) could have taught Radcliffe less to distinguish the imaginary from the real than to explore how prepossessions filter every subject's experience of the world and how to represent these genres or stories that prepossess us. Before pursuing this contention, however, we should note that the critical position sketched above responds to *Udolpho*'s own frequent critique of Emily's "imagination," a critique that does invoke the language of normative quixote tales. Often the text blames Emily's "imagination," quick to become "inflamed," for allowing "the terrors of superstition" to "[pervade] her mind" (371). Emily herself worries that she has "suffer[ed] her romantic imagination to carry her so far beyond the bounds of probability, and determined to endeavour to check its rapid flights, lest they should sometimes extend into madness" (342). These depictions of the dangers of imagination posit a mind free of imaginative distortion and guided only by reason, although they acknowledge, perhaps, the rarity of such a mind: "human reason," the narrator warns, "cannot establish her laws on subjects, lost in the obscurity of imagination." Many times Emily's "reason told" her that her "superstitions" are no more than "wild conjecture," but repeatedly her "imagination guides [her] thoughts" and leads her to "wild" beliefs (330–31).

The effort to discipline Emily's overactive imagination is pursued within the novel by Emily's father. Early on in the novel Emily and her father encounter some flickering lights as they return home through the dark woods: "Ah!," Emily exclaims, "what light is yonder? But it is gone. And now it gleams again, near the root of that large chestnut" (15). St. Aubert's quick, naturalistic explanation for these flickering lights—"Are you such an admirer of nature," he asks Emily, "and so little acquainted with her appearances as not to know that for the glow-worm?"—appears at first to rebuke Emily, who has just identified the "sweeping sound over the wood-tops" with "the voice of some supernatural being." But rather than repress Emily's supernatural imagination, St. Aubert encourages it by prompting Emily to envision the "fairies" that "are often companions" to the glow-worm ("Do you see nothing tripping yonder?"). This tease elicits from Emily an admission that, long before her father's suggestion, she had imagined a supernatural explanation—"fairies so gay / Tripping through the forest-walk"—for the flickering lights. Emily deftly eludes her father's latent ridicule by positing these fairies as part of the glow-worm's world, not her own: in the poem she recites to her father, she adopts the character of "the glow-worm" itself, speculating only on its experiences and thus stopping short from contending that "tiny elves" register on human senses. This interest in perspective is characteristic of *Udolpho* as a whole. Here I want to note that, since Emily's poem is replete with specific descriptions of natural phenomena, her father, is wrong to accuse her of not being "acquainted with [nature's] appearances": her poem does not so much see differently as offer a different explanation for phenomena that she and her father seem to share in common.

The text hints that St. Aubert makes sense of these flickering lights quite differently than Emily. "Whatever St. Aubert might think of the stanzas," the narrator notes, "he would not deny his daughter the pleasure of believing that he approved them" (17). While precisely what he *does* "think of the stanzas" remains mysterious, masked by his public "commendation" of the verses, he seems to disown Emily's supernaturalism. He has earlier labeled Emily's other poetic productions "vagaries," departures from settled understanding. That St. Aubert considers Emily's account of the phenomenon of the flickering lights to depart unnecessarily from common sense is confirmed by the verses, immediately following Emily's recital, that appear to characterize the content of the "reverie" into which St. Aubert "sunk" (though they are quoted from James Thomson's *Summer* [1727]):

> A faint erroneous Ray,
> Glanc'd from th' imperfect Surfaces of Things,
> Flings half an Image on the straining Eye;
> While wavering Woods, and Villages, and Streams,
> And Rocks, and Mountain-tops, that long retain'd
> Th' ascending Gleam, are all one swimming Scene,
> Uncertain if beheld.[16]

These lines invoke a Newtonianism—in which the sun's "Ray" interacts with particularized "Surfaces" of objects to produce the "Image[s]" registered by the human "Eye"—that seems to explain all phenomena by means of natural or mechanical descriptions. In *Summer* these lines directly follow an account of the glow-worm ("Among the crooked Lanes, on every Hedge, / The Glow-Worm lights his Gem; and, thro' the Dark, / A moving Radiance twinkles"[17]), and thus in *Udolpho* they function to revise Emily's "vagarie" by proposing a nonsuperstitious explanation of the odd lights. St. Aubert's ridicule, a gentle deployment of the quixote trope, places Emily's account of the flickering lights in competition with his own close attention to "appearances," to things as they are, a competition that positions her perceptions as quixotic.

Even Emily occasionally deploys the quixote trope, scorning others' superstition and thus upholding a commonsense apprehension of a shared "reality." She calls Annette a "ridiculous girl" who "indulge[s] . . . fancies" and believes "silly tales," and she repeatedly "smiles" (231, 247, 391) at her "simple" servant's "superstitious weakness" (392). But, the text notes ironically, although Emily "could smile at" superstition "when apparent in other persons," she "sometimes felt its influence herself" (247). (This, we have seen repeatedly, is a characteristic common to female quixotes.) Emily even comes to ridicule herself, "smil[ing]" at the recollection of how "she had suffered herself to be led away by superstition" (490). The fact that her "determin[ations]" to "resist its contagion" (490) often fail merely affords her further chances to display shame that mundane occurrences "had given her so much superstitious terror" (635). The many readings that argue that Emily does not grow or learn register suspicion that, since superstition persists in mediating her experience even late in the novel, Emily never surmounts her superstitious quixotism.[18] But Emily's learning curve seems less important than the novel's consistent ridicule of the quixotism of superstition. In this effort it enlists not only Count de Villefort, whose daughter, Blanche, like Emily, credits "superstitious tales" until "the ridicule in her father's glance" makes her blush (550), but also Montoni himself, who rebukes Emily with the very language with which she had rebuked Annette. When Emily reveals that she "had seen an apparition," Montoni demands that she "conquer" such "idle whims" and "release [her]self from the slavery of these fears" (243–44). After Udolpho's other inhabitants join Emily in the fear that "the north side of the castle [is] haunted," Montoni "employ[s] ridicule and then argument to convince them they had nothing to apprehend from supernatural agency" (543).

In all these instances, *Udolpho* seems to counter quixotism with a chastened empiricism that demands that subjects respond without distortion to the "given" world of objects. This account, however, neglects significant moments of the text. At these moments, *Udolpho* exposes that *any* way of construing the world enacts a quixotic practice of making rather than finding. The novel may ridicule Emily's superstition, but it does not establish as its alternative a clear-sighted perception of the "real," of objects as they "really are." Instead, *Udolpho* moves readers from one filter that produces the "given" to another, from one "description," to use Richard Rorty's term, to another.[19] The filter it advocates spiritualizes the landscape, a way of reading popularized by Thomson's *The Seasons* (1730) and by later texts on the "picturesque," from William Gilpin's series of *Observations* (1786–1808), his *Remarks on Forest Scenery* (1791), and *Three Essays on Picturesque Beauty* (1792) to Uvedale Price's several *Essays on the Picturesque* (1794–1810).[20] We have seen above that St. Aubert seems to think by means of Thomson's text, despite the fact that neither he nor Emily, of course, could have read Thomson (one suspects that *The Seasons* was among the sublime English poets St. Aubert recommends to Emily in 1584). Nor, for that matter, could either have seen the art of Salvator Rosa, although the fact that both father and daughter frequently "expected" to "see banditti start from behind some projecting rock" (30: cf. 54, 302, 312) or, at one point, that "in her imagination, [Emily] saw them lurking under the brow of some protecting rock" (402) testifies to a close acquaintance with Rosa's canvases and the fad for banditti they, along with Schiller's *The Robbers* (1781), generated.[21] Critics have typically identified such moments—whether incidental, such as the coffee that Emily drinks or the forks she uses ("not introduced into Western Europe until the mid-seventeenth century," "not common in England and France until the seventeenth century" [681]), or more central, such as Emily's sensibility—as Radcliffe's carelessness about anachronism. But the presence of this particular anachronism is crucial to *Udolpho*'s project.

Thomson's *Seasons* popularized a way of seeing that finds God's presence in all his works. It is a Newtonian world that escapes its apparent mechanism by insisting that we read nature's order and regularity and its beauty as signs of God's immanent presence. Speaking both of the natural cycle of seasons and *The Seasons* itself, Thomson's concluding "Hymn" begins with these lines: "These, as they change, ALMIGHTY FATHER, these, / Are but the *varied* GOD. The rolling Year / Is full of Thee." The speaker of Thomson's *Summer*, having wondered how "to sing of HIM, / Who, LIGHT HIMSELF, in uncreated Light / Invested deep, dwells awfully retir'd / From mortal Eye," solves this problem by reading *through* nature to the invisible God.[22] Thomson admits that he models this practice on Robert Boyle's writing. Boyle's *Occasional Reflections upon Several Subjects* (1665), for instance, teaches a way of reading that inspects "mysterious Nature" to "discover there so much of the Wisdom, Power, and Goodness of [its] Author."[23] Boyle explicitly describes this "way of Thinking" (77) as a "Custom" (77), "Practice" (31), or "habit" (29) that requires "frequent Exercise" (78): the "World is the great Book, not so much of Nature, as of the God of nature, which we should find ev'n crowded with instructive Lessons, if we had but the Skill, and would take the Pains, to extract and pick them out" (47). Individuals, that is, need to practice and thus accustom themselves to this way of reading. Boyle promises that one who has "by long practice, accustom'd [one's] self to spiritualize all the Objects" (80) one encounters will "live almost surrounded either with Instructors, or Remembrancers" (b2).

Describing Boyle in *Summer* as one who the "great Creator sought" "Amid the dark recesses of his works," Thomson testifies that he, too, has learned to read "Nature's Volume broad-display'd, / And to peruse its all-instructing Page, / Or, haply catching Inspiration thence, / Some easy Passage, raptur'd, to translate."[24] Thomson teaches his readers to "translate" nature into God, to make an "easy Passage" from one to the other. This rhetorical strategy works by assimilating and (to borrow Boyle's word) "spiritualizing" *all* phenomenon, whether a beautiful flower, a sublime mountain, or a lightening-bolt that destroys the happiness of a young couple; indeed, the method is built to explain the otherwise inexplicable. Emily St. Aubert, her father, her friend Blanche, and the narrator are the novel's primary practitioners of this "spiritual reading of the landscape."[25] Nature's appearances frequently prompt St. Aubert's "thoughts" to "ascend to the Great Creator," and Emily's mind, too, often "arose" from "the consideration of His works" to "the adoration of the Deity": "wherever [Emily] turned her view," the text notes, "the sublimity of God, and the majesty of His presence appeared" (36, 47–48). Emily is repeatedly "most disposed" to "[raise] her thoughts in prayer . . . when viewing the sublimity of nature" (242). However improbably, these characters have internalized Thomson: skilled hermeneuts, they perform what Stanley Fish calls, in another context, a "continual exercise in translation, a seeing through the literal contexts of things (objects, events, persons) to the significance they acquire in the light of a larger perspective."[26] This "larger perspective" demands that *all* "appearances" tell the *same* story: if Emily cannot find "the Deity" in "His works," she must look harder. *Udolpho*'s exhaustive (and exhausting) natural descriptions—the novel reads like a "how to" manual of such readings that spiritualize nature—reveals the need to teach that which, the novel implies, ought to occur naturally. (Boyle's writings, as I have noted, openly acknowledge that one must develop a "habit, produced by the practice of Occasional meditating," to "accustom" oneself to this way of seeing [29].) *Udolpho* tries to interpellate its readers into this way of seeing, one quixotism, one way to produce objects taken as "given," to replace another.

The text itself may be unaware of the quixotism of the way of seeing it adopts from Thomson and others. As we have seen, the discourse of quixotism exposes, above all, the tendency to consider the beliefs we hold (pragmatists would say the beliefs that "hold us") as accurate reflections of the "real" itself, as found rather than made. Quixotes must be blind to their own imaginative projection, must misrecognize the power they bestow *on* objects as inherently *in* objects, if the objects thus created are to become "real" enough to exert pressure back on the subject. Slavoj Žižek illustrates this process of misrecognition with the example of a monarch and his subjects: "We, the subjects, think that we treat the king as a king because he is in himself a king, but in reality a king is a king because we treat him like one. And this fact that the charismatic power of a king is an effect of the symbolic ritual performed by his subjects must remain hidden: as subjects, we are necessarily victims of the illusion that the king is already in himself a king."[27] Žižek's contention that the king's "power" is the "effect" of subjects' activity does not diminish this power's "reality" to subjects still trapped in "illusion." The act of believing in an object empowers it, as Karl Marx argued in his doctoral dissertation (1841): "*all gods*, the pagan as well as the Christian ones," he proposed, "possessed a real existence. Did not the ancient Moloch reign? Was not the Delphic Apollo a real power in the life of the Greeks?" (Marx glosses "real power" as "something that works on me").[28] John Dryden's image in *Absalom and Achitophel* (1681) of rebellious Jews who "wondered why, so long, they had obey'd / An Idoll Monarch which their hands had made" describes similarly an object created by subjects that exercises "real power" over them.[29] This behavior resembles fetishism, which I explored briefly in chapter 1 and whose resemblance to quixotism I discuss more fully below. Here I mean to emphasize that such objects gain power only to the extent that perception is quixotic, blind to its own activity: "if we come to 'know too much,' " Žižek argues, "this reality would dissolve itself."[30] The moment quixotes recognize that their imagination has played a role in creating an object, the delusion loses its power—as the cures at the conclusions of typical quixote tales recognize. One might think, then, that *Udolpho*'s success in leading readers to adopt its way of seeing would depend on masking the quixotism—the structure of making rather than finding—that can produce such spiritualized landscapes. What is remarkable about *Udolpho*, however, is that it often exposes the quixotic structure of this way of seeing, and in so doing the novel not only endorses the *content* of a particular quixotism (seeing a spiritualized landscape) but also embraces the *structure* of making rather than finding that representations of quixotism typically disown.

III. Quixotism Preserved

Udolpho often depicts the process of discovering "the Deity" in "His Works" as an operation subjects must perform *on* the real, and not as something that the real does *to* properly configured subjects. Take, for instance, the natural scenery it describes with so much energy. The text encourages readers to judge characters, as critics have noted, "by their responses to natural scenery,"[31] repeatedly contrasting sensible with insensible responses. When Emily and her aunt travel through the Alps to Udolpho itself, the Countess "only shuddered as she looked down precipices near whose edge the chairmen trotted lightly and swiftly," but Emily's experience differs. Filtered through Burke's aesthetics (the "solitary grandeur of the objects that immediately surrounded her ... received a higher character of sublimity from the reposing beauty of the Italian landscape below"), the landscape captivates her: "with [Emily's] fears were mingled such various emotions of delight, such admiration, astonishment, and awe, as she had never experienced" (166). The novel repetitively stages such scenes that include competing responses to landscape. As the Villeforts travel across the Pyrennes, the text contrasts Blanche's delighted response to their castle with her mother's, who "reflecting, with regret, upon the gay parties she had left at Paris, surveyed, with disgust, what she thought the gloomy woods and solitary wildness of the scene; and, shrinking from the prospect of being shut up in an old castle, was prepared to meet every object with displeasure" (468). The text systematically undermines the Countess's perceptions: it notes that she was "prepared" to be displeased and inserts qualifiers ("she thought") that imply that the woods and forest seem "gloomy" and "solitary," and the castle merely "old," *only* in her mind. While such scenes demonstrate that the novel clearly privileges one response to natural scenery over another, the question more difficult to answer is how the novel explains these competing responses. Is one a form of quixotism and the other an unmediated encounter with the real?

One way to explain these divergent perceptions, of course, would be to invoke the ideology of sensibility, to which, as many critics have noted, *Udolpho* is devoted. While some persons, due to insensible bodies or acquired prejudice, might fail to register the impressions given off by the scenery "itself," others' bodily sensibility registers properly the impressions of the "real."[32] Uvedale Price's writings on the picturesque deploy this very model, borrowing the mechanistic epistemology of Edmund Burke's *Philosophical Enquiry into the Origin of our Ideas of the Sublime and Beautiful* (1757), which had insisted, as we saw in chapter 1, that our response to the beautiful and sublime "arise from the mechanical structure of our bodies, or from the natural frame and constitution of our minds."[33] Price contended that our response to the picturesque, similarly, arises from certain "qualities" that "exist in" objects. Drawing an "analogy" between the way "certain qualities" of objects "uniformly produce the same effects" on our sense of "hearing" and "the other senses," his *Essay on the Picturesque, as Compared with the Sublime and Beautiful* (1796) insists that certain "inherent qualities of objects" provoke certain "operation[s] on the mind": "each object," Price's *Dialogue on the Distinct Characters of the Picturesque and the Beautiful* (1801) repeats, is "composed of qualities" that produce in us specific responses "independently of our being . . . accustomed to them."[34] When *Udolpho* describes individuals as passive before natural scenery (noting, for instance, "the delight [Emily] received from the beautiful scenery around" [495]), the text invokes this mechanical model in which a body's sensibility causes it to respond automatically to natural objects, precisely in the way it recoils from heat or salivates in response to certain foods. Sensible subjects, such as Emily, her father, or Blanche, respond to landscape as they do because of the configuration of their bodies; others, such as Emily's aunt or Blanche's mother, fail to respond because of acquired prejudices.

This is, as I say, one way that *Udolpho* might explain the divergent perceptions that it so often exposes. Indeed, this explanation would jibe well with the critique of quixotism and superstition I have outlined above. Both accounts differentiate a proper—natural, inevitable, necessary, passive—response to scenery from an improper one, caused by a subject's quixotic devotion to particular ideas, superstitions, or prejudices. It is crucial to note, however, that Radcliffe's text *does not* contrast the Countess's *mis*construction of the landscape due to her prepossessions with Blanche's delight that is prompted by accurate perception of and automatic response to the objects themselves. Instead, it suggests that Blanche's delight is no less "prepared," noting that she "had once or twice obtained" access to "reliques of romantic fiction" while in her convent and so now "fancied herself approaching a castle, such as is often celebrated in early story, where the knights look out from the battlements on some champion below" (468). By invoking the narratives imbedded in Blanche's head, the text suggests that her privileged and sensible perceptions—hearing the "melancholy dashing of oars" or the "low murmur of the waves"—depend on the representations through which she perceives: only her "preparation" by "romantic fiction" enables the scenery to affect her and to produce her "pensive mood." This landscape affects subjects differently, this alternate account implies, not because of empirical bodily differences but because of different internalized representations.

Udolpho's exposure of these internalized representations resembles the account offered by writers on the picturesque who disputed that responses to scenery were as mechanical as Burke and Price claimed. The discourse of the picturesque, that is, fractured over the question of how the objects that powerfully affect us gain their power. Richard Payne Knight, whose *Landscape: A Didactic Poem in Three Books. Addressed to Uvedale Price* (1794) had provoked Price's *Dialogue*, countered Price's theories again in his *Analytical Inquiry into the*

Principles of Taste (1805). Knight insists that our pleasure in beauty, sublimity, and the picturesque results not "solely from the eye, but must involve the intervention of the mind."[35] Drawing on the associationist theories of Archibald Alison's *Essays on the Nature and Principles of Taste* (1790), Knight contends that responses arise from a learned "association of ideas," which becomes "so spontaneous and rapid" that "it *seems to be* a mechanical operation of the mind."[36] The very term "picturesque" acknowledges that it is painters who have *taught us* to respond to particular types of landscape, our responses occurring not because of an object's "intrinsic" qualities but because we have consumed a series of visual representations. As Christopher Hussey wrote, the picturesque involved an "education of the eye" by which "pictures were . . . taken as the guide for how to see." "The picturesque object," Kim Ian Michasiw notes, "is so to the degree that it conforms to prior objects lodged in memory, and these objects are likely to be or to have been mediated by representative works of art." The "trains of thought" set in motion by the images we have consumed, Knight contends, "will continue to haunt us in spite of all we can do to free ourselves from them."[37] A natural scene that we register as "picturesque," that is, has been made picturesque "through the medium of the imagination."[38] An identical process, Knight notes, gives the "most trivial of objects" sentimental value. Such an account positions Emily's intense response to landscape, her spiritualized aesthetics, less as an "accurate" decoding of the "real" itself—imagined as immediately available, the "given" that exists before subjects attempt to know it—than as the result of a practice of quixotism, of passing the real through an internalized mediation that produces a "given" that affects subjects in desirable ways.

If at moments *Udolpho* shows that characters find in nature powerful objects that affect them, then, at other times it suggests that they make these objects powerful by means of their imagination. The landscape's sublimity moves Emily, and its beauty soothes her, because Burke's aesthetics, Thomson's poetry, and Gilpin's travelogues have taught her to be moved and soothed: the landscape can affect her because she—or the aesthetic categories that she has internalized and through which she perceives—has endowed it with such power. Emily resembles the eighteenth-century landscape writers who, as John Barrell writes, so internalized paintings by Claude Lorrain and Salvator Rosa that they "would have seen . . . a landscape as if it were already composed into the accepted structure." "The contemplation of landscape," says Barrell, "was not . . . a passive activity; it involved reconstructing the landscape in the imagination, according to principles of composition" that were "learned so thoroughly that in the later eighteenth century it became impossible for anyone with an aesthetic interest in landscape to look at the countryside without applying them, *whether or not he knew he was doing so or not*." In denying that this process involves an observer's "deliberate distortion of what he really saw into what he really did not see," Barrell collapses what he calls the "unimaginable antithesis" (what I have described as an epistemological two-step described by Bacon) between an initial commonsense perception ("what he really saw") and a subsequent interpretation ("deliberate distortion"). Rather, Barrell insists, observers were "so saturated in Claude's way of seeing and composing landscape" that they "could see it . . . in no other way."[39] On her tour in 1794 Radcliffe traveled, as Rictor Norton records, "well equipped with books to reinforce the sublime scenery," but it seems as likely, as I have argued above, that her books helped produce the scenery as sublime.[40] Gilpin taught her how to see, much as *Udolpho* itself taught others how to see. In his *Lectures on the English Comic Writers* (1818), William Hazlitt confessed that "part of the impression with which I survey the full-orbed moon shining in the blue expanse of heaven, or hear the wind sighing through autumnal leaves . . . is owing to a repeated perusal of the 'Romance of the Forest,' and the 'Mysteries of Udolpho.' "[41] Hazlitt's words undermine Burke's mechanical account by suggesting that the prior consumption of texts controls the "impression[s]" one registers—indeed, that one misrecognizes—as immediate. Perception *is* interpretation; more crucially, to perceive an object or landscape is to endow it with powers that enable it to act upon you.

Radcliffe's landscapes function, we might say, like a fetish. We have seen that Terry Castle has suggested that *Udolpho* leaves the supernatural not so much "explained" as "rerouted . . . into the realm of the everyday": the "spectral images of those one loves," rather than "old-fashioned ghosts," haunt us.[42] But this novel seems more interested in our investments in inanimate objects than in our relations with human (spectral or otherwise) others. Deidre Lynch has noted that in mid-eighteenth-century fictions "the emotional attachments that people form with possessions . . . can seem as freighted with consequence as the emotional attachments that people form with each other."[43] The landscapes through which Emily travels comfort her more than any person with whom she comes into contact after her parents' deaths. *Udolpho* is obsessed about our obsession with objects. Its opening pages promise to explore our "attachment to objects" (4), and in its persistent attempt to show "how much the heart becomes attached even to inanimate objects" (119) *Udolpho* teems with objects that resemble fetishes: the chestnut tree over which St. Aubert mourns; the books, pictures, chairs, and trees that the errant Valancourt comes to embrace because memories of Emily seem to inhere in them (this return to fetishism marks his return to virtue [594]); the "plane tree" that Emily and Valancourt sacramentalize, endowing it with power to make them remember their shared history and thus to knit them together. If, as critics suggest, the novel depicts Emily as both poet and artist, this plane tree is her supreme fiction, a representation valued not because it corresponds to a prior-existing "real" but for what it does to subjects in the present.

The mechanistic, Burkean model would contend that Emily bestows on an object such as the plane tree a layer of personal associations that might be pealed off to reveal the "real" object beneath. But *Udolpho* shows, on the contrary, that the plane tree only *becomes* an object for Emily as she uses it in her effort to memorialize her experiences with Valancourt. For Emily and Valancourt, this "memorial of the past" (582) pressures them to perform future actions. While the tree reminds them of "the dangers and misfortunes they had each encountered, since last they sat together beneath its broad branches," it demands as well future performances. It is "on this spot . . . beneath its broad branches," that Emily and Valancourt "solemnly vowed" to "imitate [St. Aubert's] benevolence" and to offer to those around them "the example of lives passed in happy thankfulness to GOD, and, therefore, in careful tenderness to his creatures" (671). That their fiction concerning the tree invokes religious discourse ("sacred," "solemnly vowed," "thankfulness to GOD") suggests the object's power: earlier, when Emily had revisited the "well-known scene" of the "high trees, that used to wave over the terrace," which she and Valancourt "had often admired together," the scene's effect on her is so powerful that she is "obliged to stop, and lean upon the wall of the terrace" (583). It is this same power that enables these objects to prompt and, they hope, ensure their future behavior. It is beside the point whether Emily and Valancourt create the aura that they experience as an external force that pressures them; the essential nature of the plane tree becomes less important than the rules for living it generates for them. Their fictional plane tree, which makes demands of them, ought to be described not in the language of Plato but in the language of Darwin or Dewey: it works to knit Emily and Valancourt together. Emily's aesthetic "spectacles" systematically assimilate objects and produce them as "interesting"—a term, empty to modern ears, that identifies an object's capacity to elicit a subject's concern.

An "interesting" object—one that causes subjects to interest themselves in it—provokes subjects to escape the narrow concern with self.[44] Like Radcliffe herself at Hardwick, Emily experiences such objects as if they inherently captured her "interest," as if they caught her in their spell: frequently she feels "she could [not] turn from this interesting object, and, even when she again moved onward, she often sent a look back" (402). *Udolpho* implies, however, that Emily's aesthetic sensibility produces such objects *as* interesting. These objects, like classic fetishes, exert pressure from the moment of their creation back on the subjects who create them.

Texts typically invoke fetishists (or quixotes), as we have seen in chapter 1, to insist on their cure, using such figures to police the boundary between the "real" and imaginative distortions of that "real." *Udolpho*'s representation of fetishistic behavior, however, is striking in that the novel surrounds the perceptions it most wants to privilege with phrases that expose the perceiver as actively making, rather than passively finding, the real. *Udolpho* refrains from explaining differential responses to scenery, as we have seen, by invoking a "real" that puts properly sensible observers through certain paces: instead, the prior consumption of texts controls the impressions one (mis)recognizes as immediate. From its opening pages, when St. Aubert discovers the "improvements" his brother-in-law Quesnel will visit upon his boyhood home, *Udolpho* exposes the omnipresence of fetishism, the "social and personal value[s]" with which we invest "material objects," without trying to cure it. Quesnel, who values only "œconomical prudence" and "pecuniary advantage" (195), plans to cut down a chestnut tree that St. Aubert loves both because of his personal history ("How often, in my youth, have I climbed among its broad branches, and sat embowered amidst a world of leaves" [13]) and transcendent taste (the replacement trees belong "on the banks of the Brenta," not "near a heavy gothic mansion" [13–14]). Radcliffe may have borrowed this emblem of lost childhood objects from Lee's *Recess*, in which, Ellinor tells us, Lord Arlington (whom she has reluctantly married) "resolved to exterminate those ruins where I had owned I passed my childhood, and which, he thought still kept alive embittered remembrances time would otherwise erase."[45] St. Aubert recognizes that Quesnel cannot "comprehend" his personal "feelings" about the tree, which, he suspects, must look "as old-fashioned as the taste that would spare that venerable tree" (13). St. Aubert loses this battle because Quesnel's power (he owns the tree) ensures that his economic evaluation of this object triumphs over St. Aubert's sentimental evaluation of it. Or so it seems: by insisting that Quesnel is blind when it comes to taste, *Udolpho* itself awards St. Aubert the victory he cannot achieve within the novel. What is crucial here is that the novel stages a competition between two vocabularies (economic vs. sentimental) to reject a rationalism that strips from objects the auras bestowed on them by romantic and quixotic minds like St. Aubert's.[46] Wolfram Schmidgen explores a similar structure in Radcliffe's *Romance of the Forest*, in which La Luc, the benevolent patriarch who offers the heroine Adeline refuge, reveals his "intense sentimental relationship to a certain 'spot' around which a small object"—an urn—"gathers his energies." Schmidgen notes that this urn, having "acquired powers of its own," "acts on La Luc," who "needs the actual physical and visual presence of the urn to activate his feelings": La Luc creates, in effect, a personal fetish that functions as a "life-giving force that sustains" him. Radcliffe never implies, Schmidgen adds, that "La Luc's dependence on this spot" is "the folly of an aging or effeminate man,"[47] and *Udolpho* similarly protects St. Aubert's fetishistic devotion to his tree from the debunking force of the quixote trope. Indeed, it is the *un*superstitious or *un*quixotic mind, such as Quesnel's, about which *Udolpho* worries.

Udolpho goes even further in exploring the structure of perception that underlies the quixotic mind it hopes to produce. Immediately after the text endorses St. Aubert's perceptions of objects and rejects the rationalist Quesnel's, St. Aubert exclaims that he is "not yet wholly insensible of that high enthusiasm, which wakes the poet's dream: I can linger, with solemn steps, under the deep shades, send forward a transforming eye into the distant obscurity, and listen with thrilling delight to the mystic murmuring of the woods" (15). When Emily first "listen[s] in deep silence to the lonely murmur of the woods," the text describes her, too, as "wrapt in high enthusiasm" (37). By the late eighteenth-century, writers had begun to free the word "enthusiasm" from the pejorative connotations it possessed in seventeenth-century writing, which deployed it to demean those who, while religiously inspired, claimed to hear or see things unavailable to ordinary senses.[48] The speaker of Joseph Warton's *Enthusiast: Or The Lover of Nature* (1744) claims no special perceptual gift, his "enthusiasm" merely marking his preference for "Nature's simple charms" over cultivated or civilized forms ("coldly correct" art or "smoaky cities").[49] But while in eighteenth-century discourse "enthusiasm" rarely gestured toward political transgressions, it continued often to signify delusory visions, as Emily's aunt's dismissal of "ridiculous enthusiasm" (112) shows; indeed, Emily herself associates her own "pensive enthusiasm" with a "beautiful illusion" (89). When *Udolpho* describes Emily's and her father's "high enthusiasm," then, it cannot avoid the suspicions that still dogged that word: are the objects such enthusiasts encounter "real or imaginary" (535), found or made?[50]

Conventional quixote tales, as we have seen, insist that to know the "real" subjects must resist "enthusiasm," purge their heads of "dreams," and discipline the "eye" from "transforming" (so it can passively register) the real. But here the phrases "high enthusiasm" or "poet's dream" do not undercut St. Aubert's perceptions: one *should* hear the woods murmur. It is crucial, too, that these passages link the capacity to hear the "mystic murmuring of the woods" not only to "high enthusiasm" and a "dream" but to a "transforming eye," an eye, that is, that makes rather than finds what it perceives. The novel does not use these phrases to insist that St. Aubert's enthusiasm discovers a truth hidden from ordinary sight, the sort of vision Wordsworth regularly claimed: in hearing the woods murmur, Wordsworth "see[s] into the life of things" or discovers "knowledge, to the human eye / Invisible."[51] *Udolpho*'s phrasing, on the contrary, implies that St. Aubert's "transforming eye" *produces* this "knowledge." These phrases simultaneously expose *and authorize* the subject's active role in producing objects or phenomenon he or she takes to be "given." *Udolpho* shows that such a "transforming eye" mediates between what Rorty calls the "physical thrust of the stimulus upon the organ" and the subject's perceptions of it.[52] Such supplementary phrases unmoor the way of seeing that Radcliffe privileges from a correspondence, or subordinate relationship, to the "real." Emily and Blanche can be moved and comforted by the landscape because they have fetishistically appointed it to play that role: St. Aubert's "transforming eye" suggests that one needs to be a quixote to hear the waves or the trees murmur.

I have been arguing that *Udolpho* aims to produce (rather than cure) quixotes, but it is perhaps more accurate to say that it exposes that all perceptions inevitably involve the practice of quixotism. The text, in effect, directs attention to the different quixotisms available. *Udolpho* shows that our perceptions always encounter difficulties, whose resolution requires imaginative activity, some hypothesis to make sense of— to make up—the confusions and ambiguities of reality. Emily repeatedly encounters "doubts" (343, 357, 373), "uncertaint[ies]" (7, 151, 386), and "myster[ies]" (234, 303, 387, 571) that leave her "utterly unable to decide" (392, 511) or "no means of ascertaining" (357) the true nature of what she encounters. The novel's "suspense" (156, 243, 319, 342, 403, 438, 442, 511, 512, 664) offers the purest form of this perceptual problem. Emily always desires desperately to "conclude her present state of torturing suspense" (388), but the opacity of experience ensures that she is persistently "compelled to remain in uncertainty . . . where suspense is almost intolerable" (156, 386). This suspense, which typically centers less on an object's meaning than, more fundamentally, on its actual form, occurs because experience offers only inevitably partial views of things we encounter.

Rarely offering "prospects"—the "commanding view" from atop a hill that reveals an entire landscape[53]—*Udolpho* instead depicts characters moving through landscapes that block them from seeing very much at all. The "parting foliage" offers only "doubtful gleams [of] the mountain's hoary head" (74); "the deep twilight . . . admitted only imperfect images to the eye" (175); the "distant landscape . . . gleamed beneath the dark foliage of the foreground" (213); "the immense pine-forests . . . excluded all view but of the cliffs aspiring above" (224); "dusky vapour" often "overspread" the "landscape" with a "veil" of "sweet obscurity" (242); the "faint and uncertain light" of the moon revealed only "partial features of the castle" (373); the "opening woods" enable Emily to catch only "partial glimpses of the castle above" (401); only the "outlines" of a mountain "were distinguishable through the dusk" (408); the "luxuriant shade . . . afforded" only "partial views" of the Mediterranean (539). This lengthy catalog gathers only a small fraction of the instances in which the landscape "prevent[s] Emily from] distinguishing, with any degree of accuracy, the form before her" (367). Such "partial views" were commonplace in the discourse of the picturesque, which denies viewers "access to the god's eye view," "resist[s] perceptual practices based on discerning or forging unity," and uses these obscured views to suggest that human perception achieves only an "inevitably partial" understanding.[54] Without the privilege of an "extensive prospect" from which "to observe" (401), *Udolpho*'s characters must choose and act on the basis of such partial knowledge: Emily's unceasing "enquiries" and "conjectures" (205, 331, 335, 387, 424), efforts that constitute her primary activity in the novel, aim to gain her enough knowledge that she may act prudently or safely. Emily must make enough sense of these "obscure" situations to make choices and to take actions, but her only way of doing so is to fit her partial knowledge of things into a larger framework that helps her make sense of them. Like the characters in Sarah Fielding's *The Adventures of David Simple* (1744), discussed in chapter 3, Emily cannot wait to act or to judge until she has accurately observed her surroundings. Her only way to conclude suspense is to project a meaning on ineradicably ambiguous situations.

The nature of the "reality" Emily confronts—frustratingly incomplete, dangerously incoherent, inevitably partial—requires, that is, that she practice quixotism. She does not have the luxury, as the traditional model of perception demands, to be passive before experience. Her "imagination" must participate in making sense. "From the parts she saw," the text notes at one point, Emily "judged . . . the whole" (227). She errs, then, not by practicing quixotism, not by using the texts in her head to make sense of—or to complete—a "reality" that is frustrating and dangerously incoherent. She errs by practicing a form of quixotism, superstition, that repeatedly disempowers her. Too often she "resolves" uncertainty by reading superstitiously: a lamp's "gloomy light" and "uncertain rays" lead Emily to "fanc[y] she saw shapes flit past her curtains" (241), in the darkness produced by "the long shadows of the pillars" she "imagin[es] she saw some person, moving in the distant obscurity" (343). One of the text's most extended moments traces Emily's struggles to make out an "object" in the "faint twilight, which . . . did not enable her to distinguish" clearly: after first "scarcely doubting, that she had witnessed a supernatural experience," she then "looked round for some other explanation," "dismiss[es] . . . her first surmise," but her continued "enquiry only perplexed her" and, finally having "no means of ascertaining" the truth, "imagination again assumed her empire, and roused the mysteries of superstition" (356–57).

The text seems here to imply that the involvement of Emily's "imagination" marks the moment that this process veers off track: her overreading converts simple or natural objects into supernatural ones. But, as I have argued above, the way of reading the novel privileges—in direct contrast to the way of reading rejected in the above passage—also involves the practice of quixotism. St. Aubert seems to admit this resemblance when he notes that "Futurity is much veiled from our eyes, and faith and hope are our only guides concerning it" (67): restricted to "partial" views and understandings, human understanding must make use of some pattern—some "guide"—to contextualize the "partial" available information. When Emily's thoughts move from the sublime landscape to the deity behind it (when she "contemplate[s] His power in the sublimity of His works" [48]), she similarly deploys her "imagination" to place in context the little that she can see or understand. At these moments, too, it is Emily's "imagination" that, "soar[ing] through the regions of space," enables her to use the landscape or particular objects to contemplate "that Great First Cause" (114). What seems crucial about these moments is that they comfort Emily, a making sense that leaves her better off than she was before: "divine complacency stole over her heart, and, hushing its throbs, inspired hope and confidence and resignation to the will of the Deity, whose works filled her mind with adoration" (114). Here, again, reading for the large (and invisible) plan that links all the visible "works" generates comfort for Emily. This practice of quixotism, in effect, improves the subject.

Emily's friend Blanche finds similarly that whenever she looks out at "the face of living nature," the "shadowy earth, the air, and ocean," "her thoughts ar[i]se involuntarily to the Great Author of the sublime objects she contemplated," and she quickly "breath[es] a prayer of finer devotion, than any she had ever uttered beneath the vaulted roof of a cloister" (475). The pages that precede Blanche's devout prayer describe her "enthusiastic soliloquy" (472), prompted by her view of an "extensive" prospect she sees through her window—or, as the text notes more precisely, prompted by her creation of the prospect out of darkness and gloom:

> The windows . . . afforded a very extensive, and what Blanche's fancy represented to be, a very lovely prospect; and she stood for some time, surveying the grey obscurity and depicturing imaginary woods and mountains, valley and rivers, on this scene of night. (471)

Radcliffe's peculiar gerund—"depicturing"—exposes the active work of Blanche's imagination that makes out of "obscurity" a landscape that not only "elevate[s] the unaccustomed mind of Blanche to enthusiasm" (472) but produces the "prayer of finer devotion" and then "sweet slumbers." *Udolpho* shows, similarly, that the "beloved landscape" (580) that so moves Emily has first been created by her: while at Udolpho, she "took her instruments for drawing, and placed herself at a window, to select into a landscape some features of the scenery without" (276). When the text notes that Emily's "eyes . . . wandered from the page to the landscape, whose beauty gradually soothed her mind into a gentle melancholy" (416), it seems less to differentiate a human-made product (the "page") from a natural one (the "landscape") than to show how a product of Emily's own making can affect her so strongly in such salutary ways. The practice of quixotism, far from marking the doings of an imagination that must be cured, seems necessary to produce the very sorts of "landscapes" that so often sooth Blanche and Emily.

It is remarkable, especially in light of the typical uses of the quixote trope this study has explored, how comfortable *Udolpho* is in exposing the quixotism necessary to produce the very sort of perceptions it most admires. A moment at the novel's start when St. Aubert watches his daughter and Valancourt stroll ahead of him through forest scenery reveals the same phenomenon. St. Aubert sighs "at the romantic picture of felicity his fancy drew; and sighed again to think, that nature and simplicity were so little known in the world, as that their pleasures were thought romantic" (49). At one level, this scene, and the long meditation into which these "sublime charms of nature" launch St. Aubert, enacts the "romantic" defense of the content of quixotism we explored in chapter 2: St. Aubert's complaint that the world "ridicules a passion which it seldom feels" (49) exposes the depravity of the "world" that refuses to value the qualities that quixotes embody. This trope repeats often in the novel, as when Emily's aunt counsels Emily to "get rid of all those fantastic notions about love, and this ridiculous pride, and be something like a reasonable creature" (221). Although "reason" is the mark at which many conventional quixote texts aim, the novel does not ask readers to endorse this notion of the "reasonable": dismissed as "fantastic" by the world, simplicity and romantic love are realities within *Udolpho*. But this scene does not just embrace the content of quixotism: it, like the other scenes we have been analyzing, also embraces its practice.

The narrative exposes, that is, that St. Aubert's aestheticized morality, in which the novel deeply invests (critics treat St. Aubert's famous conclusion to this meditation, in which he insists that "virtue and taste are nearly the same" [49], as authoritative), is itself quixotic. A moment later, as the group continues its journey through the forest, the narrator notes that "[s]ometimes, the thick foliage excluded all views of the country; at others, it admitted some partial catches of the distant scenery, which gave hints to the imagination to picture landscapes more interesting, more impressive, than any that had been presented to the eye. The wanderers often lingered to indulge in these reveries of fancy" (50). The landscapes the travelers "picture," then, are the products of their "fancy," not merely the "real" that external nature "present[s] to the eye." This open acknowledgment positions the "romantic picture" of Emily and Valancourt that, moments earlier, St. Aubert's "fancy drew" as equally imaginative, more St. Aubert's creation than a simple discovery of his "eye." What is crucial to note is that the suggestion that these "romantic pictures" are made rather than found does not function, as in orthodox quixotic narratives, to expose them as fraudulent, or invalid, or less real. Here as elsewhere, *Udolpho* at once authorizes certain perceptions *and* betrays the process, far different than passive perception, that has produced them.

I have been arguing, in effect, that the novel shows that Emily's routine perceptions, rather than just her superstitious ones, engage in the practice of quixotism. They enact, often (though not always) visibly, a structure of making rather than of finding. Critics have tended to notice only when Emily transforms Montoni into a sublime god or Udolpho itself into a prison: these moments stand out because the text, aiming to critique Emily's superstitions, surrounds them with marks of excess that help us see the difference between the object as it (ostensibly) is and the feelings or perceptions with which Emily supplements it. Critics have not seen Emily's routine perceptions (of the landscape, for instance) as quixotic precisely because the text does not subject them to critique, and, as we know from countless quixote stories, critique and then cure constitute the expected trajectory for perceptions marked as quixotic. The many deployments of the quixote tale having taught us that perception must not make, but only find, we assume that any moments that *Udolpho* privileges must involve a sensitive subject encountering the "real" in all its sublimity. But *Udolpho* exposes at times the quixotic structure that underlies the perceptions that constitute Emily's normal experience, exemplified here by her descriptions of scenery: "as [Emily] gazed, the light died away on [the castle's] walls, leaving a melancholy purple tint, which spread deeper and deeper, as the thin vapour crept up the mountain, while the battlements above were still tipped with splendour" (227). Such descriptions so successfully suture us into Emily way of seeing, her spiritualized aestheticism, that they may pass as objective descriptions, and the apparent objectivity of this way of seeing is only strengthened by the fact that the narrative voice shares Emily's tendency to encounter landscapes precisely as Claude Lorrain and James Thomson had taught: noting the play of colors (the "grey tints were well contrasted by the bright hues"), the movement of the spectator's vision ("the eye passed abruptly" from "the steeps" to the "valley below"), and the way elements are linked and divided (the mountains were "united" with the Mediterranean waters, while a distant sail "mark[s] the line of separation between the sky and the waves") (54–55). The difficulty at times of knowing whether or not to ascribe descriptions of natural scenery to Emily's consciousness[55] only exposes how deeply this novel itself embraces Emily's way of seeing, which, with the help of eighteenth-century aesthetics, makes a world in which the divine looms behind or within sublime landscapes.

The text thus legitimizes not merely the perceptions themselves but the process by which subjects and the representations they have consumed make the objects that captivate them: the practice of quixotism itself. James Watt argues that "[i]nstead of presenting her as a female Quixote," Radcliffe "authorizes Emily's experience."[56] I have argued here, on the contrary, that Radcliffe *both* presents Emily as a female quixote *and* authorizes her experience. The text simultaneously exposes and licenses Emily's "transformative eye," which manifests a quixotism so necessary that it places questions of cure entirely to one side. Despite the critical desire to make *Udolpho* confess its commitment to the "real," Radcliffe's text stages the replacement of one habit, superstition, with another, the spiritualized reading of the landscape. *Udolpho* frees us from one "picture" that "held us captive" not to land us in the "real" itself but so another "picture" can captivate us.[57]

Epilogue: Beyond Quixotism?: Quixotism and Contemporary Theory

I. Beyond Quixotism?

Recent critical thinking bears an ambiguous relationship to the legacy of quixotism that this study has traced. Much theoretical discourse is deeply suspicious of the Enlightenment "appeal" to "Reason, conceived of as a transcultural human ability to correspond to reality," on which the quixote trope so thoroughly depends.[1] Georg Lukács, for instance, began a tradition of describing "modern rationalism" itself as quixotic. According to Lukács, modern rationalism displays "unlimited confidence" in its "ability . . . to comprehend the 'true' essence of all things" and claims to have "discovered the *principle* which connects up all phenomena which in nature and society are found to confront mankind." Although this rationalism depicts every other practice as "no more than a *partial system*," Lukács insists that it is this "rationalism" itself that is "partial," blind to the way it quixotically assimilates or "regularly transforms" all experience into its "system," unaware that it does not have "direct access to immediate reality." (We have seen, in chapter 1, that quixotes are routinely indicted for "converting" or "translating" all things into a preexisting pattern or "system.") Approaching this issue not from a Marxist but from an "anarchist" perspective, Paul Feyerabend similarly depicts the "well-trained rationalist" as quixotic: like a "well-trained pet," his willingness always to "obey the mental image of *his* master" and to "conform to the standards of argumentation he has learned" leaves the rationalist unable to see that "what he regards as the 'voice of reason' is but a *causal after-effect* of the training he has received."[2] Both Lukács and Feyerabend, then, depict the rationalist himself as bound by a "mental image" he has earlier consumed ("learned" through "training"), an image that disables this ostensibly privileged knower from knowing the "real" at all. These arguments do double work: they both dismantle the value of universal reason on which the quixote trope depends and, as a further turn of the screw, they depict those who believe in this value as themselves quixotic, incapable of knowing things as they are.[3]

The capacity to redirect the quixote trope against the very value of rationality it commonly serves demonstrates not only the flexibility of the trope but also the lure of the position of objectivity it holds out for its users. The reverberating accusations that often characterize recent scholarship—Marx accuses classical political economists of fetishizing commodities, Baudrillard accuses Marx of fetishizing use value, Sut Jhally accuses Baudrillard of fetishizing consumption—show that quixotism is the booby prize that each critic tries to pass off on others, grasping for themselves the trophy of objectivity.[4] Indeed, it seems impossible for any discourse to protect itself against this charge of quixotism. The vulnerability, it seems, of any discourse to this charge enrolls the quixote trope in the category of "metalanguage" discussed by Baudrillard, which seems to its users to identify the "thinking of others" as "magical" but very often "turns against those who use it." These charges and countercharges of quixotism persist because of the resilience of the Enlightenment fantasy of what William Pietz calls "a man without fetishes," a quixote cured.[5]

Continuing to claim objective or superior vision by depicting his opponents as quixotes, Lukács himself works *within* the quixote trope. His effort to depict bourgeois rationalism as quixotic conforms to what Baudrillard calls the "subtle trap of a rationalistic anthropology," present in any "critical analysis (liberal or Marxist)," that implies *both* a "false consciousness" *and* "presupposes the existence, somewhere, of a non-alienated consciousness of an object in some 'true,' objective state." Lukács does not, that is, just deprivilege rationalist knowledge as quixotic; he reprivileges a different group as authorized knowers—and, in so doing, reaffirms the quixote trope's stark opposition between those who can see clearly and those who cannot. For Lukács, the nonalienated consciousness impossible for the bourgeoisie can be found in the proletariat. If "illusion blinds [the bourgeoisie] to the true state of affairs," this "true state of affairs" can be recognized by the proletariat, whose "standpoint" enables this class to begin, Lukács insists, "comprehending reality . . . without any preconceptions." "The same reality [that] employs the motor of class interests to keep the bourgeoisie imprisoned" in illusion, Lukács writes, "forc[es] the proletariat to go beyond it." "[D]enied the scope for such illusory activity," the proletarian worker "perceives the split in his being."[6] As Brice Wachterhauser, writing on Gadamer, summarizes: "A standpoint is precisely a point from which we *see* and not a point from which we are necessarily blinded."[7]

Lukács's argument counters the effort by dominant groups to deny subordinate groups the ability to "see" the real. Seventeenth- and eighteenth-century scientists, as we have seen in chapter 3, routinely discredited the testimony of whole "categories of people," in particular women and the "vulgar," whose faculties of sensation and thus capacity for sensibility were thought to be "poorly developed" and who, as a result, were "constitutionally prone to undisciplined and inaccurate perceptions." Lukács's model rejects this privileging of the elite by restricting the possibility of "comprehending reality . . . without any preconceptions" to those who occupy subordinate positions. This strategy to empower voices "officially" denied the capacity to perceive accurately or completely has proved extremely serviceable, perhaps most notably in the "feminist standpoint theory" developed by Nancy Hartsock and Sandra Harding. Standpoint theory contends that certain groups, because of their structural position within economies of class, gender, or race, can know the truth of social phenomena to which other groups are necessarily blind. "There are some perspectives on society from which, however well-intentioned one may be, the real relations of humans with each other and with the natural world are not visible," Hartsock writes. But the "adoption of a standpoint . . . exposes the real relations among human beings." This structural position gives those who occupy it "the ability to go beneath the surface of appearances to reveal the real but concealed social relations."[8] The power of standpoint theory can be seen in recent readings of Austen's *Northanger Abbey* (1818), which argue that Catherine Morland's "position of powerlessness and dependency give her a different perspective on the status quo": although the patriarchy, embodied in Henry Tilney, dismisses her insights, the novel as a whole confirms that Catherine's fears diagnose the dangers of patriarchal culture with "stunning accuracy."[9]

The short beast "Fable" at the end of Jane Collier's *Art of Ingeniously Tormenting; with Proper Rules for the Exercise of that Pleasant Art* (1753), which Mary Wortley Montagu, the subject of chapter 4, read (it "tormented me very much," she joked[10]), argues a similar point. In this fable a bunch of beasts discover a poem that "strongly described the misery that is endured, from the entrance of teeth and claws into living flesh." Curious to know the poem's author, the animals find on its title page only the letter "L," which limits possible candidates to "the lion, the leopard, the lynx, and the lamb" and sparks a competition in which the first three animals each claims authorship. Investigation stalls until a horse notes that none of these who "roared so loud to prove their title" could be the poem's author, since the author who so feelingly described "the tortured wretches, who are torn by savage teeth and claws, . . . must be no other than the lamb": it "is from suffering, and not from inflicting torments, that the true idea of [such ravages] is gained." This "Fable" dismisses the knowledge of the dominant animals (lion, leopard, and lynx) to privilege as "true" the understanding of the subjugated (the lamb).[11] Elizabeth Hamilton's *Memoirs of Modern Philosophers* (1800) extends this analysis by proposing that elite class positions not only "distort" the real nature of "external objects" but also blind elite subjects to their own "motives," encouraging instead a thoroughgoing "self-delusion." As Mrs. Fielding, the novel's most admired female figure, argues,

> It is the peculiar misfortune of those who move in a certain sphere, to have their worst propensities so flattered as to render it almost impossible for them to escape the snare of self-delusion. The possessors of rank and fortune are every one surrounded by a sort of atmosphere of their own, which not only distorts and obstructs the view of external objects, but which renders it difficult for them to penetrate the motives of their own hearts.

"If one would know the world," she summarizes, "it is necessary to be dependent."[12] Crucial to note, for our purposes here, is that while standpoint theory, in both eighteenth-century and more recent versions, deploys the quixote trope against the very Enlightenment rationality it initially served, identifying dominant discourse as the "blinded" position, it reaffirms the Enlightenment promise that a "non-alienated consciousness of an object in some 'true,' objective state" can be attained. Such theories imagine a space "beyond quixotism," so to speak, a place from which one can see accurately because one is not held unawares by prejudices or preconceptions.

One mark of the continued lure of this position is that it surfaces even in accounts that seem devoted to critiquing objectivity, even in work that undermines the ground on which objectivity seems to depend: a perception of the "real" that all individuals *should* share in common. The "radical doctrine that all scientific statements are historical fictions made facts through the exercise of power," Donna Haraway notes, "produces trouble when feminists want to talk about producing *feminist* science which is more *true*." Often, Haraway shows, critics who insist on "the difficulty of reconstructing the past" will insert nevertheless "a little sentence that categorically asserts a fact," although the critical presuppositions of this work put beyond reach an "unequivocally readable" fact that "escape[s] social determination" to "become objective." The problem for feminists (to reintroduce a quotation I have used in chapter 4) who try to "insist on a better account of the world," who recognize that "it is not enough to show radical historical contingency and modes of construction for everything," is "how to have *simultaneously* an account of radical historical contingency for all knowledge claims and knowing subjects . . . *and* a no-nonsense commitment to faithful accounts of a 'real' world." Stanley Fish makes a similar point as Haraway when he asserts that the "insight of historicity—of the fashioned or constructed nature of all forms of thought and organization—is too powerful a weapon for those who appropriate it to attack the project of others; for it turns against them when they attempt to place their own project on a footing that is *different*." This "different" footing would rely on the solidity of objectivity itself, whose attractions are revealed by Sandra Harding's question: "how can [we] not want to say *the way things really are* to 'our rulers' as well as to ourselves, in order to voice opposition to the silences and lies emanating from the patriarchal discourses and our own partially brainwashed consciousnesses?"[13]

A further indication of the attraction of the notion that we can occupy a prejudice-free position, "beyond quixotism," is the frequency with which we continue to endow the literatures or genres we most admire with this capacity to distance us from our own beliefs, which seems a prerequisite to remove prejudices and gain true knowledge. Michael Bell's *Literature, Modernism and Myth* (1997) suggests that the "characteristic feature of modernity" is a "double consciousness of living in a world view *as* a world view," and he identifies modernist writers as the first generation fully "aware" that one's "deepest commitments and beliefs are part of a world view" that "cannot be transcendentally grounded or privileged over other possible world views." Contemporaneous with modernist texts, Mikhail Bahktin's "Discourse in the Novel" (1934–35) valorized the novel by claiming that its "primary stylistic project" is to "create images of languages": the novel initiates "the process of coming to know one's own language as it is perceived in someone else's language, coming to know one's own horizon within someone else's horizon."[14] Such discourse seems to reinscribe the quixote trope itself by implying that those who are made aware of these forms, those who are capable of reflecting upon them, can then abandon them. We have seen that John Locke offers a

"Cure" for the "*Prejudices*" that pose "a hindrance to Knowledge": "the only way to remove this great Cause of Ignorance and Error out of the World, is, *for every one impartially to examine himself.*"[15] These accounts value particular literary forms (whether modernist innovations or the novel itself) precisely to the extent that they can provoke this sort of reflection, which enables one to transcend one's given beliefs or prejudices and occupy a space "beyond quixotism."

II. Universal Quixotism?

Recent critical writing, however, challenges *both* the confidence that reflection enables us to distance ourselves from our own beliefs, prejudices, and presuppositions *and* the contention that subaltern subject-positions offer an unmediated view of the "real" itself. This challenge undermines the quixote trope itself, since it implies the impossibility of *ever* occupying the space of clear vision—the "prospect" from which one can, unencumbered, see the entire scene[16]—that the quixote trope requires and guarantees. Much recent theory implies that we are all inevitably and ineradicably quixotes, seeing the world through cultural lenses of which we are largely (and necessarily) unaware. The neopragmatism of Donald Davidson, Richard Rorty, and Stanley Fish embraces Dewey's notion that "we are always biased beings, tending in one direction rather than another": "we see what we want to see, we obscure what is unfavorable to a cherished, probably unavowed, wish. We dwell upon favoring circumstances till they become weighted with reinforcing considerations." Despite our conviction that we hold or choose our beliefs, our beliefs actually "hold" us, as Fish insists: "any framework you have will have *you*, in the sense of limiting in advance what you can see and think." As historian Keith Jenkins argues, "the world/past comes to us always already as stories" and "we cannot get out of these stories (narratives) to check if they correspond to the real world/past."[17] Many of these claims derive from Ludwig Wittgenstein's contention, invoked at the close of chapter 6, that "a *picture* held us captive. And we could not get outside it, for it lay in our language and language seemed to repeat it to us inexorably," which Gadamer echoes: "in all our knowledge of ourselves and in all knowledge of the world, we are always already encompassed by the language that is our own."[18] Wittgenstein's claim surfaces, among other places, as the epigraph to Donna Haraway's *Primate Visions: Gender, Race, and Nature in the World of Modern Science* (1989), which tests his theory against the accounts of the "reality" produced by practicing scientists. Haraway contends that scientists' perceptions "ha[ve] been pervasively determined by borrowings from human social science," "borrowings" of which these scientists themselves are unaware (and often deny). Primatologists do not deliberately construe the behavior of free-ranging monkeys and apes they study through the lens of prevailing social theories; they believe they observe patterns and organizations *in* the objects they analyze. "But these objects," Haraway suggests, "are radically mediated for us" by the social theories that education and experience have deposited in our heads; as these social theories change (dominance hierarchy, semiotics, ergonomics), differently educated primatologists "discover" different "facts" about primate life. As Helen Longino summarizes, Haraway shows that a scientific field as rigorous as primatology is "characterized by metaphoric systems" that "both direct observations and serve to interpret them"; such metaphors "mediate researchers' interactions with their objects of study."[19]

Haraway's "us" here is crucial: in depicting contemporary primatologists as quixotes who view the world through internalized texts or models of which they are unaware, Haraway refuses to tell a story in which, through the passage of time or the use of improved method, "we" come to see more clearly than "them." Moreover, Haraway includes herself among those whose vision—to return to a pair of terms I have used throughout this study—makes what it claims to find. In an essay on the African writer Buchi Emecheta, Haraway avoids establishing the validity of her reading by dismissing other critics' readings as quixotic. Describing her own account as a "noninnocent reading," Haraway admits that she finds in Emecheta's texts what she looks for: "enmeshed in the debates about postmodernism, the multiplicity of women's self-crafted and imposed social subjectivities," her reading "valorized" Emecheta's "heterogenous statuses as exile, Nigerian, Ibo, Irish-British feminist, black woman . . . librarian, mother on welfare, sociologist, single woman . . ." Haraway's own account, then, demonstrates her contention that "all readings are also mis-readings, re-readings, partial readings, imposed readings, and imagined readings of a text that is originally and finally never simply there."[20] Haraway refuses to lay claim to a position of objectivity or to a place from which her account might be seen as objective. She labels such a move the "god-trick," which functions (like the quixote trope) to establish one's objectivity by claiming for oneself the capacity of "seeing everything from nowhere." Michel de Certeau rejects a similar image of objectivity in *The Practice of Everyday Life* (1984), which describes the "voluptuous pleasure" of "seeing Manhattan from the

100th floor of the World Trade Center," from which height the city appears as a "text that lies before one's eyes" and seems to allow "one to read it, to be a solar Eye, looking down like a god." Once "lifted" to the World Trade Center's "summit," we believe we escape "the city's grasp"; it is the "ordinary practitioners of the city," the walkers that "follow . . . an urban 'text' . . . without being able to read it," who are "blind" to the real knowledge of the spaces they traverse. But such free, objective, or godlike vision, de Certeau insists, is a "fantasy" that offers only "*imaginary* totalizations" that fail to know the many practices that, "beneath the discourses that ideologize the city," proliferate "outside the reach of panoptic power."[21] There is no place to stand, de Certeau insists, from which one can see it all. We see only what our position allows, and we typically misrecognize these partial visions as the whole picture.

These accounts describe widespread, and inevitable, contemporary quixotism. This quixotism does not afflict only those analysts, that is, who investigate cultures temporally or culturally distant from their own, although it is this effort to analyze an "other" culture that makes most evident, perhaps, the possibility that analysts will impose or transfer the assumptions of their own culture onto an "other" one. Gadamer worries, as Georgia Warnke writes, that historians who assume that "one can understand the past in the same way that the original participants understood it" will run the risk of "substitut[ing] one's present understanding for [an] original understanding."[22] Disciplines such as history or anthropology have a long tradition of theoretical discussion designed to reassure practitioners that their analyses can avoid this form of quixotism: disciplinary methodologies, in effect, promise to secure objectivity.[23] And, in a cycle that should now be familiar, critiques within these disciplines, portraying these solutions themselves as imaginary, depict as quixotic those anthropologists or historians who believe they can see objectively the naked facts of another culture.[24]

But recent writing, at least since Roland Barthes's *Mythologies* (1957), has shown that structures of quixotism shape perceptions not only when we attempt to understand other times or other cultures but when we encounter our own. The "facts" we take as "given" have always-already passed through cultural systems that have silently but necessarily established them as facts. Londa Schiebinger's work on eighteenth-century science, for instance, depicts Linnaeus as a quixote who "reads" nature itself through a social "lens" of which he is unaware: a "particular social structure . . . seemed so natural to Linnaeus that he inadvertently made it an organizing principle of his botanical taxonomy," his "scientific" taxonomies "read[ing] nature through the lens of social relations in such a way that the new language of botany incorporated fundamental aspects of the social world as much as those of the natural world." But, in addition to showing that the "facts" considered "objective" by one age seem to later scientists penetrated by cultural scripts, "made" by the cultural discourses "in their heads," Schiebinger's work critiques as well contemporary scientists who "assume that stripping away gender bias allows [them] to see more clearly what is 'really' going on in nature—to get closer to the truth free of gender." Refusing to deploy the quixote trope to claim for herself objective vision, Schiebinger summarizes that "we cannot free ourselves of cultural influence; we cannot think or act outside a culture."[25] Edward Said's influential *Orientalism* (1978), similarly, identifies "Orientalism"—the West's "ideas about the Orient," an "internal[ly] consisten[t]" system of representations—as the "lens" that delivers to Westerners an Orient we misrecognize as the "'real' Orient" itself. The close of Said's study invokes scholarship that is not "as blind to human reality" as the Orientalism he has analyzed, but his book as a whole, which acknowledges that "any and all representations, because they *are* representations, are embedded first in the language and then in the culture, institutions, and political ambience of the representer," shows the elusiveness of this ideal.[26] It seems no coincidence (and tragic, if true) that at the very moment that the dominant discourse of cultural studies demands, as Patrick Brantlinger has written, that "in order to understand ourselves, the discourse of 'the Other'—of all the others—is that which we most urgently need to hear," we are taught to suspect that we can always only hear ourselves.[27]

These writers insist that we cannot see the framework that "has" us; nor can we see that the world that seems to be merely waiting for us to discover it has been made by the framework itself. Moreover, they argue that frameworks, presuppositions, or prejudices are necessary to enable perception itself. This strain of recent critical and cultural theory implies, in effect, that we *must be* quixotes in order to perceive or understand anything at all. We all encounter the "real" mediated by discourses we have consumed but of which we are largely unaware: what feel like immediate experiences depend on internalized social forms that have shaped how we experience the world. And this is not, much recent critical theory asserts, a "curable" situation (contrary to the quixote trope's promise). Writing about the history of science, Thomas Kuhn describes scientific "progress" not as an ever-closer approach to accurate descriptions of the "real" but rather as a movement from one "paradigm" to another. "The decision to reject one paradigm is always simultaneously the decision to accept another," he argues: "there is no such thing as research in the absence of any paradigm." Fish claims that Theodor Adorno offers precisely the same choice: even "thought of the most dialectical kind delivers us from the grip of one system only to deposit us in the (equally frozen) grip of another." Philosophers such as Nelson Goodman argue, as we have seen, that perception, which is always partial, "participates in making what we perceive," and cultural theorists have exposed and critiqued the apparatuses by which these partialities get differentially installed and whose interests they serve.[28] Unlike those who reaffirm the quixote trope (deliberately or not) by positing a "real" that some (they) can access and from which others are blind, these theorists position all subjects as at all times quixotic: we all see the world through internalized lenses of which we are unaware. These latter claims seem to elude the ideology, central to orthodox uses of the quixote trope, that separates subjects into those who see the world "as it is" and those whose imaginations "distort" reality. Nobody, in these accounts, sees the world "as it is."

This latter alternative, it is true, runs the risk of collapse back into the very quixote trope it seems to counter if the claim that all subjects are quixotic carries with it the corollary that recognizing this fact makes a difference: does the recognition that all vision is shaped by cultural scripts enable one to change one's own vision or to see more clearly? Answering this question in the affirmative seems to posit a (now familiar) position *beyond* quixotism—a position from which one can see or reflect upon one's own beliefs and then abandon them—that reaffirms the orthodox quixote trope. The crucial question, then, is whether recognizing ourselves as a quixote, our own vision shaped by discourses of which we are unaware, enables us to occupy a different position? What would the consequences of such recognition be? Do we move from being quixotes to being self-conscious quixotes? Or is the latter position an impossibility, since self-knowledge, as we have seen in the previous chapters, is precisely that which quixotes lack? What would it mean to be a self-conscious quixote?

The varied approaches to these questions lie at the heart of the famous quarrel between Hans-Georg Gadamer and Jürgen Habermas over precisely what "reflection" achieves: Gadamer doubts that a hermeneutic practice that "mak[es] us aware" of our preconceptions is enough to dissolve them. Gadamer tries to answer the question of "what hermeneutical reflection really does" in "On the Scope and Function of Hermeneutical Reflection" (1967), which denies that "reflection" has necessarily an "emancipatory power" (that is, can free us from our quixotism). Habermas had grounded this assumption in his understanding of psychoanalysis, in which "the repression that is seen through robs the false compulsions of their power." But Gadamer contends that reflection "is not always and unavoidably a step towards dissolving prior convictions." The "act of rendering transparent the structure of prejudgments in understanding" can lead "to an acknowledgment," rather than a rejection, of "authority." For Gadamer, "recognizing the operativeness of history in our conditionedness," the aim of all hermeneutic practice, "teaches us . . . to see through the dogmatism" of positing an opposition between tradition and knowing as if we have to reject the former to achieve the latter. We always, Gadamer insists, encounter the world through some "preunderstanding," either accepted blindly or acknowledged: "The historicity of our existence entails that prejudices, in the literal sense of the word, constitute the initial directedness of our whole ability to experience. Prejudices are biases of our openness to the world. They are simply conditions whereby we experience something—whereby what we encounter says something to us."[29] John Dewey's account of "habit" functions similarly. While most philosophers and psychologists explore the "distortion introduced by habit into observation of objects," and "still cherish the illusion that [habits] can be dispensed with in the case of mental and moral acts," Dewey insists that "reason pure of all influence from habit is a fiction": "habits are conditions of intellectual efficiency." The "real opposition," he adds, is not "between reason and habit but between routine and unintelligent habit, and intelligent habit or art."[30]

This effort to recuperate prejudice and habit—Gadamer aims to "restore to its rightful place a positive concept of prejudice that was driven out of our linguistic usage by the French and the English Enlightenment"—naturalizes quixotism. "[O]ur prejudices," Gadamer declares, "constitute our being." Dewey, too, after showing that "the medium of habit filters all the material that reaches our perception and thought," describes habits as "positive agencies." The ineradicability of the practice of quixotism denies that we ever encounter objects in themselves, and any theory—whether Habermas's or Francis Bacon's, discussed in chapter 1—that promises this possibility ignores "the constant operativeness of history in [the understander's] own consciousness" and "impl[ies] that his own understanding does not enter into the event" of understanding. As Fish's critique of Habermas notes, any account that points to "reflection" as capable of mounting "a critique of the way things are" must forget that "the space of reflection" is already "occupied by what are to be its objects." It is only the theoretical separation of the object of knowledge (prejudices, tradition, superstition) from the knowing subject that allows the belief that one can reflect on the tradition—turn it into an object of knowledge, alienated from oneself—and thus know, critique, and reject it. Thomas McCarthy, the ablest analyst of the Gadamer-Habermas debate, summarizes Gadamer's position this way: "All interpretive understanding is necessarily bound to preconceptions and prejudgments." The interpreter "cannot assume a purely subject-object relation to his own cultural heritage; he is not an absolute ego for whom everything else—including his language and culture—are just so many cogitata . . . his concepts, beliefs, ideals, standards, and norms issue from the very tradition that he wishes to interpret."[31]

Gadamer's beliefs about what Georgia Warnke calls the "adequacy of ethical reflection" remain difficult to pin down, and my aim here is not to reconcile his competing desires to recuperate prejudice (a form of what I have called quixotism) and to explain how unwarranted prejudices can be overcome.[32] Many contend that, for Gadamer, whatever "reflection" accomplishes, it seems *in*capable of dispelling quixotism so subjects can encounter things in themselves, and these critics argue that his theory, which seems to permit subjects to gain awareness of the tradition that "grasps us" only so they can grasp it back willingly, leaves hermeneutics incapable of criticizing prejudices that are unwarranted. Habermas complains, for instance, that Gadamer's concept of "reflection" leaves subjects unable to "work themselves free of the form of life in which they *de facto* find themselves."[33] Gadamer would surely object to Habermas's use of the word "free" to describe the place that reflection leaves us, but he nuanced his position after *Truth and Method* (1960) so that his work no longer seemed to "deny the possibility of critical reflection, agency, and emancipation from power."[34] In a 1993 interview Gadamer insists that while his critique of the Enlightenment "war on all prejudgements whatsoever" aimed to insist that it is "possible for prejudgements to play a positive role in understanding," he did not mean to "relieve anyone of the duty to disempower, where possible, prejudices that do not prove to be positive." Gadamer contends, it seems, that one can learn to reflect upon, and even thus dispel, a particular prejudice, but this process does not leave the subject cleansed of all prejudice (the Enlightenment's promise). As David Detmer summarizes, "we can question some prejudices only from the standpoint, at least provisionally, of accepting others. We have no way of jerking ourselves free from all historical and cultural conditioning, so as to arrive at a perfectly neutral standpoint from which to subject all of our prejudices to a purely rational critique."[35]

Stanley Fish joins Gadamer in undermining the Enlightenment promise that "reflection" can vanquish quixotism and restore clear and rational sight. But unlike Gadamer, who contends that "reflection" can lead us to "acknowledge" valuable prejudices or authorities we previously accepted blindly, or reject those that have not "prove[d] to be positive," Fish contends provocatively that self-reflection makes *no* difference whatsoever. "[O]ne's beliefs do not relax their hold because one 'knows' that they are local and not universal," Fish writes. Even somebody "who is firmly convinced of the circumstantiality of his convictions will nevertheless experience those convictions as universally, not locally, true." Implying the ineradicability of quixotism, Fish contends that any conviction of being free from particular beliefs (so one can, as in the liberal fantasy, choose rationally from among competing beliefs) merely reveals a lack of awareness about how strongly one is in the "grip" of beliefs. The quixote trope, then, is merely one way in which subjects affirm their own transcendence at the expense of others' delusions. Rorty concurs: "For the pragmatist, 'knowledge' is, like 'truth,' simply a compliment paid to the beliefs which we think so well justified that, for the moment, further justification is not needed." For "those for whom" an "issue is obviously trivial," any argument about it will seem inexplicable since "nothing is at stake except the idiosyncratic views of overheated individuals." But "for those caught up in the confrontation, the accusation of triviality will proceed from persons incapable of seeing where the matters of true importance lie." Fish can only imagine an oscillation of perspective.[36] Neither position allows for any self-consciousness about the status of one's own vision, not even, in Fish's example, a self-consciousness that fails to alter the belief itself. It is *this* position of "conviction," and the absolute confidence that, for Fish, it implies, that we cannot escape. The knowledge that Fish allows about the historicity or the partiality of one's beliefs (which "do not relax their hold because one 'knows' that they are local and not universal") seems to have no consequences. The natural operation of one's ineradicable quixotism, that is, does not change even when one "knows" that one is a quixote.

III. Quixotism and Agency

The texts I have explored in the previous chapters, it seems to me, suggest that something does change if one recognizes oneself as a quixote. If, as Fish might say, one's *beliefs* do not change—knowing that we are "held" by certain beliefs does not lessen their hold on us—what does change is one's *relation* to these beliefs. Fish's analysis addresses a belief's content, its validity or invalidity: while labeling a belief as quixotic (moving its content from the category of the "real" to the category of the "imagined") may successfully alter others' attitudes, Fish suggests that we ourselves stubbornly continue to believe *what* we have always believed. But, more crucial to this study, to label a set of perceptions as quixotic also exposes the subject's role in making these perceptions. Orthodox quixote narratives, we have seen, use this exposure to identify this practice as making as illegitimate. But the other quixote texts that I have discussed present this phenomenon without condemning it; some even celebrate subjects' active role in constructing the very worlds they take to be given. To recognize that we make our beliefs does not necessarily alter these beliefs, but it does alter our relation to them: they become things for which we must be responsible rather than things that exist outside and independent of us. Rather than treating them as products of a world that one simply decodes, one comes to recognize one's agency in producing them. This is the difference that reflection makes: if it cannot lead us to cleanse our minds of the deposits left there by history, or by our reading—or if it cannot leave our minds *un*prepossessed and thus open to be impressed upon, passively (and properly) by experience itself—it can lead us to accept our beliefs and perceptions as our own (rather than as imposed on us).

This activity or agency is obscured by the many of the contemporary theorists who depict all subjects as quixotes. While these arguments show that the "real" always arrives mediated by cultural forms, the emphasis on beliefs grasping, holding, or gripping subjects replaces attention to the process by which subjects, like quixotes, actively make the world they ostensibly find. Most critical arguments that the "real" *always* arrives mediated by some cultural form depict social actors as what Anthony Giddens has called "structural dopes," and these accounts, by depicting subjects as "simply subjected to social formations" or to beliefs that *choose them*, leave "little room," as Paul Smith has argued, "for an elaboration of a theory of human agency."[37] Eighteenth-century accounts, of course, model this assumption that we are passive before a world of objects, our perceptions and beliefs *forced* upon us by "Nature" itself. The disciplinary assumptions of the natural sciences that solidified in the seventeenth century depended on what Dewey called a "dualistic partitioning" that separates "mind," which is "wholly open and empty," from a "nature wholly fixed" that makes impressions upon it.[38] We have seen that Locke's *Essay Concerning Human Understanding* (1690), describing how objects "obtrude their particular *Ideas* upon our minds, whether we will or no," proposes that "the mind can no more refuse" these impressions "than a mirror can refuse, alter, or obliterate the Images or *Ideas*, which, the Objects set before it, do therein produce."[39] Thomas Reid's *Inquiry into the Human Mind on the Principles of Common Sense* (1764) insists, similarly, that Nature places a wide range of beliefs beyond doubt, no matter what contemporary skeptical philosophers claim. Disputing philosophers whose "system of skepticism" challenged the foundation of common beliefs such as the reality of external objects or of causation, Reid's *Inquiry* insists that it is impossible *not* to hold these beliefs: "by the constitution of our nature, we are under a necessity of assenting to them." Reid admits that he does not "pretend to know" *how* "a sensation should instantly make us conceive and believe the existence of an external thing altogether unlike it," but he insists that "by a law of our nature, such a conception and belief constantly and immediately follow the sensation." Ridiculing philosophers devoted to Descartes's "theory of ideas" (which held that we cannot know real objects but only "ideas" of them in our mind), Reid depicts these philosophers as quixotes "seduced by some received hypothesis" or by "an idol of their own imagination."[40] Reid's effort to differentiate one set of beliefs, guaranteed by Nature itself and thus held by all in common, from another set, which, when believed, mark those who hold them as ridiculous, enacts the quixote trope. Reid guarantees the validity of one set of competing beliefs by locating their origin in "a law of our nature" that "immediately" produces certain "conception[s] and belief[s]" that "constantly and immediately follow the sensation." We are passive before "Nature," which unavoidably produces certain ideas—sensations and their consequent beliefs—within those who are not quixotically devoted to others. Of course the quixote believes that his perceptions occur identically: neither quixote nor rational subject admits their own activity in producing the world they encounter.

For some theorists, however, the inevitable omnipresence of quixotism serves to recuperate (rather than dissolve) the subject's agency. Donna Haraway's work, as we have seen, moves from recognizing the activity of perception to insisting on subjects' responsibility in making the world they encounter: she "insists on the constructed quality of politics and meanings and holds readers responsible for their constructions." As we saw above, Haraway surrounds her reading of Buchi Emecheta's *Joys of Motherhood* (1979) with two competing readings, but she does so *not* to privilege her own and to dismiss the others as partial or deluded. On the contrary, she positions each reading, including her own, as a "non-innocent reading" that has real "stakes." The "highly political practices called reading" produce "inclusions and exclusions, identifications and separations," for which those who deploy these reading practices in different ways are "accountable."[41]

This effort to make readers or critics "accountable" for their claims about texts (or descriptions of the "real") depends on denying that the text can (and does) speak for itself. This metaphor carries the implication that critics or readers must reproduce a language that is not their own: they are accountable, that is, not for the language itself but only for the accuracy with which they reproduce it. For Francis Bacon, as we have seen, the successful scientist's account of nature "echoes most faithfully the voices of the world itself, and is written as it were at the world's own dictation; being nothing else than the image and reflexion thereof, to which it adds nothing of its own, but only iterates and gives it back."[42] It is this model of a "nature wholly fixed" and complete that Dewey's pragmatism challenges, precisely because it demands "subjection" (accurate reproduction or correspondence) rather than "responsibility."[43] Empiricism, Dewey wrote in 1917, which is "tied up to what has been, or is, 'given,'" limits each subject's role in knowledge to reproducing this preexisting "given"; "empirical philosophy" assigns "thought" only the "secondary and retrospective" role of "the gathering together and tying of items already completely given." Such theories deny "thinking" any "constructive power": "genuine projection of the novel, deliberate variation and invention, are idle fictions in such a version of experience. If there ever was creation, it all took place at a remote period. Since then the world has only recited lessons."[44] Pragmatism, which Dewey describes as "inherently forward-looking," refuses to merely "recite lessons": it aims to rewrite reality or to share in the writing of reality. This requires one to "surrender" any concern "with ultimate reality, or with reality as a complete (i.e., completed) whole," or with "the notion of a static universe" in which "Reality is neatly and finally tied up in a packet without loose ends." One must recognize instead that "reality" is "itself in transition," is changing, flexible, and contested, and that we can "influence" and "modify" it.[45] Dewey believed that with this "single move" he had "flanked" orthodox philosophy, rejecting its obsession with distinguishing a proper "copying" of reality from "an improper but unavoidable modification of reality through organic inhibitions and stimulations" (this opposition underlies the quixote trope). Instead, Dewey emphasized distinguishing "the right, the economical, the effective, and if one may venture, the useful and satisfactory reaction" to reality from "the wasteful, the enslaving, the misleading, and the confusing reaction." "The only question," he insisted, is "whether the *proper* reactions take place": the goal should be "to make a *certain* difference in reality, but *not* to make any old difference." The whole point of this "new logic," Dewey stated in 1909, was to "[introduce] responsibility into the intellectual life."[46]

It is, in short, by refusing to subordinate subjects to merely reproducing or registering a "Real" that Dewey manages to build back in each subject's "responsibility." "A world that is . . . indeterminate enough to call out deliberation and to give play to choice to shape its future is a world in which the will is free."[47] More recent critics are unlikely to follow Dewey's confident invocation of a "free" will, but Haraway similarly establishes "accountability" by so deauthorizing the text itself (typically considered authoritative) that it seems almost to disappear: "All readings are also mis-readings, re-readings, partial readings, imposed readings, and imagined readings of a text that is originally and finally never simply there." Because Haraway's deauthorization of the text brackets off the question of whether her reading corresponds or is faithful to a prior "real" (or the author's intention), she can focus on the "stakes" of her own reading, which, like the text it construes, is "enmeshed in contending practices and hopes."[48] Offering a similar description of historical writing, Keith Jenkins insists that historians take responsibility for their stories about a past that traditional historical writing figures as a pre-existing "given": although most believe that evidence is "there before it is used," Jenkins contends that evidence "only really becomes evidence when it has been used" and needs "to be quite literally articulated by the historian." Jenkins insists that "there is no real account, no proper history that, deep down, allows us to check all other accounts against it: there is no fundamentally correct 'text' of which all other interpretations are just variations; variations are all there are." All history, Jenkins asserts, "is always for someone": writers assert particular histories so "they can have real effects (a real say) in the world." Every narrative is of use to the present that tells it. And this insight demands, Jenkins notes, that we recognize "not only . . . the questions one asks and the answers one accepts, but why one asks and answers in the way one does and not another." To borrow (once more) Dewey's language, what is "actually at stake" in any account is "what kind of person one is to become, what sort of self is in the making, what kind of world is making."[49]

This insistence on the agency of readers or writers does not apply solely to verbal objects (literary or cultural histories). Indeed, Haraway extends this analysis to the production of those paradigmatic pre-existing "givens" in Baconian or Enlightenment thought, "objects" or "facts" themselves. In her essay "Modest Witness" (1996), Haraway openly acknowledges her effort to reverse the Baconian project of "factor[ing] out human agency from the product[ion]" of facts: her work aims instead at "unmasking the labor required to produce a fact." As early as "Situated Knowledges" (1988), Haraway rejects Bacon's position (without naming him) when she insists that "[t]he world neither speaks itself nor disappears in favour of a master decoder. The codes of the world are not still, waiting only to be read." Instead, Haraway contends, we help construct the very objects we investigate, embrace, consume, reject, analyze. Indeed, the "boundary" of an object materializes within social interaction. "Boundaries are drawn by mapping practices; 'objects' do not pre-exist as such."[50] This assault on the Baconian project constitutes, I have been arguing, an "embrace" of the practice of quixotism. Haraway not only reveals but also accepts the subjects' role in producing the very "givens" that exert real pressures upon them. This embrace opens up, rather than forecloses, a recognition of our agency in producing the world we typically think we passively encounter.

This embrace of quixotism differs, of course, from the way orthodox quixote tales make use of the figure of quixote. Such tales, which I have discussed in chapter 2, contend that only by rejecting quixotic perceptions can we can encounter things as they really are: privileging the "real" or the "given" as that which exists prior to any subjective projection, such tales promise that the effort to cleanse our minds of all mediations will place us beyond quixotism itself. To embrace the practice of quixotism does not merely reverse this binary opposition to elevate value over fact, interpretation over the given, the subjective over objective: rather, such an embrace exposes that each member of these common pairs of opposites assumes the subject's *absence* from the process of perception. An embrace of quixotism, viewing neither of these polar opposites as pure as the theories I have described above require them to be, repositions the subject as an active agent in perception itself. By an embrace of the practice of quixotism, then, I mean a recognition that we make, rather than just find, the "real" that surrounds us.[51]

Theories that imagine a space beyond quixotism (like orthodox quixote narratives that deploy the quixote trope) reify *a* "real" in which all must eventually be brought to share; those who do not recognize it are deluded, mistaken, partial, interested. Such theories (or narratives) position subjects—ideally, when "cured"—as free from the hold of history. Traditional historical writing, for instance, conceals "the whole working process of making history," which involves historians with "presuppositions," by "prioriti[zing] the original source" and "fetishiz[ing] documents." These narratives (to borrow Michel de Certeau's words) "conceal the complex laws of production that govern" the "fabrication" of discourse by implying that proper or accurate perceptions and beliefs reproduce without mediation the "real" itself: the role such tales imagine for subjects requires resolute passivity.[52] The practice of quixotism exposes, rather than "conceal[s]," such laws by revealing the histories behind behaviors, attitudes, or perspectives that, for the subject, seem immediate. Doubting that experience resolves neatly into "givens" and "interpretations," into primary "facts" and secondary "evaluations," the practice of quixotism suspects that we may make what it feels like we find, that the very features of textual objects that seem "empirically given or presented, existentially vouched for," attain that status only through our acts of making and interpreting. This does not make our readings any less real or valid or persuasive. It does demand that we be "accountable" for them and consider their consequences, consider, as Dewey said, what "changes" such readings might produce "in prior existing things."[53]

Notes

Introduction: The Quixote Trope

1. As my Epilogue explores more fully, these terms stem from Nelson Goodman's *Ways of Worldmaking* (Indianapolis: Hackett, 1978), 14 and *passim*.
2. Frederick Crews, *Postmodern Pooh* (New York: North Point Press, 2001), xv; Phyllis Trible, review of Leon Kass, *The Beginning of Wisdom: Reading Genesis*, in *The New York Times Book Review* (October 19, 2003): 28; Roger Kimball: *The Rape of the Masters: How Political Correctness Sabotages Art* (San Francisco: Encounter Books, 2004), 100, 152.
3. Surprisingly (or perhaps not), there has been little scholarly attention to "over-reading." But see "Over-Reading, Overreading, Over Reading: Implications for Teaching and Learning," ed. Jason Snart and Dean Swinford, a special issue of *Inventio: Creative Thinking and Learning* 5, 1 (2003).
4. Wendy Motooka, *Age of Reasons: Quixotism, Sentimentalism and Political Economy in Eighteenth-Century Britain* (London: Routledge, 1998), 27.
5. Jonathan Swift, *A Tale of a Tub*, ed. S. C. Guthkelch and D. Nichol Smith, second edition (Oxford: Clarendon Press, 1958), 52.
6. See Barbara Johnson, "Melville's Fist: The Execution of *Billy Budd*," in *The Critical Difference: Essays in the Contemporary Rhetoric of Reading* (Baltimore: Johns Hopkins University Press, 1980), 79–109.
7. J. L. Austin, *How to Do Things with Words*, second edition (Cambridge: Harvard University Press, 1975), 117.
8. Bernard Mandeville, *Free Thoughts on Religion, The Church and National Happiness*, ed. Irwin Primer (New Brunswick: Transaction Publishers, 2001), 134. I am grateful to Irwin Primer for this reference.
9. John Dewey, *Human Nature and Conduct* (1922) in *John Dewey: The Middle Works, 1899–1924*, ed. Jo Ann Boydston, 14 vols. (Carbondale: Southern Illinois University Press, 1976–1983), 14: 59.
10. Richard Graves, *The Spiritual Quixote*, ed. Clarence Tracy (Oxford: Oxford University Press, 1967), 435–36, 448.
11. Elizabeth Hamilton, *Memoirs of Modern Philosophers*, 3 vols. (New York: Garland Press, 1974), 2: 125.
12. Mandeville, *Free Thoughts*, 187.

13. Hans-Georg Gadamer, "On the Scope and Function of Hermeneutic Reflection" (1967) in *Philosophical Hermeneutics*, ed. and trans. David E. Linge (Berkeley: University of California Press, 1976), 18–43, quotation at 32–33; Gadamer, "On The Problem of Self-Understanding" (1962) in *Philosophical Hermeneutics*, 44–58, quotation at 51; Priestley quoted in Jenny Uglow, *The Lunar Men: The Friends Who Made the Future* (New York: Farrar, Straus and Giroux, 2002), 76–77.
14. Georg Lukács, "Reification and the Consciousness of the Proletariat" (1920) in *History and Class Consciousness: Studies in Marxist Dialectics* (Cambridge: MIT Press, 1971), 83–222, quotation at 163.
15. Fred Parker, *Scepticism and Literature: An Essay on Pope, Hume, Sterne, and Johnson* (New York: Oxford University Press, 2003), 1.
16. Christopher Norris, *Uncritical Theory: Postmodernism, Intellectuals, and the Gulf War* (Amherst: University of Massachusetts Press, 1992), 14–15. Jean Baudrillard explores these notions in *For a Critique of the Political Economy of the Sign*, trans. Charles Levin (St. Louis: Telos Press, 1981) and *Simulations*, trans. Paul Foss, Paul Patton, and Phillip Beitchman (New York: Semiotext[e], 1983). Don DeLillo's account in *White Noise* (New York: Viking, 1985) of the most photographed barn in America ("Once you've seen the signs about the barn, it becomes impossible to see the barn": 12) has led many critics to propose that "the distinction between the real and fictional cannot be sustained" (Frank Lentricchia, "Don DeLillo," *Raritan* 8 [1989]: 1–29, quotation at 6) and to explore "representations which are . . . lived as real" (John Frow, "The Last Things Before the Last: Notes on *White Noise*," in *Introducing Don DeLillo*, ed. Frank Lentricchia [Durham: Duke University Press, 1991], 175–91, quotation at 180).
17. A. J. Close, *Don Quixote* (Cambridge: Cambridge University Press, 1990), 12; Leo Spitzer, "Linguistic Perspectivism in the *Don Quixote*," in *Linguistics and Literary History: Essays in Stylistics* (Princeton: Princeton University Press, 1945), 41–85; John J. Allen, *Don Quixote: Hero or Fool? A Study in Narrative Technique* (Gainesville: University Presses of Florida, 1969), 21–22.
18. Debra Malina, "Rereading the Patriarchal Text: *The Female Quixote, Northanger Abbey*, and the Trace of the Absent Mother," *Eighteenth-Century Fiction* 8, 2 (1996): 271–92, quotation at 282.
19. See A. P. Burton, "Cervantes the Man Seen Through English Eyes in the Seventeenth and Eighteenth Centuries," *Bulletin of Hispanic Studies* 45, 1 (1968): 1–15; Stuart M. Tave, *The Amiable Humorist: A Study in the Comic Theory and Criticism of the Eighteenth and Early Nineteenth Centuries* (Chicago: University of Chicago Press, 1960), 141–63; Homer Goldberg, *The Art of Joseph Andrews* (Chicago: University of Chicago Press, 1969), 27–43; Susan Staves, "Don Quixote in Eighteenth-Century England," *Comparative Literature* 24, 3 (1972): 193–215; John Skinner, "*Don Quixote* in 18th-Century England: A Study in Reader Response," *Cervantes: Bulletin of the*

Cervantes Society of America 7, 1 (1987): 45–57; Ronald Paulson, *Don Quixote in England: The Aesthetics of Laughter* (Baltimore: Johns Hopkins University Press, 1998); Heinz-Joachim Müllenbrock, "*Don Quixote* and Eighteenth-Century English Literature," in *Intercultural Encounters: Studies in English Literatures*, ed. Heinz Antor and Kevin L. Cope (Heidelberg: Universitätsverlag C. Winter, 1999), 197–209.

20. Stanley Fish, "Interpreting the *Variorum*" (1976) in *Is There a Text in this Class? The Authority of Interpretive Communities* (Cambridge: Harvard University Press, 1980), 147–80, argues that, although we typically think that "formal structures . . . call forth different interpretive strategies," actually one's "predisposition to execute different interpretive strategies will *produce* different formal structures" (169): these "interpretive strategies . . . exist prior to the act of reading and therefore determine the shape of what is read" (171).
21. Donna Haraway, "Reading Buchi Emecheta: Contests for 'Women's Experience' in Women's Studies" (1988) in *Simians, Cyborgs, and Women: The Reinvention of Nature* (New York: Routledge, 1991), 109–24.

Chapter 1 Historicizing Quixote and the Scandal of Quixotism

1. Susan Staves, "Don Quixote in Eighteenth-Century England," *Comparative Literature* 24, 3 (1972): 193–215, quotation at 193.
2. Maria Edgeworth, *Angelina; Or, L'amie Inconnue*, in *The Parent's Assistant and Moral Tales*, ed. Elizabeth Eger and Clíona ÓGallchoir, in *The Novels and Selected Tales of Maria Edgeworth*, 12 vols. (Brookfield, VT: Pickering & Chatto, 1997–2003), 10: 257–302, quotation at 285; Elizabeth Hamilton, *Memoirs of Modern Philosophers*, 3 vols. (New York: Garland Press, 1974), 3: 164. Subsequent references to Hamilton's text will be parenthetical.
3. Samuel Johnson, *Rambler* 115 (April 23, 1751) in *The Rambler*, ed. W. J. Bate and Albrecht B. Strauss, 3 vols., in *The Yale Edition of the Works of Samuel Johnson*, 15 vols. to date (New Haven: Yale University Press, 1958–2005), 4: 252.
4. Richard Popkin, *The High Road to Pyrrhonism*, ed. Richard A. Watson and James E. Force (1980; Indianapolis: Hackett, 1993), 55.
5. For more on quixotism and common sense, see Wendy Motooka, *The Age of Reasons: Quixotism, Sentimentalism and Political Economy in Eighteenth-Century Britain* (London: Routledge, 1998), 91–92.
6. Frederick R. Karl, *The Adversary Literature: The English Novel in the Eighteenth Century: A Study in Genre* (New York: Farrar, Straus, Giroux, 1974), 59–60, 67.

7. Eric J. Ziolkowski, *The Sanctification of Don Quixote: From Hidalgo to Priest* (University Park: Pennsylvania State University Press, 1991), 3–4; Homer Goldberg, *The Art of Joseph Andrews* (Chicago: University of Chicago Press, 1969), 74; Ronald Paulson, *Don Quixote in England: The Aesthetics of Laughter* (Baltimore: Johns Hopkins University Press, 1998), 19. The continued concern to separate the "hero" from the "deluded comic fool" is evident in Pedro Javier Pardo Garcia, "Romantic and Quixotic Heroes in Detective Fiction," *Exemplaria* 2, 1 (1998): 117–23. Susan C. Greenfield, "Money or Mind? *Cecilia*, the Novel, and the Real Madness of Selfhood," *Studies in Eighteenth-Century Culture* 33 (2004): 49–70, is a recent reading that treats the quixote figure as "expos[ing]" the "painful inadequacy of the world" (49).
8. Oscar Mandel, "The Function of the Norm in *Don Quixote*," *Modern Philology* 55, 3 (1958): 154–63, quotation at 157; Anthony Close, *The Romantic Approach to "Don Quixote": A Critical History of the Romantic Tradition in "Quixote" Criticism* (Cambridge: Cambridge University Press, 1978), 2, 223; Close, "Theory vs. the Humanist Tradition Stemming from Américo Castro," in *Cervantes and His Postmodern Constituencies*, ed. Anne J. Cruz and Carroll B. Johnson (New York: Garland Press, 1999), 1–21, quotations at 5, 14; Close, *Don Quixote* (Cambridge: Cambridge University Press, 1990), 2.
9. Ziolkowski, *Sanctification*; Alexander Welsh, *Reflections on the Hero as Quixote* (Princeton: Princeton University Press, 1981); Henry Fielding, *Covent-Garden Journal* 24 (March 24, 1752) in *The Covent-Garden Journal and a Plan of the Universal Register-Office*, ed. Bertrand A. Goldgar (Middletown: Wesleyan University Press, 1988), 154–61, quotation at 160.
10. Rosalie Colie, *The Resources of Kind: Genre-Theory in the Renaissance* (Berkeley: University of California Press, 1973), 31.
11. Recent critics often use the term "translation" to describe quixotic activity. See David Marshall, "Writing Masters and 'Masculine Exercises' in *The Female Quixote*," *Eighteenth-Century Fiction* 5, 2 (1993): 105–35: "Arabella manages to translate" Miss Groves's scandalous history "into the conventions of romance in order to read its protagonist as an afflicted heroine rather than a sexually transgressive juvenile delinquent" (106).
12. Harold Bloom, *The Anxiety of Influence: A Theory of Poetry* (New York: Oxford University Press, 1973) and *A Map of Misreading* (New York: Oxford University Press, 1975).
13. John Richetti, "Introduction," in *The Cambridge Companion to the Eighteenth-Century Novel*, ed. John Richetti (Cambridge: Cambridge University Press, 1996), 1–8, quotation at 5.
14. John J. Allen, *Don Quixote: Hero or Fool? A Study in Narrative Technique* (Gainesville: University Presses of Florida, 1969), 41. John Farrell, *Freud's Paranoid Quest: Psychoanalysis and Modern Suspicion*

(New York: New York University Press, 1996) offers an extended exploration of the relations between Cervantes's Quixote and the psychoanalyst's paranoid.
15. Philip K. Dick, "Shell Game" (1954) in *The Collected Stories of Philip K. Dick*, 5 vols. (New York: Citadel, 1991), 3: 189–202, quotation at 3: 195; Paul Smith, *Discerning the Subject* (Minneapolis: University of Minnesota Press, 1988), 87, 96.
16. Michael McKeon, *The Origins of the English Novel, 1600–1740* (Baltimore: Johns Hopkins University Press, 1987), 279.
17. Fred Parker, *Scepticism and Literature: An Essay on Pope, Hume, Sterne, and Johnson* (Oxford: Oxford University Press, 2003). For skepticism, see Popkin, *High Road*; Popkin, *The History of Scepticism from Erasmus to Spinoza*, revised and enlarged edition (Berkeley: University of California Press, 1979) and "Theories of Knowledge," in *The Cambridge History of Renaissance Philosophy*, ed. Charles B. Schmitt and Quentin Skinner (Cambridge: Cambridge University Press, 1988), 668–84. These studies of skepticism ignore Cervantes.
18. Parker Woodward, "Don Quixote," *Baconiana* 14 [No. 56] (1916): 173–86, quotations at 173, 179. Scholars credit Thomas Shelton with *The history of the valorous and wittie knight-errant Don Quixote of the Mancha* (1612) and *The second part of The history of the valorous and knight-errant, Don Quixote of the Mancha* (1620), the first complete translation into any language of Cervantes's *El ingenioso hidalgo Don Quixote de le Mancha* (1605, 1615). See also Edwin Durning-Lawrence, "Did Bacon Write 'Don Quixote'?" *Baconiana* 12 [No. 47] (1914): 169–70; S. A. E. Hickson, "Review of Bacon-Shakespeare-Cervantes," *Baconiana* 17 [No. 64] (1923): 50–61 and *Baconiana* 17 [No. 65] (1923): 136–44; Horace Nickson, "The Authorship of 'Don Quixote,'" *Baconiana* 20 [No. 78] (1931): 271–85; R. Langdon-Down, "Observations on Shelton's *Don Quixote*," *Baconiana* 36 [No. 143] (1952): 58–67; Nieves Mathews, *Francis Bacon: The History of Character Assassination* (New Haven: Yale University Press, 1996), 388.
19. "Introduction," in *The Enlightenment and its Shadows*, ed. Peter Hulme and Ludmilla Jordanova (London: Routledge, 1990), 1–15, quotation at 3–4; Frederick C. Beiser, *The Sovereignty of Reason: The Defense of Rationality in the Early English Enlightenment* (Princeton: Princeton University Press, 1996), 3.
20. Francis Bacon, *Advancement of Learning*, in *The Works of Francis Bacon*, ed. James Spedding, Robert Leslie Ellis, and Douglas Denon Heath, 14 vols. (London: Longman, 1857–1874), 3: 255–491, quotation at 3: 397; Bacon, *Valerius Terminus*, in *Works*, 3: 199–252, quotation at 3: 219.
21. Bacon, *New Organon*, in *Works*, 4: 39–248, quotations at 4: 54–62; Bacon, *Natural and Experimental History*, in *Works*, 5: 131–36, quotation at 5: 132.

22. Bacon, *Great Instauration*, in *Works*, 4: 7–43, quotation at 4: 27.
23. Bacon, *De Augmentis*, in *Works*, 4: 275–498, quotation at 4: 431.
24. Bacon, *Advancement*, 3: 395; Bacon, *Great Instauration*, 4: 27; James Bono, *The Word of God and the Languages of Man: Interpreting Nature in Early Modern Science and Medicine. Volume 1: Ficino to Descartes* (Madison: University of Wisconsin Press, 1995), 226–27; Donna Haraway, "Modest Witness: Feminist Diffractions in Science Studies," in *The Disunity of Science: Boundaries, Contexts, and Power*, ed. Peter Galison and David J. Stump (Stanford: Stanford University Press, 1996), 428–41, quotation at 431.
25. Bacon, *Great Instauration*, 4: 27; Bacon, *New Organon*, 4: 70; Bacon, *Natural and Experimental History*, 5: 132; Bacon, *De Augmentis*, 4: 327.
26. John Locke, *An Essay Concerning Human Understanding*, ed. Peter Nidditch (Oxford: Clarendon Press, 1975), 118; William Congreve, *The Mourning Bride*, in *The Complete Plays of William Congreve*, ed. Herbert Davis (Chicago: University of Chicago Press, 1967), 317–85, quotation at 345; Edmund Burke, *A Philosophical Enquiry into the Origin of our Ideas of the Sublime and Beautiful*, ed. J. T. Boulton (London: Routledge, 1958), 45.
27. Francis Ferguson, *Solitude and the Sublime: Romanticism and the Aesthetics of Individuation* (New York: Routledge, 1992), 40; Thomas Wieskel, *The Romantic Sublime: Studies in the Structure and Psychology of Transcendence* (Baltimore: Johns Hopkins University Press, 1976), 14.
28. Bacon, *Natural and Experimental History*, 5: 132; Bacon, *Great Instauration*, 4: 30.
29. Robert Hooke, *General Scheme*, in *The Posthumous Works of Robert Hooke* (1705), intro. Richard Westfall (New York: Johnson Reprint Corporation, 1969), 1–70, quotations at 9–10.
30. Jonathan Swift, *A Tale of a Tub*, ed. S. C. Guthkelch and D. Nichol Smith, second edition (Oxford: Clarendon Press, 1958), 166–67. Adam Smith called the "System" of Cartesian philosophy "one of the most entertaining Romances that has ever been wrote," because it "deduce[s]" all "phaenomena" from "some principle . . . and all united in one chain": see Smith, *Lectures on Rhetoric and Belles Lettres*, ed. H. C. Bryce (1983; rept. Indianapolis: Liberty Press, 1985), 146.
31. Bono, *Word of God*, 245.
32. Steven Shapin and Simon Schaffer, *Leviathan and the Air-Pump: Hobbes, Boyle, and the Experimental Life* (Princeton: Princeton University Press, 1985), 67, 23; Lorraine Daston, "Introduction: The Coming into Being of Scientific Objects," in *Biographies of Scientific Objects* (Chicago: University of Chicago Press, 2000), 1–14, quotation at 4; see also Daston, "Baconian Facts, Academic Civility, and the Prehistory of Objectivity," in *Rethinking Objectivity*, ed. Allan Megill (Durham: Duke University Press, 1994), 37–64.

33. Bacon, *Great Instauration*, 4: 27.
34. Bacon, *Great Instauration*, 4: 26–27.
35. John Dewey, "What Pragmatism Means by Practical" (1908) in *John Dewey: The Middle Works, 1899–1924*, ed. Jo Ann Boydston, 14 vols. (Carbondale: Southern Illinois University Press, 1976–1983), 4: 98–115, quotation at 102.
36. Motooka, *Age of Reasons*, 6, 92.
37. Mandel, "Function of the Norm," 155. Close concurs that "Cervantes invites us to measure irrationality . . . against a prudent norm," adding that readers miss this since "literature's canonical texts have been teaching us for over two and a half centuries to question the system presupposed by Cervantes: one which treats imaginative excess or individualistic truancy as being, ultimately, an offence to reasonable, socially acceptable norms of behavior" (*Don Quixote*, 87, 114).
38. John Dewey, "The Need for a Recovery of Philosophy," (1917) in *John Dewey: The Middle Works*, 10: 3–48, quotation at 10: 25.
39. I quote Egerton's "The Liberty," published in *Poems on Several Occasions, together with a Pastoral* (London: J. Nutt, 1703), from David Fairer and Christine Gerrard, ed., *Eighteenth-Century Poetry: An Annotated Anthology*, second edition (Oxford: Blackwell, 2004), 11–12 (subsequent parenthetical references will cite line numbers). For Egerton, see Jeslyn S. Medoff, " 'My Daring Pen': The Autobiographical Poetry of Sarah Fyge (1688–1723)" (Ph.D. diss., Rutgers University, 1994); Carol Barash, " 'The Native Liberty . . . of the Subject': Configurations of Gender and Authority in the Works of Mary Chudleigh, Sarah Fyge Egerton, and Mary Astell," in *Women, Writing, History: 1640–1799*, ed. Isobel Grundy and Susan Wiseman (Athens: University of Georgia Press, 1992), 55–69. The best discussion of the poem occurs in a long footnote in Fredric V. Bogel, *The Difference Satire Makes: Rhetoric and Reading from Jonson to Byron* (Stanford: Stanford University Press, 2001), 210 n 33.
40. Edgeworth, *Angelina*, 10: 287.
41. Raymond Williams, *Culture and Society, 1780–1950* (New York: Columbia University Press, 1960), 300; Stanley Fish, "A Wolf in Reason's Clothing" (1997) in *The Trouble with Principle* (Cambridge: Harvard University Press, 1999), 187–210, quotation at 206. See also Fish, "Introduction: That's Not Fair," in *There's No Such Thing as Free Speech and It's a Good Thing, Too* (New York: Oxford University Press, 1994), 3–28, esp. 3–11; Barbara Herrnstein Smith, "The Unquiet Judge: Activism without Objectivism in Law and Politics," in *Rethinking Objectivity*, ed. Allan Megill (Durham: Duke University Press, 1994), 289–311.
42. Paul Hammond, *Figuring Sex Between Men from Shakespeare to Rochester* (Oxford: Clarendon Press, 2002), 9; Leo Bersani, *The Culture of Redemption* (Cambridge: Harvard University, 1990), 179.

43. Alexander Welsh, "The Influence of Cervantes," in *The Cambridge Companion to Cervantes*, ed. Anthony J. Cascardi (Cambridge: Cambridge University Press, 2002), 80–99, quotation at 83; Richard L. Predmore, "El problema de la realidad en el *Quijote*," *Nueva Revista de Filología Hispánica* 7 (1953): 491–92, re-quoted in Predmore's *The World of Don Quixote* (Cambridge: Harvard University Press, 1967), 54–55. Predmore qualifies this view in the later text.
44. For an account of an eighteenth-century text (not discussed in this study) that does allow the "scandal" of quixotism to surface, see Pedro Javier Pardo Garcia, "Novel, Romance and Quixotism in Richardson's *Pamela*," *Atlantis* 18 (1996): 306–36. A more conventional account of *Pamela* is offered in Florian Stuber, "Pamela II: 'Written in Imitation of the Manner of Cervantes,' " in *New Essays on Samuel Richardson*, ed. Albert J. Rivero (New York: St. Martin's Press, 1996), 53–68.
45. Fish, "Wolf in Reason's Clothing," 207.
46. Considering quixotism in early American literature, Gillian Brown, "The Quixotic Fallacy," *Novel* 32, 2 (1999), 250–73, notes: "For a democratic society, where the perennial problem is agreement upon the fundamental general rules to which individuals should conform, narratives about the quixotic fallacy furnish a perfect medium for exploring individual differences and measures for resolving them" (251).
47. Mary Poovey, *A History of the Modern Fact: Problems of Knowledge in the Sciences of Wealth and Society* (Chicago: University of Chicago Press, 1998), 114; George M. Fredrickson, *Racism: A Short History* (Princeton: Princeton University Press, 2002). See Kwame Anthony Appiah's review of Fredrickson's book in *The New York Times Book Review* (August 4, 2002), 11.
48. Locke, *Essay Concerning Human Understanding*, 101; John Milton, *Areopagitica*, in *Complete Prose Works of John Milton*, gen. ed. Don M. Wolfe, 8 vols. (New Haven: Yale University Press, 1953–80), 2: 484–570, quotation at 2: 543.
49. Joel Weinsheimer, *Eighteenth-Century Hermeneutics: Philosophy of Interpretation in England from Locke to Burke* (New Haven: Yale University Press, 1993), 28; John P. Wright, "Association, Madness, and the Measures of Probability in Locke and Hume," in *Psychology and Literature in the Eighteenth Century*, ed. Christopher Fox (New York: AMS Press, 1987), 103–27, quotation at 105; see also Martin Kallich, *The Association of Ideas and Critical Theory in Eighteenth-Century England: A History of a Psychological Method in English Criticism* (The Hague: Mouton, 1970). Greenfield, "Money or Mind?," notes that when "Locke insists that all knowledge is empirically derived from sensory experience, he inevitably (if unwittingly) raises the skeptical possibility" that individuals never encounter reality itself (51).

50. Brown, "Quixotic Fallacy," 260.
51. Mandel, "Function of the Norm," 159.
52. Edwin B. Knowles first gathered seventeenth-century allusions to *Don Quixote* in "Don Quixote through English Eyes," *Hispania* 23, 2 (1940): 103–15; "Allusions to *Don Quixote* before 1660," *Philological Quarterly* 20, 4 (1941): 573–86; "Cervantes and English Literature," *Cervantes Across the Centuries*, ed. Angel Flores and M. J. Benardete (1948; rept. New York: Gordian Press, 1969), 277–303; for additional allusions, see Edward M. Wilson, "Cervantes and English Literature of the Seventeenth Century," *Bulletin Hispanique* 50, 1 (1948): 27–52, Johannes Hartau, "Don Quixote in Broadsheets of the Seventeenth and Early Eighteenth Centuries," *Journal of the Warburg and Courtauld Institutes* 48 (1985): 234–38, and Gustav Ungerer, "Recovering Unrecorded Quixote Allusions in Ephemeral English Publications of the late 1650s," *Bodleian Library Record* 17, 1 (2000): 65–69. For general accounts of Cervantes in England, see (in addition to the studies cited in Introduction, note 19) James Fitzmaurice-Kelly, "Cervantes in England," *Proceedings of the British Academy* 2 (1906): 11–29; Edgar Allison Peers, "Cervantes in England," *Bulletin of Spanish Studies* 24, 4 (1947): 226–38.
53. Edmund Gayton, *Pleasant Notes Upon Don Quixot* (London: William Hunt, 1654), *2[ii]; John Taylor, *Swarme of Sectaries, and Schismatiques* (1641) in *Images of English Puritanism: A Collection of Contemporary Sources, 1589–1646*, ed. Lawrence A. Sasek (Baton Rouge: Louisiana State University Press, 1989), 297–99, quotation at 299; Bernard Mandeville, *Free Thoughts on Religion, The Church and National Happiness*, ed. Irwin Primer (New Brunswick: Transaction Publishers, 2001), 133.
54. For a more positive evaluation of the link between quixotism and enthusiasm, see Ziolkowski, *Sanctification*, 38–44.
55. Henry More, *Enthuasiasmus Triumphatus* (1662), intro. M. V. DePorte, Augustan Reprint Society, Publication Number 118 (Los Angeles: William Andrews Clark Library, 1966), 2, 14.
56. *A Breife Description or Character of the Religion and Manners of the Phanatiques in Generall* (London, 1660); John Philips, *Montelion, 1660, or, The Prophetical Almanack being a True and Exact Accompt of All the Revolutions that are to Happen in the World this Present Year 1660* ([London], 1660), B[8]r.
57. *Midsummer Moon: or, Lunacy Rampant* in *J. Cleaveland Revived: Poems, Orations, Epistles, and Other of His Genuine Incomparable Pieces* (London: Nathaniel Brooke, 1660), 181; *We have Brought our Hoggs to a Fair Market* (London: Thomas Mills, 1660); John Cleveland, *The Character of a London Diurnall* ([London], 1647), 3. For Cheynell, see Nicholas Tyacke, "Religious Controversy During the Seventeenth Century: The Case of Oxford," in *Aspects of English Protestantism, c. 1530–1700* (Manchester: Manchester University Press, 2001), 262–319.

58. Cleveland, *London Diurnall*, 5–6; Joad Raymond, *The Invention of the Newspaper: English Newsbooks 1641–1649* (Oxford: Clarendon Press, 1996), 227. The passages from *Mercurius Britanicus* can be found in Raymond, *Invention*, 224, 227.
59. John Cleveland, *A character of a diurnal-maker by J.C* (London, 1654), 3.
60. Pietz, "The problem of the fetish, II: The origin of the fetish," *Res* 13 (1987): 23–45, quotation at 35. See also Pietz, "The problem of the fetish, I," *Res* 6 (1985): 5–17; Pietz, "The problem of the fetish, IIIa: Bosman's Guinea and the enlightenment theory of fetishism," *Res* 16 (1988): 105–23; and Pietz, "Fetishism and Materialism: The Limits of Theory in Marx," in *Fetishism and Cultural Discourse*, ed. Emily Apter and William Pietz (Ithaca: Cornell University Press, 1993), 119–51. See also Michael Rosen, *On Voluntary Servitude: False Consciousness and the Theory of Ideology* (Cambridge: Harvard University Press, 1996), 78–80.
61. Astley quoted in Pietz, "The problem of the fetish, II," 40.
62. Eliza Haywood, *The Female Spectator*, ed. Kathryn R. King and Alexander Pettit, vols. 3–4 of *Selected Works of Eliza Haywood II* (London: Pickering and Chatto, 2001), 3: 198 (my emphases); Daniel Defoe, *The Compleat English Gentleman*, ed. Karl D. Bülbring (London: David Nutt, 1890), 16–17.
63. Karl Marx, *Capital*, trans. Samuel Moore and Edward Aveling, 3 vols. (New York: International Publishers, 1967), 1: 72–74; Sigmund Freud, *Three Essays on the Theory of Sexuality* (New York: Basic Books, 1962), 20 and "Fetishism," in *The Standard Edition of the Complete Psychological Works of Sigmund Freud*, ed. James Strachey, 24 vols. (London: Hogarth Press, 1953–1974), 21: 149–59.
64. In Jean Baudrillard's words, traditional quixote stories "provide . . . the guarantee of the real, the lived, the concrete . . . of an objective reality": *For a Critique of the Political Economy of the Sign*, trans. Charles Levin (St. Louis: Telos Press, 1981), 137.
65. Ruth El Saffar, "Cervantes and the Games of Illusion," in *Cervantes and the Renaissance*, ed. Michael D. McGaha (Easton, PA: Juan de la Cuesta, 1980), 141–56, notes "the isolation, the unfulfillment, and the separation of the main character from his community"; Quixote "bursts past the bonds of his nameless village" (145).
66. Kristen Poole, *Radical Religion from Shakespeare to Milton: Figures of Nonconformity in Early Modern England* (Cambridge: Cambridge University Press, 2000), 109.
67. Lawrence E. Klein, "Sociability, Solitude, and Enthusiasm," in *Enthusiasm and Enlightenment in Europe, 1650–1850*, ed. Lawrence E. Klein and Anthony J. La Vopa (San Marino: Huntington Library, 1998), 153–77, quotation at 162–63; Jan Goldstein, "Enthusiasm or Imagination? Eighteenth-Century Smear Words in Comparative National Context," in *Enthusiasm and Enlightenment*, 29–49, quotation at 30.

68. Peter Dear, *Discipline and Experience: The Mathematical Way in the Scientific Revolution* (Chicago: University of Chicago Press, 1995), 23. Subsequent references will be parenthetical.
69. Recent studies of the history of reading oddly ignore Don Quixote and his descendants: see *Manners of Reading: Essays in Honor of Thomas R. Edwards*, ed. Adam Potkay and Robert Maccubbin, a special issue of *Eighteenth-Century Life* 16, 3 (1992); *The Practice and Representation of Reading in England*, ed. James Raven, Helen Small, and Naomi Tadmor (Cambridge: Cambridge University Press, 1996); *A History of Reading in the West*, ed. Gugleilmo Cavallo and Roger Chartier, trans. Lydia G. Cochrane (Amherst: University of Massachusetts Press, 1999); Cecile M. Jagodzinski, *Privacy and Print: Reading and Writing in Seventeenth-Century England* (Charlottesville: University Press of Virginia, 1999); Kevin Sharpe, *Reading Revolutions: The Politics of Reading in Early Modern England* (New Haven: Yale University Press, 2000); *Reading, Society and Politics in Early Modern England*, ed. Kevin Sharpe and Steven N. Zwicker (Cambridge: Cambridge University Press, 2003).
70. Blanford Parker, "Reconsidering Eighteenth-Century Poetry," *The Age of Johnson: A Scholarly Annual* 13 (2002): 437–55, quotation at 445.
71. Thomas W. Laqueur, "Credit, Novels, Masturbation," in *Choreographing History*, ed. Susan Leigh Foster (Bloomington: Indiana University Press, 1995), 119–28, quotations at 124, 126. See also Greenfield, "Money or Mind?" 51–52.
72. Henry Fielding, *The Coffee-House Politician*, in *Plays: Volume One, 1728–1731*, ed. Thomas Lockwood (Oxford: Clarendon Press, 2004), 405–98, quotation at 458; Richard Steele, Number 178 (May 30, 1710) in *The Tatler*, ed. Donald F. Bond, 3 vols. (Oxford: Clarendon Press, 1987), 2: 468; Peter Motteux, "The Translator's Preface," *The History of the Renown'd Don Quixote De La Mancha*, 4 vols. (London: Sam. Buckley, 1712), 1: A5.
73. John Locke, *Of the Conduct of the Understanding* (1706), intro. John Yolton (Bristol: Thoemmes Press, 1996), 39. Motooka, *Age of Reasons*, suggests that the "inhabitants" of eighteenth-century England "feared" their "world . . . to be universally quixotic" (51).
74. Laqueur, *Solitary Sex: A Cultural History of Masturbation* (New York: Zone Books, 2003), 340, 341–43 (Laqueur cites many claims that imaginative excess affected women particularly: see 18, 54, 94, 200, 260, 298, 320); Catherine Ingrassia, *Authorship, Commerce, and Gender in Early Eighteenth-Century England: A Culture of Paper Credit* (Cambridge: Cambridge University Press, 1998), 20.
75. Harry Levin, "The Quixotic Principle: Cervantes and Other Novelists" (1970) in *Grounds for Comparison* (Cambridge: Harvard University Press, 1972), 224–43, quotation at 239. See also Paulson, *Don Quixote in England* : by the middle of the eighteenth century "it is the woman who is most likely . . . to have imitated a literary text" (62).

76. Debra Malina, "Rereading the Patriarchal Text: *The Female Quixote, Northanger Abbey*, and the Trace of the Absent Mother," *Eighteenth-Century Fiction* 8, 2 (1996): 271–92, quotation at 274; Jacqueline Pearson, *Women's Reading in Britain, 1750–1835: A Dangerous Recreation* (Cambridge: Cambridge University Press, 1999), 5 (see also 84, 196, 198).
77. William B. Warner, "Licensing Pleasure: Literary History and the Novel in Early Modern Britain," in *Columbia History of the British Novel*, ed. John Richetti (New York: Columbia University Press, 1994), 1–22, 16; Mary D. Sheriff, "Passionate Spectators: On Enthusiasm, Nymphomania, and the Imagined Tableau," in *Enthusiasm and Enlightenment*, 51–83, esp. 54–55.
78. As Ingrassia says in a different context: "Scholars have appropriated an eighteenth-century fiction as fact" (*Authorship*, 8). See also McKeon, *Origins of the English Novel*, 52.
79. See Jan Fergus, "Women Readers: A Case Study," in *Women and Literature in Britain, 1700–1800*, ed. Vivien Jones (Cambridge: Cambridge University Press, 2000), 155–76; "Provincial Servants' Reading in the Late Eighteenth Century," in *Practice and Representation of Reading in England*, 202–25; "Eighteenth-Century Readers in Provincial England: The Customers of Samuel Clay's Circulating Library and Bookshop in Warwick, 1770–72," *Papers of the Bibliographical Society of America* 78, 2 (1984): 155–213; *Provincial Readers in Eighteenth-Century England* (Oxford: Oxford University Press, 2006). See also Terry Lovell, "Subjective Powers? Consumption, the Reading Public, and Domestic Woman in Early Eighteenth-Century England," in *The Consumption of Culture, 1660–1800: Image, Object, Text*, ed. Ann Bermingham and John Brewer (New York: Routledge, 1995), 23–41.
80. For "Lady Credit," see Paula R. Backscheider, "Defoe's Lady Credit," *Huntington Library Quarterly* 44, 2 (1981): 89–100; John F. O'Brien, "The Character of Credit: Defoe's 'Lady Credit,' *The Fortunate Mistress*, and the Resources of Inconsistency in Early Eighteenth-Century Britain," *ELH* 63, 3 (1996): 603–631; Ingrassia, *Authorship*, 24–27.
81. Sheriff, "Passionate Spectators," 68.
82. For this shift, see Ernest Lee Tuveson, *The Imagination as a Means of Grace: Locke and the Aesthetics of Romanticism* (Berkeley: University of California Press, 1960); M. H. Abrams, *The Mirror and the Lamp: Romantic Theory and the Critical Tradition* (New York: Oxford University Press, 1953); G. S. Rousseau, "Science and the Discovery of the Imagination in Enlightened England," *Eighteenth-Century Studies* 3, 1 (1969): 108–135, esp. 129–30; James Engell, *The Creative Imagination: Enlightenment to Romanticism* (Cambridge: Harvard University Press, 1981); Frederick Burwick, *Poetic Madness and the Romantic Imagination* (University Park: Penn State University Press, 1996).

83. Colin Campbell, *The Romantic Ethic and the Spirit of Modern Consumerism* (Oxford: Blackwell, 1987), 89, 143, 176, 203. See also Charlotte Sussman, *Consuming Anxieties: Consumer Protest, Gender and British Slavery, 1713–1833* (Stanford: Stanford University Press, 2000), 34–35.
84. E. J. Clery, *Women's Gothic: From Clara Reeve to Mary Shelley* (Horndon: Northcote House, 2000), 14 (see also 23, 61); Sheriff, "Passionate Spectators," 68; Adriana Craciun, *Fatal Women of Romanticism* (Cambridge: Cambridge University Press, 2003), 123; see also Pearson, *Women's Reading*, 57.
85. Claudia Johnson, *Equivocal Beings: Politics, Gender, and Sentimentality in the 1790s: Wollstonecraft, Radcliffe, Burney, Austen* (Chicago: University of Chicago Press, 1995), 12, 14.
86. Johnson, *Rasselas*, in *Rasselas and Other Tales*, ed. Gwin J. Kolb, in *Yale Edition of the Works of Samuel Johnson*, 16: 3–176, quotation at 16: 150. *Rasselas* itself does not gender what it calls "disorders of intellect": "If we speak with rigorous exactness," Imlac says, "no human mind is in its right state. There is no man whose imagination does not sometimes predominate over his reason" (150).
87. See also Roy Porter, *Mind-Forg'd Manacles: A History of Madness in England from the Restoration to the Regency* (Cambridge: Harvard University Press, 1987), 58; Paul-Gabriel Boucé, "Imagination, pregnant women, and monsters, in eighteenth-century England and France," in *Sexual Underworlds of the Enlightenment*, ed. G. S. Rousseau and Roy Porter (Chapel Hill: University of North Carolina Press, 1988), 86–100; Lester S. King, "The Power of the Imagination," in *The Philosophy of Medicine: The Early Eighteenth Century* (Cambridge: Harvard University Press, 1978), 152–81.
88. Fielding, *Covent-Garden Journal*, 160.
89. Eliza Haywood, *Love in Excess*, ed. David Oakleaf, second edition (Peterborough: Broadview Press, 2000), 173.
90. The many satiric representations of Edmund Burke as Don Quixote show as well the continued pejorative connotations of quixotism: see Frans De Bruyn, "Edmund Burke the Political Quixote: Romance, Chivalry, and the Political Imagination," *Eighteenth-Century Fiction* 16, 4 (2004): 695–733, and Nicholas Robinson, *Edmund Burke: A Life in Caricature* (New Haven: Yale University Press, 1996).
91. For the eighteenth-century assumption that "women are *essentially* sexual beings," see Mary Poovey, *The Proper Lady and the Woman Writer: Ideology as Style in the Works of Mary Wollstonecraft, Mary Shelley, and Jane Austen* (Chicago: University of Chicago Press, 1984), 71 (also 19, 23, 35); Ellen Pollak, *The Poetics of Sexual Myth: Gender and Ideology in the Verse of Swift and Pope* (Chicago: University of Chicago Press, 1985), 92.
92. Delarivier Manley, *New Atalantis*, ed. Ros Ballaster (New York: Penguin, 1992), 223–24.

93. Samuel Johnson, *Rambler* 115 (April 23, 1751) in *Yale Edition of the Works of Samuel Johnson*, 4: 252.
94. Jane Barker, *The Galesia Trilogy and Selected Manuscript Poems*, ed. Carol Shiner Wilson (New York: Oxford University Press, 1997), 239; Clara Reeve, *The Progress of Romance* (1785), facsimile reprint, 2 vols. in one, ed. Esther M. McGill (New York: Facsimile Text Society, 1930), 2: 78.
95. John Tinnon Taylor, *Early Opposition to the English Novel: The Popular Reaction from 1760 to 1830* (New York: King's Crown Press, 1943), 53. See also Deidre Lynch, "Personal Effects and Sentimental Fictions," *Eighteenth-Century Fiction* 12, 2–3 (2000): 345–68, esp. 346–47.
96. William Wycherley, *The Country Wife*, in *The Plays of William Wycherley*, ed. Arthur Friedman (Oxford: Clarendon Press, 1979), 241–355, quotation at 283 (3.1.5–6).
97. Mary Wollstonecraft, Letter to Everina Wollstonecraft (October 9, 1786) in *The Collected Letters of Mary Wollstonecraft*, ed. Janet Todd (New York: Columbia University Press, 2003), 82; Wollstonecraft, *Vindication of the Rights of Woman*, in *A Vindication of the Rights of Men* and *A Vindication of the Rights of Woman*, ed. Sylvana Tomaselli (Cambridge: Cambridge University Press, 1995), 65–303, quotation at 193–94.

Chapter 2 Charlotte Lennox's *Female Quixote* and Orthodox Quixotism

1. Mitzi Myers, "Quixotes, Orphans, and Subjectivity: Maria Edgeworth's Georgian Heroism and the (En)Gendering of Young Adult Fiction," *The Lion and the Unicorn: A Critical Journal of Children's Literature* 13, 1 (1989): 21–40.
2. Amy Pawl, "Feminine Transformations of the *Quixote* in Eighteenth-Century England: Lennox's *Female Quixote* and Her Sisters," in *Echoes and Inscriptions: Comparative Approaches to Early Modern Spanish Literatures*, ed. Barbara Simerka and Christopher B. Weimer (Lewisburg, PA: Bucknell University Press, 2000), 142–59, suggests that Tenney's and Barrett's female quixotes, who undergo "repeated humiliation[s]" and suffer the sort of physical abuse "usually reserved for male quixotes," are "treated less sympathetically" than Lennox's or Edgeworth's (155–57): I suggest here a stronger likeness between these texts than Pawl accepts.
3. For the British response during the 1790s to the French Revolution, see M. O. Grenby, *The Anti-Jacobin Novel: British Conservatism and the French Revolution* (Cambridge: Cambridge University Press, 2001); Andrew McCann, *Cultural Politics in the 1790s: Literature, Radicalism, and the Public Sphere* (New York: St. Martin's, 1999); Paul Keen, *The*

Crisis of Literature in the 1790s: Print Culture and the Public Sphere (Cambridge: Cambridge University Press, 1999); Chris Jones, *Radical Sensibility; Literature and Ideas in the 1790s* (London: Routledge, 1993); Gary Kelly, *Women, Writing and Revolution 1790–1827* (Oxford: Oxford University Press, 1993).

4. Tabitha Gilman Tenney, *Female Quixotism*, ed. Cathy N. Davidson, Jean Nienkamp, and Andrea Collins (New York: Oxford University Press, 1992), 4–5. Subsequent references will be parenthetical.

5. See Debra Malina, "Rereading the Patriarchal Text: *The Female Quixote, Northanger Abbey*, and the Trace of the Absent Mother," *Eighteenth-Century Fiction* 8, 2 (1996): 271–92.

6. Charlotte Lennox, *The Female Quixote*, ed. Margaret Dalziel (Oxford: Oxford University Press, 1989), 6 (subsequent references will be parenthetical); Mary Hays, *Memoirs of Emma Courtney*, ed. Eleanor Ty (New York: Oxford University Press, 1996), 10, 14–15; Eaton Stannard Barrett, *The Heroine*, intro. Michael Sadler (New York: Frederick A. Stokes, Co., [1929]), 29 (subsequent references will be parenthetical); Jane Austen, *Northanger Abbey*, ed. John Davie, intro. Terry Castle (New York: Oxford University Press, 1990), 1.

7. Elizabeth Hamilton, *Memoirs of Modern Philosophers*, 3 vols. (New York: Garland Press, 1974), 1: 146–47. Subsequent references will be parenthetical.

8. Maria Edgeworth, *Angelina; Or, L'amie Inconnue*, in *The Parent's Assistant and Moral Tales*, ed. Elizabeth Eger and Clíona ÓGallchoir, in *The Novels and Selected Tales of Maria Edgeworth*, 12 vols. (Brookfield, VT: Pickering & Chatto, 1997–2003), 10: 257–302, quotations at 10: 263, 277. Subsequent references will be parenthetical.

9. Gary Kelly, "Unbecoming a Heroine: Novel Reading, Romanticism, and Barrett's *The Heroine,*" *Nineteenth-Century Literature* 45, 2 (1990): 220–41, quotation at 235.

10. Pawl, "Feminine Transformations," briefly discusses the romance trope "in which a lover's silence or denial is as revealing as a declaration" of love (145). Thomas H. Schmid, " 'My Authority': Hyper-Mimesis and the Discourse of Hysteria in *The Female Quixote,*" *Rocky Mountain Review of Language and Literature* 51, 1 (1997): 21–35, offers a psychoanalytic account of Arabella's "taking the very *absence* of signs of nobility as absolute *confirmation* of nobility and overwhelming desire" (27).

11. Gillian Brown, "The Quixotic Fallacy," *Novel* 32, 2 (1999), 250–73, quotation at 264.

12. Wendy Motooka, *The Age of Reasons: Quixotism, Sentimentalism and Political Economy in Eighteenth-Century Britain* (London: Routledge, 1998), 6, 92.

13. William Shakespeare, *Othello*, in *The Riverside Shakespeare*, second edition, ed. G. Blakemore Evans with J. J. M. Tobin (Cambridge: Houghton Mifflin, 1997), 1246–96, quotation at 1271 (3.3.323–24).

14. Ellen Pollak, *The Poetics of Sexual Myth: Gender and Ideology in the Verse of Swift and Pope* (Chicago: University of Chicago Press, 1985), 92; Mary Poovey, *The Proper Lady and the Woman Writer: Ideology as Style in the Works of Mary Wollstonecraft, Mary Shelley, and Jane Austen* (Chicago: University of Chicago Press, 1984), 19, 23, 35, 71.
15. Avril Horner and Sue Zlosnik, "Dead Funny: Eaton Stannard Barrett's *The Heroine* as Comic Gothic," *Cardiff Corvey: Reading the Romantic Text* 5 (Nov 2000): Online: Internet (7/1/2006): <http://www.cf.ac.uk/encap/corvey/articles/cc05_n02.html>, argue that as a "parody" Barrett's *Heroine* displays an "ideological ambivalence" and is less "reactionary" than critical accounts suggest. But while they claim that Cherry gains "freedom and power" by "play[ing] the part of the heroine," they admit that text "undermines this escape fantasy" and leaves Cherry married to "her father's choice." Kelly, "Unbecoming a Heroine," also notes that "Cherry willingly undergoes reeducation under the tuition of Stuart" (234).
16. Stanley Fish, *Surprised by Sin: The Reader in Paradise Lost* (1967), second edition (Cambridge: Harvard University Press, 1998).
17. William Shakespeare, *King Lear*, in *Riverside Shakespeare*, 1297–1354, quotation at 1342 (5.3.264).
18. Most critics now think Lennox did write it: see O M Brack, Jr. and Susan Carlile, "Samuel Johnson's Contributions to Charlotte Lennox's *The Female Quixote*," *Yale University Library Gazette* 77, 3–4 (2003): 166–73. David Marshall offers the most sophisticated reading of the novel's concern with authorship in "Writing Masters and 'masculine Exercises' in *The Female Quixote*," *Eighteenth-Century Fiction* 5, 2 (1993): 105–35.
19. George Haggerty, *Unnatural Affections: Women and Fiction in the Later 18th Century* (Bloomington: Indiana University Press, 1998), 124, 127–28; Laurie Langbauer, *Women and Romance: The Consolations of Gender in the English Novel* (Ithaca: Cornell University Press, 1990), 84–85.
20. Michel Foucault, *Madness and Civilization*, trans. Richard Howard (New York: Random House, 1965), 201, 205; "Preface," in *Histoire de la folie* (1961), trans. and quoted in David Macey, *The Lives of Michel Foucault* (New York: Pantheon, 1994), 95.
21. Margaret Doody, "Introduction," in *The Female Quixote*, ed. Dalziel, xxv.
22. Marshall, "Writing Masters," 120; Langbauer, *Women and Romance*, 85; Haggerty, *Unnatural Affections*, 136. See also Catherine A. Craft, "Reworking Male Models: Aphra Behn's *Fair Vow-Breaker*, Eliza Haywood's *Fantomina*, and Charlotte Lennox's *Female Quixote*," *Modern Language Review* 86, 4 (1991): 821–38, esp. 834; Pawl, "Feminine Transformations," 142; Motooka, *Age of Reasons*, 133.
23. Deborah Ross, "Mirror, Mirror: The Didactic Dilemma of *The Female Quixote*," *SEL* 27, 3 (1987): 455–73, quotation at 466.

24. Haggerty, *Unnatural Affections*, 124; Kate Levin, "'The Cure of Arabella's Mind': Charlotte Lennox and the Disciplining of the Female Reader," *Women's Writing* 2, 3 (1995): 271–90, quotation at 277–78; Elizabeth Kraft, *Character and Consciousness in Eighteenth-Century Comic Fiction* (Athens: University of Georgia Press, 1992), 87.
25. Francis Bacon, *The Great Instauration* (1620) in *The Works of Francis Bacon*, ed. James Spedding, Robert Leslie Ellis, and Douglas Denon Heath, 14 vols. (London: Longman, 1857–74), 4: 7–43, quotation at 4: 27.
26. Pawl, "Feminine Transformations," 143–44; Michael McKeon, *The Origins of the English Novel, 1660–1740* (Baltimore: Johns Hopkins University Press, 1987), 280; see also Paul Lewis, "Gothic and Mock Gothic: The Repudiation of Fantasy in Barrett's *Heroine*," *English Language Notes* 21, 1 (1983): 44–52, esp. 46.
27. John J. Allen, *Don Quixote: Hero or Fool?: A Study in Narrative Technique* (Gainesville: University Presses of Florida, 1969), 41.
28. Thomas S. Kuhn, *The Structure of Scientific Revolutions*, second edition, enlarged (1962; Chicago: University of Chicago Press, 1970), 7, 24, 63. See also Peter Dear, *Discipline and Experience: The Mathematical Way in the Scientific Revolution* (Chicago: University of Chicago Press, 1995), 13; Thomas Laqueur, *Making Sex: Body and Gender from the Greeks to Freud* (Cambridge: Harvard University Press, 1990), 99.
29. Marshall, "Writing Masters," 120; Ronald Paulson, *Satire and the Novel in Eighteenth-Century England* (New Haven: Yale University Press, 1967), 276.
30. Pawl, "Feminine Transformations," 146. Marshall, "Writing Masters," argues similarly that Arabella's "absolute power is a fiction, a fantasy, because she is only a character in a prescripted plot that dictates her words and actions" (121).
31. John Locke, *An Essay Concerning Human Understanding*, ed. Peter Nidditch (Oxford: Clarendon Press, 1975), 131. Samuel Johnson's *Dictionary of the English Language* (London: W. Strahan, 1755), cites this quotation from Locke in its fourth definition of "Power."
32. Kraft, *Character and Consciousness*, 98, my emphases.
33. Motooka, *Age of Reasons*, 126.
34. Charlotte Lennox, *The Life of Harriot Stuart*, ed. Susan Kubica Howard (London: Associated University Presses, 1995), 66. Subsequent references will be parenthetical.
35. Patricia Meyer Spacks, *Desire and Truth: Functions of Plot in Eighteenth-Century English Novels* (Chicago: University of Chicago Press, 1994), 15–16. See also John Tinnon Taylor, *Early Opposition to the English Novel* (New York: King's Crown Press, 1943), 59–69.
36. Charlotte Lennox, "The Art of Coquetry," in *Poems on Several Occasions Written by a Lady* (1747), rept. in Miriam Rossiter Small, *Charlotte Ramsay Lennox: An Eighteenth-Century Lady of Letters*

(New Haven: Yale University Press, 1935), 233–36, quotation at 235 (lines 107–108).

37. An apostrophe (which eighteenth-century texts routinely use both for genitive singulars and nominative plurals) follows each proper name in the first and second edition.
38. James J. Lynch, "Romance and Realism in Charlotte Lennox's *The Female Quixote*," *Essays in Literature* 14, 1 (1987): 51–63, quotation at 51; Ross, "Mirror, Mirror," 457–58; see also Spacks, *Desire and Truth*, 28–29; Pawl, "Feminine Transformations," 150. For a contrary view, see Langbauer, *Women and Romance*: "*The Female Quixote* shows that romance is excessive fiction, so excessive that *it* is nonsensical, ultimately mad" (63).
39. The novel punishes those who act self-interestedly, such as Sir George, who manipulates the "Laws of Romance": having "meditat[ed] on the Means he should use" to trap Arabella, Sir George "furnish[es] his Memory with all the necessary Rules of making Love in *Arabella*'s Taste" and "served himself with her Foible, to effect his Designs" (130). Leaving Sir George "entangled in his own Artifices" (383), the text rewards Arabella and Glanville with a traditional romance conclusion, "united . . . in every Virtue and laudable Affection of the Mind" (383).
40. See Scott Paul Gordon, "The Space of Romance in Lennox's *Female Quixote*," *SEL* 38, 3 (1998): 499–516. Both Henry Fielding's *History of Amelia* (1751) and Frances Burney's *Evelina, Or, A Young Lady's Entrance into the World* (1778) invoke the category of "*Quixotte*" to erase the possibility that certain characters act by "Design": calculation cannot coexist with delusion. See Fielding, *Amelia*, ed. Martin Battestin (Middletown: Wesleyan University Press, 1987), 424; Burney, *Evelina*, ed. Edward and Lillian Bloom (London: Oxford University Press, 1968), 369.
41. Haggerty, *Unnatural Affections*, 136; Levin, "The Cure," 275. Anne Hall Bailey, "Charlotte Lennox's *The Female Quixote*: The Reconciliation of Enlightenment Philosophies," *Tennessee Philological Bulletin: Proceedings of the Annual Meeting of the Tennessee Philological Association* 38 (2001): 9–18, agrees that the ending "merely pays 'lip service' to the stereotypical concluding formula for an eighteenth-century novel" (14).
42. Levin, "The Cure," 272–73, 275. See also Eric Rothstein "Woman, Women, and *The Female Quixote*," in *Augustan Subjects: Essays in Honor of Martin C. Battestin*, ed. Albert J. Rivero (Newark: University of Delaware Press, 1997), 249–75; and Poovey, *Proper Lady*, on Mary Shelley: "After composing the novels that show most clearly the influence of her mother's self-confidence . . . Mary Shelley began to use her literary career both to defend her [own] behavior and, more significantly, to so characterize it that it would need no defense" (116–17).

43. Catherine Gallagher, *Nobody's Story: The Vanishing Acts of Women Writers in the Marketplace, 1670–1820* (Berkeley: University of California Press, 1994), 176, 179, 192–94. Schmid, "Hyper-Mimesis," agrees that "Arabella's surrender," which has "disturbed feminist readers," is "a grimly fitting ending to the saga of the female hysteric that the novel tells" (33).
44. Kraft, *Character and Consciousness*, 86.
45. Alan Sinfield, "Cultural Materialism, *Othello*, and the Politics of Plausibility," in *Faultlines: Cultural Materialism and the Politics of Dissident Reading* (Berkeley: University of California Press, 1992), 29–51, quotation at 49; Sinfield, "How to read *The Merchant of Venice* without being heterosexist," in *Alternative Shakespeares, Volume 2*, ed. Terence Hawkes (New York: Routledge, 1996), 122–39, esp. 136.
46. Craft, "Reworking Male Models," 832; Patricia Meyer Spacks, *Privacy: Concealing the Eighteenth-Century Self* (Chicago: University of Chicago Press, 2003), 42.
47. This fact begins to answer David Marshall's query about "what sort of instruction or warning daughters and granddaughters were meant to receive from *The Female Quixote*" ("Writing Masters," 133). Christine Roulston, "Histories of Nothing: Romance and Femininity in Charlotte Lennox's *The Female Quixote*," *Women's Writing* 2, 1 (1995): 25–42, claims that Henry Fielding, too, believed that *The Female Quixote* would lead women to "identify with Arabella and hence learn from her errors" (29). See also Brian Hanley, "Henry Fielding, Samuel Johnson, Samuel Richardson, and the Reception of Charlotte Lennox's *The Female Quixote* in the Popular Press," *ANQ: A Quarterly Journal of Short Articles, Notes, and Reviews* 13, 3 (2000): 27–32.
48. Sigmund Freud quoted in John Farrell, *Freud's Paranoid Quest: Psychoanalysis and Modern Suspicion* (New York: New York University Press, 1996), 100.
49. Farrell, *Freud's Paranoid Quest*, 33.

Chapter 3 Suspicion and Experience in Sarah Fielding's *David Simple*

1. A notable exception is Elizabeth Janeway's *Powers of the Weak* (New York: Knopf, 1980), which identifies "suspicion" or what she calls "disbelief" as a "power of the weak" (an "attitude on the part of the ruled" that the "powerful" usually demonize by means of "unpleasant name[s]" such as "*mistrust*," "*cynicism*," "*alienation*, or *disaffection*"). Janeway, however, contends that "disbelief" is "so easy and common that we may tend to disbelieve in the power of disbelieving": eighteenth-century novels display instead the difficulty of disbelief for characters, largely female, who seem all-too-ready to credit what they hear (161, 167).

2. Steven Shapin, *A Social History of Truth: Civility and Science in Seventeenth-Century England* (Chicago: University of Chicago Press, 1994), 291. See also Shapin, *The Scientific Revolution* (Chicago: University of Chicago Press, 1996).
3. Simon Schaffer, "Defoe's Natural Philosophy and the Worlds of Credit," in *Nature Transfigured: Science and Literature, 1700–1900*, ed. John Christie and Sally Shuttleworth (Manchester: Manchester University Press, 1989), 13–44, quotation at 22. The interest in "credit" was high in the 1990s: see, for instance, Julian Hoppit, "Attitudes to Credit in Britain, 1680–1790," *The Historical Journal* 33, 2 (1990): 30–22; John F. O'Brien, "The Character of Credit: Defoe's 'Lady Credit,' *The Fortunate Mistress*, and the Resources of Inconsistency in Early Eighteenth-Century Britain," *ELH* 63, 3 (1996): 603–631; Sandra Sherman, *Finance and Fictionality in the Early Eighteenth Century: Accounting for Defoe* (Cambridge: Cambridge University Press, 1996); Catherine Ingrassia, *Authorship, Commerce, and Gender in Early Eighteenth-Century England: A Culture of Paper Credit* (Cambridge: Cambridge University Press, 1998).
4. Shapin, *Social History of Truth*, 267–68. See also 351: "To require very great rigor, precision, and certainty might be to put too great a strain upon conversation; it was to endanger its continuance. Certain conceptions of truth and precision were not worth that price."
5. Scott Paul Gordon, *The Power of the Passive Self in English Literature, 1640–1770* (Cambridge: Cambridge University Press, 2002). As I discussed briefly in chapter 2 of this study, I explore similar questions in "The Space of Romance in Lennox's *Female Quixote*," *SEL* 38, 3 (1998): 499–516.
6. See Ludmilla Jordanova, *Sexual Visions: Images of Gender in Science and Medicine between the Eighteenth and Twentieth Centuries* (Madison: University of Wisconsin Press, 1989), 19–42.
7. Max Weber, *The Protestant Ethic and the Spirit of Capitalism* (New York: Scribners, 1948); J. Douglas Canfield, *Tricksters and Estates: On the Ideology of Restoration Comedy* (Lexington: University Press of Kentucky, 1997); Ben Ross Schneider, Jr., *The Ethos of Restoration Comedy* (Urbana: University of Illinois Press, 1971), esp. 21–71.
8. Michel Foucault, *Discipline and Punish: The Birth of the Prison*, trans. Alan Sheridan (New York: Vintage, 1977).
9. Peter Stallybrass and Allon White, *The Politics and Poetics of Transgression* (Ithaca: Cornell University Press, 1986), 21–22, 97–98.
10. J. C. Flügel, *The Psychology of Clothes* (London: Hogarth Press, 1950); see also Erin Mackie, *Market à la Mode: Fashion, Community, and Gender in the Tatler and the Spectator* (Baltimore: Johns Hopkins University Press, 1977), 190.
11. Norbert Elias, *The History of Manners: The Civilizing Process: Volume 1*, trans. Edmund Jephcott (New York: Pantheon, 1978), 200.

12. Claude Rawson, "Henry Fielding," in *The Cambridge Companion to the Eighteenth-Century Novel*, ed. John Richetti (Cambridge: Cambridge University Press, 1996), 120–52, quotation at 126.
13. Janet Todd, *Sensibility: An Introduction* (New York: Methuen, 1986), 97; see also Linda Bree, *Sarah Fielding* (New York: Twayne, 1996), 34–35.
14. For this debate over Fielding's evaluation of prudence, see Martin C. Battestin, "Fielding's Definition of Wisdom: Some Functions of Ambiguity and Emblem in *Tom Jones*," *ELH* 35, 2 (1968): 188–217, rept. in *Providence of Wit: Aspects of Form in Augustan Literature and the Arts* (Oxford: Clarendon Press, 1974), 164–92. Others on the pro-prudence side include Eleanor N. Hutchens, " 'Prudence' in *Tom Jones*: A Study of Connotative Irony," *Philological Quarterly* 39, 4 (1960): 496–507, rept. in *Irony in Tom Jones* (Alabama: University of Alabama Press, 1965), 101–19; Glenn Hatfield, *Henry Fielding and the Language of Irony* (Chicago: University of Chicago Press, 1968), 179–96; Frederick G. Ribble, "Aristotle and the 'Prudence' Theme in *Tom Jones*," *Eighteenth-Century Studies* 15, 1 (1981): 26–47; Wolfgang Iser, "The Role of the Reader in Fielding's *Joseph Andrews* and *Tom Jones*," in *The Implied Reader: Patterns of Communication in Prose Fiction from Bunyan to Beckett* (Baltimore: Johns Hopkins University Press, 1974), 29–56.
15. Henry Fielding, *Joseph Andrews*, ed. Martin C. Battestin (Oxford: Clarendon Press, 1967), 23.
16. George Sherburn, "Introduction," in *The History of Tom Jones* (New York: Modern Library, 1950), v–xiv, quotation at x; Wolfgang Iser, *The Implied Reader*, 34, 43, 54. On the incapacity of Fielding's "paragons" to perceive hypocrisy, see also Patrick Reilly, "Fielding's Magisterial Art," in K. G. Simpson, ed., *Henry Fielding: Justice Observed* (New York: Barnes and Noble, 1985), 75–100, esp. 81; Andrew Wright, *Henry Fielding: Mask and Feast* (Berkeley: University of California Press, 1966), 159–62; John Preston, *The Created Self: The Reader's Role in Eighteenth-Century Fiction* (New York: Barnes and Noble, 1970), 124–29; Treadwell Ruml II, "*Jonathan Wild* and the Epistemological Gulf between Virtue and Vice," *Studies in the Novel*, 21, 2 (1989): 114–27.
17. Hutchens, *Irony in Tom Jones*, 101.
18. Sarah Fielding, *The Adventures of David Simple* and *Volume the Last*, ed. Peter Sabor (Lexington: University Press of Kentucky, 1998), 253. Subsequent references will be parenthetical.
19. Hutchens, *Irony in Tom Jones*, 110.
20. Mark Kinkead-Weekes, "Out of the Thicket in *Tom Jones*," in *Henry Fielding*, ed. Simpson, 137–57, quotations at 146, 148; C. J. Rawson, "Order and Misrule: Eighteenth-Century Literature in the 1970's" (1975), rept. as "More Providence than Wit: Some Recent Approaches to Eighteenth-Century Literature," in *Order from Confusion Sprung: Studies*

in *Eighteenth-Century Literature from Swift to Cowper* (London: Allen and Unwin, 1985), 383–418, esp. 397–98, and also Rawson, "Henry Fielding," 140–41.
21. See Gerard A. Barker, "*David Simple*: The Novel of Sensibility in Embryo," *Modern Language Studies* 12, 2 (1982): 69–80; Todd, *Sensibility*, 88–109; Carolyn Woodward, "Sarah Fielding's Self-Destructing Utopia: *The Adventures of David Simple*," in *Living by the Pen: Early British Women Writers*, ed. Dale Spender (New York: Teachers College Press, 1992), 65–81, esp. 73–74; Felicity Nussbaum, "Effeminacy and Femininity: Domestic Prose Satire and *David Simple*," *Eighteenth-Century Fiction* 11, 4 (1999): 421–44, esp. 436. But see G. A. Starr, "Aphra Behn and the Genealogy of the Man of Feeling," *Modern Philology* 87, 4 (1990): 362–72, esp. 367.
22. G. A. Starr, "'Only a Boy': Notes on Sentimental Novels," *Genre* 10 (1977): 501–27, quotations at 502, 506, 509–10, 517–18; almost all these phrases reoccur verbatim in Starr, "Sentimental Novels of the Later Eighteenth Century," in *The Columbia History of the British Novel*, ed. John Richetti (New York: Columbia University Press, 1994), 181–98 quotations at 181–82, 189–90.
23. Barker, "Novel of Sensibility in Embryo," 77. Barker states that *Volume the Last* "converts *David Simple* into a novel of education," but what Barker suggests David learns—he "recognizes the exceptional nature of his temperament . . . and the role it has played in bringing about his tragedy" (78)—positions David less as educatable than as still "fixed," although he "recognizes" his fixity. See also Wendy Motooka, *The Age of Reasons: Quixotism, Sentimentalism and Political Economy in Eighteenth-Century Britain* (London: Routledge, 1998), 113.
24. Aphra Behn, *Oroonoko*, in *The Fair Jilt and Other Short Stories*, Volume 3 of *The Works of Aphra Behn*, 7 vols., ed. Janet Todd (Columbus: Ohio State University Press, 1995), 3: 51–119, quotation at 3: 85, 109. Michael McKeon, *The Origins of the English Novel, 1600–1740* (Baltimore: Johns Hopkins University Press, 1987), notes that Oroonoko experiences a "rueful conversion to Western skepticism" (113).
25. One might call this education into what the Marquis de Stainville calls "Considerations of Prudence," did not the word "prudence" and its cognates (prudent, prudently, prudential) appear only twelve times in the full three volumes of *David Simple*, while the word "suspicion" and its cognates (suspicious, suspiciously, suspect, suspects, suspecting, suspected) appear seventy-four times. (This ratio, six to one, contrasts markedly with other eighteenth-century texts: Henry Fielding's *Joseph Andrews* and *Tom Jones* each use "suspicion" and its cognates only three times more than "prudent" and its cognates, while Richardson's *Pamela* displays the reverse, with prudent and its cognates appearing

twice and much as suspicion and its cognates, and his *Clarissa* features a nearly precise equality of usage.)
26. Terri Nickel, " 'Ingenious Torment': Incest, Family, and the Structures of Community in the Work of Sarah Fielding," *The Eighteenth Century: Theory and Interpretation* 36, 3 (1995): 234–47, quotation at 235.
27. Ann Jessie Van Sant, *Eighteenth-Century Sensibility and the Novel: The Senses in Social Context* (Cambridge: Cambridge University Press, 1993), 60–82; R. S. Brissenden, *Virtue in Distress: Studies in the Novel of Sentiment from Richardson to Sade* (London: Macmillan, 1974).
28. Eliza Haywood, *The British Recluse*, in *Popular Fiction by Women, 1660–1730: An Anthology*, ed. Paula Backscheider and John J. Richetti (New York: Oxford University Press, 1996), 153–224, quotation at 182.
29. Henry Fielding, *Tom Jones*, ed. Martin Battestin (Middletown: Wesleyan University Press, 1975), 614–16.
30. Preston, *The Created Self*, 129.
31. Patricia Meyer Spacks, *Privacy: Concealing the Eighteenth-Century Self* (Chicago: University of Chicago Press, 2003), 67.
32. Henry Fielding, "An Essay on the Knowledge of Characters of Men," in *Miscellanies, Volume One*, ed. Henry Knight Miller (Middletown: Wesleyan University Press, 1972), 153–78, quotations at 155–57.
33. See Robert Markley, *Fallen Languages: Crises of Representation in Newtonian England, 1660–1740* (Ithaca: Cornell University Press, 1993), esp. 104–116, 141–44, 159.
34. Markley, *Fallen Languages*, 113, 122.
35. Shapin, *Social History of Truth*, 201, 287, 77–78, 219.
36. Sarah Fielding, *The Cry*, intro. Mary Anne Schofield, 3 vols. in 1 (Delmar: Scholars' Facsimiles and Reprints, 1986), 1: 52. Subsequent references will be parenthetical.
37. Portia exposes, too, the language used to mask the unpalatable practice of suspicion: "notwithstanding the esteem which they profess'd for suspicion, yet did they think it proper to veil it under the name of caution" (1: 31).
38. For the politics of these revisions, see Janine Barchas, "Sarah Fielding's Dashing Style and Eighteenth-Century Print Culture," *ELH* 63, 3 (1996): 633–56, rept. in *Graphic Design, Print Culture, and the Eighteenth-Century Novel* (Cambridge: Cambridge University Press, 2003), 153–72, and Robert S. Hunting, "Fielding's Revisions of *David Simple*," *Boston University Studies in English* 3 (1957): 117–21.
39. *The Adventures of David Simple.*, ed. Malcolm Kelsall (London: Oxford University Press, 1969), 26–27; compare *David Simple*, ed. Sabor, 20–21.
40. Max Byrd, *Tristram Shandy* (London: Allen and Unwin, 1985), 37–38, 56, 62.

41. Haywood, *The British Recluse*, 155, 210.
42. Toni Bowers, "Sex, Lies, and Invisibility: Amatory Fiction from the Restoration to Mid-Century," in *The Columbia History of the British Novel*, ed. Richetti, 50–72, quotation at 67.
43. Haywood, *Fantomina*, in *Popular Fiction by Women*, ed. Backscheider and Richetti, 227–48, quotation at 239.
44. Seventeenth- and eighteenth-century texts tend to attach the adjective "believing" to female characters: in Aphra Behn's *The Rover, or, The Banish'd Cavaliers* (1677), Angellica Bianca wonders "How many fond believing Fools" Wilmore has seduced (*The Rover*, in *The Plays: 1671–1677*, Volume 5 of *Works of Aphra Behn*, 5: 445–521, quotation at 5: 512), while in Haywood's *Love in Excess, or The Fatal Enquiry* (1719–1720), Camilla contends that since women know that men's "inconstancy is the fault of nature," "we, the fond believers only are to blame" (*Love in Excess*, ed. David Oakleaf [Peterborough: Broadview Press, 2000], 227).
45. Haywood, *The British Recluse*, 211.
46. Mary Davys, *The Reform'd Coquet*, in *The Reform'd Coquet, Familiar Letters Betwixt a Gentleman and a Lady, and The Accomplish'd Rake*, ed. Martha F. Bowden (Lexington: University Press of Kentucky, 1999), 1–84, quotations at 21, 34. Subsequent references will be parenthetical.
47. Behn, *Oroonoko*, 84.
48. Adam Smith, *An Inquiry into the Nature and Causes of the Wealth of Nations*, ed. R. H. Campbell and A. S. Skinner, 2 vols. (1976; rept. Indianapolis: Liberty Press, 1981), 1: 26–27.
49. Janet Todd, *The Sign of Angellica: Women, Writing, and Fiction, 1660–1800* (New York: Columbia University Press, 1989), 102; Todd, *Sensibility*, 102; Woodward, "Sarah Fielding's Self-Destructing Utopia," 74; Nussbaum, "Effeminacy and Femininity," 439; Alexander Pettit, "*David Simple* and the Attenuation of 'Phallic Power,'" *Eighteenth-Century Fiction* 11, 2 (1999): 169–84, esp. 169, 176; see also Bree, *Sarah Fielding*, 32–36.
50. For a revisionist account of the relation between amatory fiction and the fictions typically credited with originating the novel, see William B. Warner, "Licensing Pleasure: Literary History and the Novel in Early Modern Britain," in *Columbia History of the British Novel*, ed. Richetti, 1–22 and *Licensing Entertainment: The Elevation of Novel Reading in Britain, 1684–1750* (Berkeley: University of California Press, 1998).
51. Mary Wortley Montagu, "Written ex tempore in Company in a Glass Window the first year I was marry'd" (1712–1713), in *Essays and Poems and Simplicity, A Comedy*, ed. Robert Halsband and Isobel Grundy (Oxford: Clarendon Press, 1977), 179 (lines 9–11). Haywood's later fiction, such as *The History of Miss Betsy Thoughtless* (1751), represents this ideology in Betsy's brothers, who solve Betsy's

public vulnerability to predatory men by quickly (and prudently) marrying her off. Deborah Nestor, "Virtue Rarely Rewarded: Ideological Subversion and Narrative Form in Haywood's Later Fiction," *SEL* 34, 3 (1994): 579–98, however, questions whether *Betsy Thoughtless* endorses this ideology that it represents.

Chapter 4 Mary Wortley Montagu and the Quixotic Dream of Objectivity

1. John Gay, "Mr Popes Welcome from Greece," in *Poetry and Prose*, ed. Vinton A. Dearing and Charles E. Beckwith, 2 vols. (Oxford: Clarendon Press, 1974), 1: 254–60, quotation at 1: 256 (line 61).
2. Mary Wortley Montagu, *Complete Letters*, ed. Robert Halsband, 3 vols. (Oxford: Clarendon Press, 1965–1967), 2: 14, see also 2: 4, 10–11, 21, 31. Details in this paragraph can be found in Halsband, *The Life of Lady Mary Wortley Montagu* (Oxford: Clarendon Press, 1956), 106–108, and Isobel Grundy, *Lady Mary Wortley Montagu: Comet of the Enlightenment* (Oxford: Clarendon Press, 1999), 226–30.
3. Grundy, *Lady Mary Wortley Montagu*, 229.
4. Headnote to "Epistle From Arthur G[ray] to Mrs M[urra]y," in Mary Wortley Montagu, *Essays and Poems and Simplicity, A Comedy*, ed. Robert Halsband and Isobel Grundy (Oxford: Clarendon Press, 1977), 221.
5. Mary Wortley Montagu, "Epistle From Arthur G[ray] to Mrs M[urra]y," in Montagu, *Essays and Poems*, 221–24, lines 15–23. Subsequent references to Montagu's poetry will be cited parenthetically by line numbers.
6. Robert Halsband, "Virtue in Danger: The Case of Griselda Murray," *History Today* 17, 10 (1967): 692–700, quotation at 700.
7. Stanley Fish, *Surprised by Sin: The Reader in Paradise Lost* (1967), second edition (Cambridge: Harvard University Press, 1998).
8. Cynthia Lowenthal, *Lady Mary Wortley Montagu and the Eighteenth Century Familiar Letter* (Athens: University of Georgia Press, 1994), 169.
9. Lowenthal, *Lady Mary Wortley Montagu*, 36.
10. Montagu, *Complete Letters*, 2: 147–48; 3: 132. Translation of the letter from 1739 from Montagu, *Selected Letters*, ed. Isobel Grundy (New York: Penguin, 1997), 249–50.
11. E. C. Riley, *Don Quixote* (London: Allen and Unwin, 1986), 162; Christopher Braider, *Refiguring the Real: Picture and Modernity in Word and Image, 1400–1700* (Princeton: Princeton University Press, 1993), 102.
12. Jonathan Swift, *The Poems of Jonathan Swift*, ed. Harold Williams, 3 vols. (Oxford: Clarendon Press, 1937), 2: 524–30 (lines 11, 25, 45,

51–52, 118). Subsequent parenthetical references to Swift's poetry cite line numbers from this edition.
13. Ronald Paulson, *Don Quixote in England: The Aesthetics of Laughter* (Baltimore: Johns Hopkins University Press, 1998), 95.
14. Thomas B. Gilmore, Jr., "The Comedy of Swift's Scatalogical Poems," *PMLA* 91, 1 (1976): 33–43, quotation at 33; see also Harry M. Solomon, " 'Difficult Beauty': Tom D'Urfey and the Context of Swift's 'The Lady's Dressing Room,' " *SEL* 19, 3 (1979): 431–44, esp. 431.
15. Donald Greene, "On Swift's 'Scatalogical' Poems," *Sewanee Review* 75 (1967): 672–89, quotation at 677; Gilmore, "Comedy," 36, 39; see also "Forum," *PMLA* 91, 3 (1976): 464–67.
16. William Freedman, "Dynamic Identity and the Hazards of Satire in Swift," *SEL* 29, 3 (1989): 473–88, quotation at 477.
17. Fredric V. Bogel, *The Difference Satire Makes: Rhetoric and Reading from Jonson to Byron* (Stanford: Stanford University Press, 2001), 12, 21, 42, 46, 49, 79 (cf. 71).
18. Jonathan Swift, "A Meditation upon a Broom-stick," in *Prose Works*, ed. Herbert Davis, 14 vols. (Oxford: Blackwell, 1939–1968), 1: 237–40, quotation at 1: 240.
19. Bogel, *Difference*, 131. See also Bogel's admission that the "decision to prefer either of these meanings over the other cannot be scripted by the text but is a matter of interpretive activity" (67).
20. Bogel's account, of course, does not reproduce this logic: see *Difference*, 113–20.
21. As Sarah Franklin, "Making Transparencies: Seeing Through the Science Wars," in *Science Wars*, ed. Andrew Ross (Durham: Duke University Press, 1996), 151–67, notes, "the privilege accorded the value of objectivity is based heavily on a conflation between seeing and knowing" (152).
22. Katherine Hayles, "Consolidating the Canon," in *Science Wars*, 226–37, quotation at 232; Keller, "Gender and Science" (1978) in *Reflections on Gender and Science* (New Haven: Yale University Press, 1985), 75–94, quotations at 79, 84.
23. See Evelyn Fox Keller, "Feminism and Science" (1982) in *Sex and Scientific Inquiry*, ed. Sandra Harding and Jean F. O'Barr (Chicago: University of Chicago Press, 1987), 233–46 and *Reflections on Gender and Science*; Susan Bordo, "The Cartesian Masculinization of Thought" (1986) in *Sex and Scientific Inquiry*, 247–64 and *The Flight to Objectivity: Essays on Cartesianism and Culture* (Albany: SUNY Press, 1987); Carolyn Merchant, *The Death of Nature: Women, Ecology and the Scientific Revolution* (San Francisco: Harper & Row, 1980); Londa Schiebinger, "The History and Philosophy of Women in Science: A Review Essay" (1987) in *Sex and Scientific Inquiry*, 7–34, esp. 33.

24. Mary E. Hawkesworth, "Knowers, Knowing, Known: Feminist Theory and Claims of Truth," *Signs* 14, 3 (1989): 533–57, quotation at 535.
25. Helen E. Longino, "Subjects, Power, and Knowledge: Description and Prescription in Feminist Philosophies of Science," in *Feminist Epistemologies*, ed. Linda Alcoff and Elizabeth Potter (New York: Routledge, 1993), 101–20, quotations at 110, 104.
26. Hawkesworth, "Knowers, Knowing, Known," 535.
27. See Catherine Wilson, *The Invisible World: Early Modern Philosophy and the Invention of the Microscrope* (Princeton: Princeton University Press, 1995).
28. Steven Shapin and Simon Schaffer, *The Leviathan and the Air-Pump: Hobbes, Boyle, and the Experimental Life* (Princeton: Princeton University Press, 1985), 37; Joseph Roach, "The Artificial Eye: Augustan Theater and the Empire of the Visible," in *The Performance of Power: Theatrical Discourse and Politics*, ed. Sue-Ellen Case and Janelle Reinelt (Iowa City: University of Iowa Press, 1991), 131–45, quotation at 132. See also Marjorie Hope Nicolson, "The Microscrope and the English Imagination" (1935), rept. in *Science and Imagination* (Ithaca: Cornell University Press, 1956), 155–234.
29. John Dryden, *Discourse Concerning the Original and Progress of Satire* (1693) in *Poems, 1693–1969*, ed. A. B. Chambers, William Frost, and Vinton A. Dearing, *The Works of John Dryden*, 20 vols. (Berkeley: University of California Press, 1956–2002), 4: 3–90, quotation at 4: 48; Byron, *Don Juan* (1818–1823) in *Byron's Don Juan: A Variorum Edition*, ed. Truman Guy Steffan and Willis W. Pratt, 4 vols. (Austin: University of Texas Press, 1957), 3: 335 (12.40.2).
30. Algarotti and Bentley quoted by Nicholson, "The Microscope," 208, 189. Dustin Griffin, *Satire: A Critical Reintroduction* (Lexington: University Press of Kentucky, 1994), explores the "paradoxical idea that it is better not to look too deeply" (49; cf. 54).
31. Griffin, *Satire*, 48; Alexander Pope, "The First Satire of the Second Book of Horace" (1733) in *Imitations of Horace*, ed. John Butt, in *The Twickenham Edition of the Poems of Alexander Pope*, 11 vols. (New Haven: Yale University Press, 1938–1968), 4: 4–21, quotation at 4: 17 (line 116).
32. Dustin Griffin, *Satire*, 146; Ricardo Quintana, "Situational Satire: A Commentary on the Method of Swift," *University of Toronto Quarterly* 17 (1947/48): 130–36, quotation at 133; Louis I. Bredvold, "The Gloom of the Tory Satirists" (1949), rept. in *Eighteenth-Century English Literature: Modern Essays in Criticism*, ed. James L. Clifford (New York: Oxford University Press, 1959), 3–20, quotation at 11.
33. Samuel Johnson, "Vanity of Human Wishes," in *Poems*, ed. E. L. McAdam, Jr., and George Milne, *The Yale Edition of the Works of*

Samuel Johnson, 15 vols. to date (New Haven: Yale University Press, 1958–2005), 6: 90–109, quotation at 6: 91–92.
34. See P. K. Elkin, *The Augustan Defence of Satire* (Oxford: Clarendon Press, 1973): satirists insist "that they had been provoked into writing satire not by malice, pique, or anger, but by righteous indignation" (91).
35. Bogel, *Difference*, 2, 10, 12, 38 (cf. 18, 49).
36. Claude Rawson, *Gulliver and the Gentle Reader: Studies in Swift and Our Time* (London: Routledge, 1993), 34.
37. Helen E. Longino, "Can There Be a Feminist Science?" in *Feminism and Science*, ed. Nancy Tuana (Bloomington: Indiana University Press, 1989), 45–57, quotation at 51; see also Ruth Hubbard, "Science, Facts, and Feminism," in *Feminism and Science*, 119–31, esp. 125–26.
38. Lorraine Cole, *What Can She Know: Feminist Theory and the Construction of Knowledge* (Ithaca: Cornell University Press, 1991), 31–32, 34.
39. Alexander Pope, *The Rape of the Lock*, in *The Rape of the Lock and Other Poems*, ed. Geoffrey Tillotson, in *The Twickenham Edition of the Poems of Alexander Pope*, 11 vols. (New Haven: Yale University Press, 1938–1968), 2: 125–206, quotation at 2: 155 (Canto 1, line 138).
40. Bogel, *Difference*, 4.
41. Basil Willey, *The Eighteenth-Century Background* (New York: Columbia University Press, 1946), 106. In "The Semiotics of Restoration Satire" (in *Cutting Edges: Postmodern Critical Essays on Eighteenth-Century Satire*, ed. James E. Gill, Tennessee Studies in Literature, Volume 37 [Knoxville: University of Tennessee Press, 1995], 23–42), Rose Zimbardo contends that we have "long believed Restoration satire to be mimetic, and have assumed in it a binary form that brings into collision an idealized antithesis and a thesis, which, however downwardly exaggerated, images the *real*" (30). For the issue of referentiality in satire, see also Griffin, *Satire*, 116–32; Bogel, *Difference*, 10.
42. Roland Barthes, "The Reality Effect," in *The Rustle of Language* (New York: Hill and Wang, 1986), 141–48, quotations at 146, 148. See also the interesting discussion in Troy Bickham, " 'A conviction of the reality of things': Material Culture, North American Indians and Empire in Eighteenth-Century Britain," *Eighteenth-Century Studies* 39, 1 (2005): 29–47, esp. 36–39.
43. For a related account of this poem, see Todd Parker, "Swift's 'A Description of a City Shower': The Epistemological Force of Filth," *1650–1850: Ideas, Aesthetics, and Inquiries in the Early Modern Era* 4 (1998): 285–304.
44. *Mundus Muliebris* (London: R. Bentley, 1690), 2–3; *Mundus Foppiensis*, ed. Michael Kimmel, Augustan Reprint Society, Publication Number 248 (Los Angeles: William Andrews Clark Library, 1988), i.

45. Barry Barnes, *Interests and the Growth of Knowledge* (London: Routledge, 1977), 2.
46. *Mundus Foppiensis*, ii, 8.
47. Bogel, *Difference*, 10.
48. Melinda Alliker Rabb, "Remembering in Swift's 'The Lady's Dressing Room,'" *Texas Studies in Language and Literature* 32, 3 (1990): 375–96, quotation at 393 n 4.
49. Robert N. Proctor, *Value Free Science? Purity and Power in Modern Knowledge* (Cambridge: Harvard University Press, 1991), 9.
50. Harry T. Solomon, "'Difficult Beauty,'" 440; Louise K. Barnett, "The Mysterious Narrator: Another Look at 'The Lady's Dressing Room,'" *Concerning Poetry* 9, 2 (1976): 29–32, quotation at 29; John M. Aden, "Those Gaudy Tulips: Swift's 'Unprintables,'" in *Quick Springs of Sense: Studies in the Eighteenth Century*, ed. Larry S. Champion (Athens: University of Georgia Press, 1974), 14–32, quotation at 21.
51. Barbara Johnson, "Melville's Fist: The Execution of *Billy Budd*," in *The Critical Difference: Essays in the Contemporary Rhetoric of Reading* (Baltimore: Johns Hopkins University Press, 1980), 79–109, quotation at 91.
52. Michel Pêcheux, *Language, Semantics, and Ideology: Stating the Obvious*, trans. Harbans Nagpal (London: Macmillan, 1982), 67.
53. Gilmore, "Comedy," 36–37.
54. Hawkesworth, "Knowers, Knowing, Known," 548; Hayles, "Consolidating the Canon," 229, 231.
55. Pêcheux, *Language, Semantics, and Ideology*, 65.
56. Mary Wortley Montagu, *Reasons*, in Montagu, *Essays and Poems*, 273–76. Subsequent references will be parenthetical, citing line numbers.
57. Donna Landry, "Reading the *Rape* and *To a Lady* with Texts by Swift, Wortley Montagu, and Yearsley," in *Approaches to Teaching Pope's Poetry*, ed. Wallace Jackson and R. Paul Yoder (New York: MLA, 1993), 134–41, quotation at 137.
58. Miss W—, "The Gentleman's Study, In Answer to [Swift's] The Lady's Dressing-Room," in *Eighteenth-Century Women Poets*, ed. Roger Lonsdale (New York: Oxford University Press, 1989), 130–34, quotation at 130–32; "Thoughts upon Reading the *Lady's Dressing-Room* and the *Gentleman's Study*," added to *Chloe Surpriz'd: or, the Second Part of the Lady's Dressing-Room* (London, 1732), 7.
59. Warren Chernaik, *Sexual Freedom in Restoration Literature* (Cambridge: Cambridge University Press, 1995), 14.
60. See Jim McGhee, "Obscene Libel and the Language of 'The Imperfect Enjoyment,'" in *Reading Rochester*, ed. Edward Burns (New York: St. Martins Press, 1995), 42–65, quotation at 59 n 49; Richard E. Quaintance, "French Sources of the Restoration 'Imperfect Enjoyment' Poem," *Philological Quarterly* 42, 2 (1963): 190–99, identifies ten poems; John H. O'Neill, "An Unpublished

'Imperfect Enjoyment' Poem," *Papers on Language and Literature* 13, 2 (1977): 197–202, prints a poem Quaintance overlooks and cites in addition "five poems on the same subject by William Wycherley in which there is no narrative, only reflection" (200 n 6).
61. The phrase "in all Heads . . . a touch of Fool" occurs in a draft, recorded in *Essays and Poems*, 275.
62. Aphra Behn, "The Disappointment," in *Poetry*, Volume 1 of *The Works of Aphra Behn*, ed. Janet Todd, 7 vols. (Columbus: Ohio State University Press, 1992–1996), 1: 65–69, quotation at 1: 69 (lines 137–38); George Etherege, "The Imperfect Enjoyment," in *The Poems of Sir George Etherege*, ed. James Thorpe (Princeton: Princeton University Press, 1963), 7–8, quotation at 8 (line 41).
63. Chernaik, *Sexual Freedom*, 17; Braudy, "Remembering Masculinity," 192–93; see also John H. O'Neill, "Rochester's 'Imperfect Enjoyment': 'The True Veine of Satyre' in Sexual Poetry," *Tennessee Studies in Literature* 25 (1980): 57–71, esp. 61.
64. Bogel, *Difference*, 125.
65. Jill Campbell, "Lady Mary Wortley Montagu and the Historical Machinery of Female Identity," in *History, Gender and Eighteenth-Century Literature*, ed. Beth Fowkes Tobin (Athens: University of Georgia Press, 1994), 64–85, quotation at 69.
66. Mary Lefkowitz, "Whatever Happened to Historical Evidence?" in *The Flight from Science and Reason*, ed. Paul R. Gross, Norman Levitt, and Martin W. Lewis (Baltimore: Johns Hopkins University Press, 1996), 301–12, quotation at 302; Proctor, *Value-Free Science?*, 10.
67. Zimbardo, "Semiotics," 30–32, 35, 39 (italics in original).
68. Pierre Bourdieu, "Introduction," in "The Economy of Linguistic Exchanges," in *Language and Symbolic Power*, ed. John B. Thompson (Cambridge: Harvard University Press, 1991), 37–42, quotations at 37–39. See also Pêcheux, *Language, Semantics, Ideology*, 111, and M. M. Bakhtin, "Discourse in the Novel" (1934/1935) in *The Dialogic Imagination: Four Essays*, ed. Michael Holquist (Austin: University of Texas Press, 1981), 259–422, esp. 277, 305.
69. For this "view from no where," which Donna Haraway calls the "god-trick," see Haraway, "Situated Knowledges: The Science Question in Feminism and the Privilege of Partial Perspective" (1988) in *Simians, Cyborgs, and Women: The Reinvention of Nature* (New York: Routledge, 1991), 183–201, quotation at 189; Thomas Nagel, *The View from Nowhere* (New York: Oxford University Press, 1986). I discuss this issue more fully in my Epilogue.
70. Nancy Vickers, "Diana Described: Scattered Woman and Scattered Rhyme" (1981) in *Writing and Sexual Difference*, ed. Elizabeth Abel (Chicago: University of Chicago Press, 1982), 95–109, esp. 107–109; Peter Stallybrass and Ann Jones, "The Politics of *Astrophil and Stella*," *SEL* 24, 1 (1984): 53–68, quotation at 54; Lisa M. Zeitz and Peter Thoms, "Power, Gender, and Identity in Aphra Behn's 'The

Disappointment,'" *SEL* 37, 3 (1997): 501–16, quotation at 511; Leo Braudy, "Remembering Masculinity: Premature Ejaculation Poetry of the Seventeenth Century," *Michigan Quarterly Review* 33, 1 (1994): 177–201, quotation at 184.
71. Jessica Munns, "'But to the touch were soft': pleasure, power, and impotence in 'The Disappointment' and 'The Golden Age,'" in *Aphra Behn Studies*, ed. Janet Todd (Cambridge: Cambridge University Press, 1996), 178–96, notes that Behn's "Disappointment" focuses on "the female experience" rather than on "penile absorption" (183).
72. These lines occur in a draft, recorded in *Essays and Poems*, 276.
73. Sarah Fielding, *The Adventures of David Simple* and *Volume the Last*, ed. Peter Sabor (Lexington: University Press of Kentucky, 1998), 30. Felicity Nussbaum, *The Brink of All We Hate: English Satires on Women, 1660–1750* (Lexington: University Press of Kentucky, 1984), traces the history of these antifeminist satires.
74. Mary E. Hawkesworth, "From Objectivity to Objectification: Feminist Objections" (1991) in *Rethinking Objectivity*, ed. Allan Megill (Durham: Duke University Press, 1994), 151–77, quotation at 166.
75. For a similar formulation about a recent and very different literary quarrel, see Kenneth Bleeth and Julie Rivkin, "The 'Imitation of David': Plagiarism, Collaboration, and the Making of a Gay Literary Tradition in David Leavitt's 'The Term Paper Artist,'" *PMLA* 116, 5 (2001): 1349–63, esp. 1350.
76. For the issue of women and satire, see Sara Gadeken, "Sarah Fielding and the Salic Law of Wit," *SEL* 42, 3 (2002): 541–57.
77. Sandra Harding, "The Instability of the Analytical Categories of Feminist Theory" (1986) in *Sex and Scientific Inquiry*, 282–302, quotation at 285. For further analysis of the "Archimedean point," see Myra Jehlen, "Archimedes and the Paradox of Feminist Criticism," *Signs* 6, 4 (1981): 575–601.
78. Haraway, "Situated Knowledges," 187.

Chapter 5 Quixotic Perception in Sophia Lee's *The Recess*

1. Kate Ferguson Ellis, *The Contested Castle: Gothic Novels and the Subversion of Domestic Ideology* (Urbana: University of Illinois Press, 1989), 68. See also Angela Wright, "Early Women's Gothic Writing: Historicity and Canonicity in Clara Reeve's *The Old English Baron* and Sophia Lee's *The Recess*," in *Approaches to Teaching Gothic Fiction: The British and American Traditions*, ed. Diane Long Hoeveler and Tamar Heller (New York: MLA, 2003), 99–104, esp. 101.
2. Barry Barnes, *Interests and the Growth of Knowledge* (London: Routledge, 1977).

3. Terry Castle, "The Spectralization of the Other in *The Mysteries of Udolpho*" (1987) in *The Female Thermometer: Eighteenth-Century Culture and the Invention of the Uncanny* (New York: Oxford University Press, 1995), 120–39, quotation at 123–24.
4. David Richter, *The Progress of Romance: Literary Historiography and the Gothic Novel* (Columbus: Ohio State University Press, 1996), 72; J. M. S. Tompkins, *The Popular Novel in England, 1700–1800* (London: Constable, 1932), 227–28; Ellis, *Contested Castle*, 69.
5. Jayne Elizabeth Lewis, " 'Ev'ry Lost Relation': Historical Fictions and Sentimental Incidents in Sophia Lee's *The Recess*," in *Eighteenth-Century Fiction* 7, 2 (1995): 165–82, quotation at 182; Jane Spencer, *Rise of the Woman Novelist: From Aphra Behn to Jane Austen* (Oxford: Blackwell, 1986), 195.
6. Lewis, "Ev'ry Lost Relation," 166–69.
7. Megan Isaac, "Sophia Lee and the Gothic of Female Community," *Studies in the Novel* 28, 2 (1996): 200–218; April Alliston, "The Value of a Literary Legacy: Retracing the Transmission of Value Through Female Lines," *Yale Journal of Criticism: Interpretation in the Humanities* 4, 1 (1990): 109–27 and *Virtue's Faults: Correspondences in Eighteenth-Century British and French Women's Fiction* (Stanford: Stanford University Press, 1996), 148–87; Anne H. Stevens, "Sophia Lee's Illegitimate History," *Eighteenth-Century Novel* 3 (2003): 231–56, esp. 240–44; Michael Dobson and Nicola H. Watson, *England's Elizabeth: An Afterlife in Fame and Fantasy* (New York: Oxford University Press, 2002), 103; E. J. Clery, *Women's Gothic: From Clara Reeve to Mary Shelley* (Horndon: Northcote House, 2000), 45–46.
8. Sophia Lee, *The Recess; or, A Tale of Other Times*, ed. April Alliston (Lexington: University Press of Kentucky, 2000), 226. Subsequent references will be parenthetical.
9. Spencer, *Rise of the Woman Novelist*, 198; Spencer also notes that "the heroines, indulging in romance, forget that masculine ambition determines history" (197).
10. Mary Wollstonecraft, *Vindication of the Rights of Woman*, in *A Vindication of the Rights of Men* and *A Vindication of the Rights of Woman*, ed. Sylvana Tomaselli (Cambridge: Cambridge University Press, 1995), 65–303, quotation at 74–75; Mary Poovey, *The Proper Lady and the Woman Writer: Ideology as Style in the Works of Mary Wollstonecraft, Mary Shelley, and Jane Austen* (Chicago: University of Chicago Press, 1984), 98. For analyses of the role of education in curing young women's quixotism, see Claudia Johnson, *Equivocal Beings: Politics, Gender, and Sentimentality in the 1790s: Wollstonecraft, Radcliffe, Burney Austen* (Chicago: University of Chicago Press, 1995), 24, 47–73; Daniel Cottom, *The Civilized Imagination: A Study of Ann Radcliffe, Jane Austen, and Sir Walter Scott* (Cambridge: Cambridge University Press, 1985), 17–18; and

Cannon Schmitt, *Alien Nation; Nineteenth-Century Gothic Fictions and English Nationality* (Philadelphia: University of Pennsylvania Press, 1997), 29.
11. Mary Wollstonecraft, *The Wrongs of Woman*, in *Mary and The Wrongs of Women*, ed. Gary Kelly (New York: Oxford University Press, 1976), 71–204, quotation at 130.
12. Wendy Motooka, *The Age of Reasons: Quixotism, Sentimentalism and Political Economy in Eighteenth-Century Britain* (London: Routledge, 1998), 37, 51.
13. Dorrit Cohn, *Transparent Minds: Narrative Modes for Presenting Consciousness in Fiction* (Princeton: Princeton University Press, 1978), 106; Margaret Doody, "George Eliot and the Eighteenth-Century Novel," *Nineteenth-Century Fiction* 35, 3 (1980): 160–91, quotation at 288.
14. What Claudia Johnson notes of Jane Austen's *Emma* (1815) applies here: "Emma's misapprehensions seem utterly plausible when we read the novel for the first time" (*Jane Austen: Women, Politics, and the Novel* [Chicago: University of Chicago Press, 1988], 133).
15. Elizabeth Napier, *The Failure of Gothic: Problems of Disjunction in an Eighteenth-Century Literary Form* (Oxford: Clarendon Press, 1987), 15.
16. Isaac, "Sophia Lee and the Gothic of Female Community," 215.
17. Alliston, *Virtue's Faults*, notes that "Ellinor's narrative . . . repeats the story that has already been read from a different point of view" (175).
18. This formulation owes much to Hayden White's "The Historical Text as Literary Artifact" (1974) in *Tropics of Discourse: Essays in Cultural Criticism* (Baltimore: Johns Hopkins University Press, 1978), 81–100, although unlike White I would stress that generic choices may determine what we register as an "event" or "fact" at all.
19. Tilottama Rajan, "Wollstonecraft and Godwin: Readings the Secrets of the Political Novel," *Studies in Romanticism* 27, 2 (1988): 221–51, quotation at 228; Joan W. Scott, "The Evidence of Experience," *Critical Inquiry* 17, 4 (1991): 773–97, quotation at 777; Wollstonecraft, *Vindication*, 78.
20. Frances Burney, *Camilla*, ed. Edward A. Bloom and Lillian D. Bloom (Oxford: Oxford University Press, 1983), 510, 655–56; Nelson Goodman, *Of Mind and Other Matters* (Cambridge: Harvard University Press, 1984), 25.
21. Motooka, *Age of Reasons*, 27.
22. Stevens, "Illegitimate History," 249.
23. Alliston, "Introduction," in *The Recess*, xix–xliv, quotation at xxiii; Jayne Lewis, " 'The *sorrow* of seeing the Queen': Mary Queen of Scots and the British History of Sensibility, 1707–1789," in *Passionate Encounters in a Time of Sensibility*, ed. Maximillian E. Novak and Anne Mellor (Newark: University of Delaware Press, 2000), 193–220, quotation at 216; see also Lewis, *Mary Queen of*

Scots: Romance and Nation (London: Routledge, 1998), 136–46, and Stevens, "Illegitimate History," 245–50.
24. Fredric Jameson, "Marxism and Historicism" (1979) in *The Ideologies of Theory: Essays, 1971–1986, Volume 2: The Syntax of History* (Minneapolis: University of Minnesota Press, 1988), 148–77, quotation at 150.
25. Charlotte Lennox, *The Female Quixote*, ed. Margaret Dalziel (Oxford: Oxford University Press, 1989), 7; Frances Sheridan, *Memoirs of Miss Sidney Bidulph*, ed. Patricia Köster and Jean Coates Cleary (Oxford: Oxford University Press, 1995), 23; Mary Hays, *Memoirs of Emma Courtney*, ed. Eleanor Ty (Oxford: Oxford University Press, 1996), 14–15; Johnson, *Equivocal Beings*, 55.
26. Eugenia C. DeLamotte, *Perils of the Night: A Feminist Study of Nineteenth-Century Gothic* (New York: Oxford University Press, 1990), 170.
27. Catherine Gallagher, *Nobody's Story: The Vanishing Acts of Women Writers in the Marketplace, 1670–1820* (Berkeley: University of California Press, 1994), 129. See also Ros Ballaster, *Seductive Forms: Women's Amatory Fiction from 1684–1740* (Oxford: Clarendon Press, 1992), 116–17; Michael McKeon, *The Origins of the English Novel, 1600–1740* (Baltimore: Johns Hopkins University Press, 1987), 54–55; and, for a different account, John Richetti, *Popular Fiction Before Richardson: Narrative Patterns, 1700–1739* (Oxford: Clarendon Press, 1969), 119–67. Some critics doubt that Manley wrote *Queen Zarah*: see John L. Sutton, Jr., "The Source of Mrs. Manley's Preface to Queen Zarah," *Modern Philology* 82, 2 (1984): 167–72; and J. A. Downie, "What If Delarivier Manley Did Not Write The Secret History of Queen Zarah?" *Library: The Transactions of the Bibliographical Society* 5, 3 (2004): 247–64.
28. Katie Trumpener's *Bardic Nationalism: The Romantic Novel and the British Empire* (Princeton: Princeton University Press, 1997) briefly discusses how the twin's "hope for political restoration rests on the preservation of family records" (111).
29. William Robertson, *The History of Scotland, During the Reigns of Queen Mary and King James VI. till his Accession to the crown of England* (New York: Harper, 1829), 312. Critics typically oppose Robertson's *History* to Lee's text (although in 1789 Hester Piozzi linked them, noting that "after Robertson's History, and [Sophia Lee's] Recess, I thought so little more could be done for Mary" [*The Piozzi Letters: Correspondence of Hester Lynch Piozzi, 1784–1821 (formerly Mrs. Thrale)*, ed. Edward A. Bloom and Lillian D. Bloom, 6 vols. (Newark: Delaware University Press, 1989), 1: 292]), but Robertson could have provoked Lee to stage competing narrative constructions. After noting that "the memory of Elizabeth is still adored in England," Robertson declares that "whoever undertakes to

write the history of Scotland, finds himself obliged, frequently, to view her in a very different and in a less amiable light" (315).
30. Hans Kellner, *Language and Historical Representation: Getting the Story Crooked* (Madison: University of Wisconsin Press, 1989), 4.
31. William Shakespeare, *The Tempest*, in *The Riverside Shakespeare*, second edition, ed. G. Blakemore Evans with J. J. M. Tobin (Boston: Houghton Mifflin, 1997), 1656–1688, quotation at 1668 (1.2.479–82).
32. David Hume, *The History of England from the Invasion of Julius Caesar to The Revolution in 1688*, 6 vols. (Indianapolis: Liberty Press, 1983), 4: 318–21.
33. Robertson, *History of Scotland*, 309.
34. Rajan, "Wollstonecraft and Godwin," 222.
35. For an alternate account see Stevens, "Illegitimate History," which contends that "by reading Matilda's letter and Ellinor's journal . . . the reader learn[s] the 'real' story hidden by Elizabeth's deceptions" (249). More generally, Stevens argues that Lee "questions the authority of historiography" only to insist that "reading a novel may be a superior means to understand the past," "resolving . . . historical controversies by substituting a certain fiction in place of an uncertain fact" (233, 247). See also Stevens, "Tales of Other Times: A Survey of British Historical Fiction, 1770–1812," *Cardiff Corvey: Reading the Romantic Text* 7 (December 2001): Online: Internet (7/1/2006): <http://www.cf.uk/encap/corvey/articles/cc07_n03.html>
36. Rajan, "Wollstonecraft and Godwin," 223.
37. Spencer, *Rise of the Woman Novelist*, 200. Stevens, "Illegitimate Histories," agrees that Ellinor is "the character who most values truth in the novel" (248), while Clery, *Women's Gothic*, asserts that Ellinor has a "more vivid imagination" than Matilda and is the "passionate core of the novel" (48).
38. Michel de Certeau, "History: Science and Fiction" (1983) in *Heterologies: Discourse on the Other* (Minneapolis: University of Minnesota Press, 1986), 199–221, quotation at 200–201.
39. Richard Maxwell, "Phantom States: *Cleveland, The Recess*, and the Origins of Historical Fiction," in *The Literary Channel: The International Invention of the Novel*, ed. Margaret Cohen and Carolyn Dever (Princeton: Princeton University Press, 2002), 151–82, notes that, like the abbé Prevost's *Cleveland* (1731–1739), Lee's novel shifts the "spotlight to a new generation in which a return to royal status seems possible, only to prove a chimera" (167).
40. James Watt, *Contesting the Gothic: Fiction, Genre and Cultural Conflict, 1764–1832* (Oxford: Clarendon Press, 1999), 62.
41. Frank Kermode, *The Sense of an Ending: Studies in the Theory of Fiction* (New York: Oxford University Press, 1967), 11; Lionel

Gossman, *Towards a Rational Historiography* in *Transactions of the American Philosophical Society* 79, 3 (1989): 1–68, quotation at 26. See also Thomas S. Kuhn, *The Structure of Scientific Revolutions*, second edition, enlarged (Chicago: University of Chicago Press, 1970) and Thomas Lacquer, *Making Sex: Body and Gender from the Greeks to Freud* (Cambridge: Harvard University Press, 1988).

42. Motooka, *Age of Reasons*, 6, 92; Hans-Georg Gadamer, "The Hermeneutics of Suspicion," in *Hermeneutics: Questions and Prospects*, ed. Gary Shapiro and Alan Sica (Amherst: University of Massachusetts Press, 1984), 53–65, quotation at 60–61.
43. Hayden White, *Metahistory: The Historical Imagination in Nineteenth-Century Europe* (Baltimore: Johns Hopkins University Press, 1973), 6 n 5.
44. Kaja Silverman, "Too Early/Too Late: Male Subjectivity and the Primal Scene" (1988) in *Male Subjectivity at the Margins* (New York: Routledge, 1992), 157–84, quotation at 165.
45. David Punter, *The Literature of Terror: A History of Gothic Fictions from 1765 to the Present Day* (London: Longman, 1980), 57; William Riggin, *Pícaros, Madmen, Näifs, and Clowns: The Unreliable First-Person Narrator* (Norman: University of Oklahoma Press, 1981), 10; Wolfgang Iser, *The Implied Reader: Patterns of Communication in Prose Fiction from Bunyan to Beckett* (Baltimore: Johns Hopkins University Press, 1974), 34–35; Rajan, "Wollstonecraft and Godwin," 223, 226, 229–30, 241.
46. William Godwin, "Original Manuscript Ending of Caleb Williams," Appendix I to *Caleb Williams*, ed. Maurice Hindle (New York: Penguin, 1988), 339–46, quotation at 345.
47. Tzvetan Todorov, *The Fantastic: A Structural Approach to a Literary Genre* (Ithaca: Cornell University Press, 1973), 25, 43.
48. Alliston, "Introduction," in *The Recess*, xxiii.
49. William Godwin, "Of History and Romance," Appendix IV to *Caleb Williams*, ed. Hindle, 359–73, quotation at 370–71.

Chapter 6 Ann Radcliffe's *The Mysteries of Udolpho* and the Practice of Quixotism

1. Ann Radcliffe, *Journey Made in the Summer of 1794 through Holland and the Western Frontier of Germany* (London: G.G. and J. Robinson, 1795), 371. See Jeanne Moskal, "Cleanliness, Dirt, and Nationalism in Ann Radcliffe's Dutch Travels," *European Romantic Review* 12, 2 (2001): 216–25; Angela Keane, *Women Writers and the English Nation in the 1790s: Romantic Belongings* (Cambridge: Cambridge University Press, 2000), 26–31.
2. Radcliffe, *Journey*, 371–75.

3. Ann Radcliffe, *The Mysteries of Udolpho*, ed. Bonamy Dobrée and Terry Castle (New York: Oxford University Press, 1998), 96. Subsequent references will be parenthetical.
4. Eugenia C. DeLamotte, *Perils of the Night: A Feminist Study of Nineteenth-Century Gothic* (New York: Oxford University Press, 1990), 46.
5. John Locke, *An Essay Concerning Human Understanding*, ed. Peter Nidditch (Oxford: Clarendon Press, 1975), 118.
6. Richard Rorty, "The World Well Lost" (1972) in *Consequences of Pragmatism: Essays, 1972–1980* (Minneapolis: University of Minnesota Press, 1982), 3–18, quotation at 4.
7. Radcliffe contrasts the "ideal" graces of Mason's tragic heroine with Mary's real tragedy: "Hardwick once veiled a form as lovely as the ideal graces of the Poet," she writes, "and conspired a fate more tragical than that, which Harewood witnessed" (371–72). *Udolpho* itself quotes *Elfrida* to emphasize how "secluded" from civilization the traveling Emily felt (402).
8. Barbara M. Benedict, *Framing Feeling: Sentiment and Style in English Prose Fiction, 1745–1800* (New York: AMS Press, 1994), 175, 181, 194; Rhoda L. Flaxman, "Radcliffe's Dual Modes of Vision," in *Fetter'd or Free: British Women Novelists, 1670–1815*, ed. Mary Anne Schofield and Cecilia Macheski (Athens: Ohio University Press, 1986), 124–33, esp. 127; Anne Williams, *Art of Darkness: A Poetics of Gothic* (Chicago: University of Chicago Press, 1995), 164; Gary Kelly, *English Fiction of the Romantic Period, 1789–1830* (Essex: Longman, 1989), 53 and " 'A Constant Vicissitude of Interesting Passions': Ann Radcliffe's Perplexed Narratives," *Ariel* 10, 2 (1979): 45–64, esp. 49–50; Fred Botting, *Gothic* (London: Routledge, 1996), 65, 67.
9. DeLamotte, *Perils of the Night*, 47.
10. Patricia Meyer Spacks, *Desire and Truth: Functions of Plot in Eighteenth-Century English Novels* (Chicago: University of Chicago Press, 1994), 165, 167–68; Kim Ian Michasiw, "Ann Radcliffe and the Terrors of Power," *Eighteenth-Century Fiction* 6, 4 (1994): 327–46, quotation at 332; Kenneth W. Graham, "Emily's Demon Lover: The Gothic Revolution and *The Mysteries of Udolpho*," in *Gothic Fictions: Prohibition/Transgression*, ed. Kenneth W. Graham (New York: AMS Press, 1989), 163–71, quotation at 167–68. See also Elizabeth Napier, *The Failure of the Gothic: Problems of Disjunction in an Eighteenth-Century Literary Form* (Oxford: Clarendon Press, 1987), 107 and David Punter, *The Literature of Terror: A History of Gothic Fictions from 1765 to the Present Day* (London: Longman, 1980), 68.
11. Coral Ann Howells, *Love, Mystery and Misery: Feeling in Gothic Fiction* (London: Athlone Press, 1978), 48.

12. As early as 1824, when the *Gentleman's Magazine*'s obituary for Lee claimed that Radcliffe was "among the warmest admirers of 'The Recess,'" Radcliffe's lineage has featured Lee's text: critics have so desired to link the two that they enrolled the young Ann Radcliffe (then Ann Ward) in the girls' school in Bath run by with Sophia Lee and her sister, a "fact" disproved by Rictor Norton, *Ann Radcliffe: Mistress of Udolpho* (London: Leicester University Press, 1998), 46–48. For similarities between Radcliffe and Lee, see E. J. Clery, *Women's Gothic: From Clara Reeve to Mary Shelley* (Horndon: Northcote House, 2000), 64–65; Norton, *Ann Radcliffe*, 83.
13. Punter, *Literature of Terror*, 68, 73, 75, 77.
14. Howells, *Love, Mystery and Misery*, 38–39.
15. Howells, *Love, Mystery and Misery*, 47.
16. James Thomson, *Summer*, in *The Seasons*, ed. James Sambrook (Oxford: Clarendon Press, 1981), 58–143, quotation at 138 (lines 1687–93).
17. Thomson, *Summer*, 136–38 (lines 1682–84).
18. See Howells, *Love, Mystery and Misery*, 48, and David S. Durant, "Ann Radcliffe and the Conservative Gothic," *SEL* 22, 3 (1982): 519–30, esp. 525.
19. Richard Rorty, "The Contingency of Selfhood" (1986) in *Contingency, Irony, and Solidarity* (Cambridge: Cambridge University Press, 1989), 23–43, quotation at 39.
20. Although the literature on the picturesque is immense, few studies explore it as a spiritualized aesthetic: a notable exception is Robert Mayhew, "William Gilpin and the Latitudinarian Picturesque," *Eighteenth-Century Studies* 33, 3 (2000): 349–66. See also Ann Bermingham, *Landscape and Ideology: The English Rustic Tradition, 1740–1860* (Berkeley: University of California Press, 1986); *The Politics of the Picturesque: Literature, Landscape and Aesthetics since 1770*, ed. Stephen Copley and Peter Garside (Cambridge: Cambridge University Press, 1994); Tim Fulford, *Landscape, Liberty, and Authority: Poetry, Criticism and Politics from Thomson to Wordsworth* (Cambridge: Cambridge University Press, 1996); Stephen Daniels, *Fields of Vision: Landscape Imagery and National Identity in England and the United States* (Princeton: Princeton University Press, 1993); Sidney K. Robinson, *Inquiry into the Picturesque* (Chicago: University of Chicago Press, 1991); Malcolm Andrews, *The Search for the Picturesque: Landscape Aesthetics and Tourism in Britain, 1760–1800* (Stanford: Stanford University Press, 1989).
21. For the "fad for stories of Banditti," see Robert Miles, "The 1790s: The Effulgence of Gothic," in *The Cambridge Companion to Gothic Fiction*, ed. Jerrold E. Hogle (Cambridge: Cambridge University Press, 2002), 41–62, quotation at 50, and Clery, *Women's Gothic*, 54–55.
22. James Thomson, "A Hymn," in *The Seasons*, 254–59, quotation at 254 (lines 1–2); Thomson, *Summer*, 68 (lines 175–78).

23. Robert Boyle, *Occasional Reflections Upon Several Subjects, Whereto is Premis'd a Discourse about such Kind of Thoughts* (London: Henry Herringman, 1665), 35. Subsequent references will be parenthetical.
24. Thomson, *Summer*, 68–69, 130 (lines 175–78, 192–95, 1553–55).
25. Mayhew, "William Gilpin," 355. See also Mayhew, "The Denominational Politics of Travel-Writing: the Case of Tory Anglicans in the 1770s," in *Enlightenment Geography: The Political Languages of British Geography, 1650–1850* (New York: St. Martin's Press, 2000), 141–67.
26. Stanley Fish, *Self-Consuming Artifacts: The Experience of Seventeenth-Century Literature* (Berkeley: University of California Press, 1972), 25.
27. Slavoj Žižek, *The Sublime Object of Ideology* (London: Verso, 1989), 146.
28. Karl Marx, "Difference Between the Democritean and Epicurean Philosophy of Nature," in Karl Marx and Frederick Engels, *Collected Works*, 47 vols. (New York: International Publishers, 1975), 1: 25–107, quotation at 1: 104.
29. John Dryden, *Absalom and Achitophel*, in *Poems, 1681–1684*, ed. H. T. Swedenberg, Jr., *The Works of John Dryden*, 20 vols. (Berkeley: University of California Press, 1956–2002), 2: 3–36, quotation at 2: 7 (lines 63–64).
30. Žižek, *Sublime Object*, 20–21.
31. Daniel Cottom, *The Civilized Imagination: A Study of Ann Radcliffe, Jane Austen, and Sir Walter Scott* (Cambridge: Cambridge University Press, 1985), 35.
32. I have explored the mechanical nature of sensibility in eighteenth-century discourse in my *Power of the Passive Self in English Literature, 1640–1770* (Cambridge: Cambridge University Press, 2002).
33. Edmund Burke, *A Philosophical Enquiry into the Origin of our Ideas of the Sublime and Beautiful*, ed. J. T. Boulton (London: Routledge, 1958), 45.
34. Uvedale Price, *An Essay on the Picturesque* (1796), facsimile rept. in Price, *On the Picturesque* (Otley: Woodstock Books, 2000), 57, 147; *Sir Uvedale Price on the Picturesque, with an Essay on the Origin of Taste*, ed. Sir Thomas Dick Lauder (Edinburgh: Caldwell, 1842), 483–88. See Christopher Hussey, *The Picturesque: Studies in a Point of View* (1927; London: Cass, 1967), 13; Andrew Ballantyne, *Architecture, Landscape, and Liberty: Richard Payne Knight and the Picturesque* (Cambridge: Cambridge University Press, 1997), 83. For a different account, see Wolfram Schmidgen, *Eighteenth-Century Fiction and the Law of Property* (Cambridge: Cambridge University Press, 2002), which contends that Radcliffe and Price "share basic assumptions about landscape aesthetic and promote related ways of seeing" (177).
35. Ballantyne, *Architecture*, 143.
36. Richard Payne Knight, *An Analytical Inquiry into the Principles of Taste*, fourth edition (London: T. Payne, 1808), 136.

37. Hussey, *Picturesque*, 4, 17; Kim Ian Michasiw, "Nine Revisionist Theses on the Picturesque," *Representations* 38 (1998): 76–100, quotation at 87; Knight, *Analytical Inquiry*, 136.
38. Richard Payne Knight, "Review of *The Life of Sir Joshua Reynolds* by James Northcote," *Edinburgh Review* 23 (1814): 292, quoted in Ballantyne, *Architecture*, 146.
39. John Barrell, *The Idea of Landscape and the Sense of Place, 1730–1840* (Cambridge: Cambridge University Press, 1972), 6, 16.
40. Norton, *Ann Radcliffe*, 190.
41. William Hazlitt quoted in *The Critical Response to Ann Radcliffe*, ed. Deborah D. Rogers (Westport, CT: Greenwood Press, 1994), 104.
42. Terry Castle, "The Spectralization of the Other in *The Mysteries of Udolpho*" (1987) in *The Female Thermometer: Eighteenth-Century Culture and the Invention of the Uncanny* (New York: Oxford University Press, 1995), 120–39, quotation at 123–24.
43. Deidre Lynch, "Personal Effects and Sentimental Fictions," *Eighteenth-Century Fiction* 12, 2–3 (2000): 345–68, quotation at 345.
44. For a different account of the word "interesting," see Patricia Meyer Spacks, *Boredom: The Literary History of a State of Mind* (Chicago: University of Chicago Press, 1995), 114–15.
45. Sophia Lee, *The Recess; or, A Tale of Other Times*, ed. April Alliston (Lexington: University Press of Kentucky, 2000), 199.
46. David S. Durant, "Aesthetic Heroism in *The Mysteries of Udolpho*," *The Eighteenth Century: Theory and Interpretation* 22, 2 (1981): 175–88, argues readers "are asked to eschew the rational faculty" (186). For a different claim, see Ian Duncan, *Modern Romance and the Transformations of the Novel: The Gothic, Scott, Dickens* (Cambridge: Cambridge University Press, 1992), which posits the "rational and scientific voice of [Emily's] absent father" (42) as *Udolpho*'s ideal.
47. Schmidgen, *Eighteenth-Century Fiction*, 182–83.
48. See Ronald Knox, *Enthusiasm: A Chapter in the History of Religion, with Special Reference to the XVII and XVIII Centuries* (New York: Oxford University Press, 1950); Clement Hawes, *Mania and Literary Style: The Rhetoric of Enthusiasm from the Ranters to Christopher Smart* (Cambridge: Cambridge University Press, 1996); *Enthusiasm and Enlightenment in Europe, 1650–1850*, ed. Lawrence E. Klein and Anthony J. La Vopa (San Marino: Huntington Library, 1998); Shaun Irlam, *Elations: The Poetics of Enthusiasm in Eighteenth–Century Britain* (Stanford: Stanford University Press, 1999).
49. Joseph Warton, "The Enthusiast: Or The Lover of Nature," in *Eighteenth-Century Poetry: An Annotated Anthology*, ed. David Fairer and Christine Gerrard, second edition (Oxford: Blackwell, 2004), 384–89, quotations at 386–88 (lines 88, 144, 169).
50. Emily asks a similar question after she rereads a poem and finds that its "visionary scenes" fail to move her as they once did. "Where did the

charm exist?" she wonders: "Was it in my mind, or in the imagination of the poet?" (383).
51. William Wordsworth, "Lines Written a Few Miles Above Tintern Abbey" (1798) in *William Wordsworth (The Oxford Authors)*, ed. Stephen Gill (Oxford: Oxford University Press, 1984), 131–35, quotation at 133 (line 50); Wordsworth, *The Prelude* (1805) in *William Wordsworth*, 375–590, quotation at 403 (II.423–24).
52. Rorty, "The World Well Lost," 3–18, quotation at 4.
53. Fulford, *Landscape, Liberty, and Authority*, 11; see also John Barrell, "An Unerring Gaze: The Prospect of Society in the Poetry of James Thomson and John Dyer," in *English Literature in History, 1730–80: An Equal, Wide Survey* (New York: St. Martins, 1983), 51–109.
54. Michasiw, "Nine Revisionist Theses," 88.
55. Countering Howells, *Love, Mystery and Misery*, who describes the novel as "registered so intensely and so exclusively from Emily's point of view" (45), Terry Castle's "Introduction" to the Oxford University Press edition of *Udolpho* notes that Emily is not "consistently the novel's presiding consciousness," since she is "absent from long stretches of narrative" and we do not always "see things from her vantage point" (vii–xxvi, quotation at xiv). For superb discussions of the presence of free indirect discourse in fiction before Austen, see Margaret Doody, "George Eliot and the Eighteenth-Century Novel," *Nineteenth-Century Fiction* 35, 3 (1980): 260–91 and "Deserts, Ruins and Troubled Waters: Female Dreams in Fiction and the Development of the Gothic Novel," *Genre* 10 (1977): 529–72.
56. James Watt, *Contesting the Gothic: Fiction, Genre and Cultural Conflict, 1764–1832* (Cambridge: Cambridge University Press, 1999), 105.
57. Ludwig Wittgenstein, *Philosophical Investigations* (New York: Macmillan, 1953), 35–36: "A *picture* held us captive. And we could not get outside it, for it lay in our language and language seemed to repeat it to us inexorably." See also Richard Rorty, "Keeping Philosophy Pure: An Essay on Wittgenstein" (1976) in *Consequences of Pragmatism*, 19–36, esp. 32.

Epilogue: Beyond Quixotism?: Quixotism and Contemporary Theory

1. Richard Rorty, "Solidarity or Objectivity" (1985) in *Objectivity, Relativism, and Truth: Philosophical Papers, Volume 1* (Cambridge: Cambridge University Press, 1991), 21–34, quotation at 28.
2. Georg Lukács, "Reification and the Consciousness of the Proletariat" (1920) in *History and Class Consciousness: Studies in Marxist Dialectics* (Cambridge: MIT Press, 1971), 83–222, quotations at

112–13, 153, 171; Paul Feyerabend, *Against Method: Outline of an Anarchistic Theory of Knowledge* (London: Verso Books, 1975), 25.
3. For a recent critique of scientific reason, see J. M. Coetzee, *The Lives of Animals* (Princeton: Princeton University Press, 1999), esp. 27–31.
4. Karl Marx, *Capital: A Critique of Political Economy*, trans. Samuel Moore and Edward Aveling, 3 vols. (New York: International Publishers, 1967); Jean Baudrillard, *For a Critique of the Political Economy of the Sign*, trans. Charles Levin (St. Louis: Telos Press, 1981); Sut Jhally, *The Codes of Advertising: Fetishism and the Political Economy of Meaning in the Consumer Society* (New York: Routledge, 1990).
5. Baudrillard, *For a Critique*, 90; William Pietz, "The problem of the fetish, I," *Res* 6 (1985): 5–17, quotation at 14.
6. Lukács, "History and Class Consciousness," 163, 164,166.
7. Brice Wachterhauser, "Getting it Right: Relativism, Realism and Truth," in *The Cambridge Companion to Gadamer*, ed. Robert J. Dostal (Cambridge: Cambridge University Press, 2002), 52–78, quotation at 72.
8. Steven Shapin, *A Social History of Truth: Civility and Science in Seventeenth-Century England* (Chicago: Chicago University Press, 1994), 77; Nancy Hartsock, "The Feminist Standpoint: Developing the Ground for a Specifically Feminist Historical Materialism," in *Discovering Reality: Feminist Perspectives on Epistemology, Metaphysics, Methodology, and Philosophy of Science*, ed. Sandra Harding and Merrill Hintikka (Dordrecht: Reidel, 1983), 283–310, quotations at 285, 304. For an excellent account of feminist standpoint theory, see Rosemary Hennessy, "The Feminist Standpoint, Discourse, and Authority: From Women's Lives to Ideology Critique," in *Materialist Feminism and the Politics of Discourse* (New York: Routledge, 1993), 67–138.
9. Claudia Johnson, *Jane Austen: Women, Politics, and the Novel* (Chicago: University of Chicago Press, 1988), 39, 47.
10. Mary Wortley Montagu, *Complete Letters*, ed. Robert Halsband, 3 vols. (Oxford: Clarendon Press, 1965–1967), 3: 67.
11. Jane Collier, *The Art of Ingeniously Tormenting*, ed. Judith Hawley (Bristol: Thoemmes Press, 1994), 233–34.
12. Elizabeth Hamilton, *Memoirs of Modern Philosophers*, 3 vols. (New York: Garland Press, 1974), 2: 302–303, 3: 220.
13. Donna Haraway, "Situated Knowledges: The Science Question in Feminism and the Privilege of Partial Perspective" (1988) in *Simians, Cyborgs, and Women: The Reinvention of Nature* (New York: Routledge, 1991), 183–201, quotation at 187; Haraway, "In the Beginning Was the Word: The Genesis of Biological Theory" (1981) in *Simians, Cyborgs, and Women*, 71–80, quotation at 79; Stanley Fish, "Critical Self Consciousness, Or Can We Know What We're Doing," in *Doing What Comes Naturally: Change, Rhetoric, and the*

Practice of Theory in Literary and Legal Studies (Durham: Duke University Press, 1989), 436–67, quotation at 455; Sandra Harding, "The Instability of the Analytical Categories of Feminist Theory" (1986) in *Sex and Scientific Inquiry*, ed. Sandra Harding and Jean F. O'Barr (Chicago: University of Chicago Press, 1987), 282–302, quotation at 285.
14. Michael Bell, *Literature, Modernism, and Myth: Belief and Responsibility in the Twentieth Century* (Cambridge: Cambridge University Press, 1997), 1, 9; M. M. Bakhtin, "Discourse in the Novel," in *The Dialogic Imagination: Four Essays*, ed. Michael Holquist (Austin: University of Texas Press, 1981), 259–422, quotation at 365.
15. John Locke, *Of the Conduct of the Understanding* (1706), intro. John Yolton (Bristol: Thoemmes Press, 1996), 39 (my emphasis).
16. John Barrell, "An Unerring Gaze: The Prospect of Society in the Poetry of James Thomson and John Dyer," in *English Literature in History, 1730–80: An Equal, Wide Survey* (New York: St. Martins, 1983), 51–109.
17. John Dewey, *Human Nature and Conduct* (1922) in *John Dewey: The Middle Works, 1899–1924*, ed. Jo Ann Boydston, 14 vols. (Carbondale: Southern Illinois University Press, 1976–1983), 4: 134, 169; Stanley Fish, "Vicki Frost Objects" (1997) in *The Trouble with Principle* (Cambridge: Harvard University Press, 1999), 153–61, quotation at 159; Keith Jenkins, *Re-Thinking History* (New York; Routledge, 1991), 9.
18. Ludwig Wittgenstein, *Philosophical Investigations* (New York: Macmillan, 1953), 35–36; Hans-Georg Gadamer, "Man and Language" (1966) in *Philosophical Hermeneutics*, ed. and trans. David E. Linge (Berkeley: University of California Press, 1976), 59–68, quotation at 62.
19. Donna Haraway, *Primate Visions: Gender, Race, and Nature in the World of Modern Science* (New York: Routledge, 1989), 4; Helen E. Longino, *Science as Social Knowledge: Values and Objectivity in Scientific Inquiry* (Princeton: Princeton University Press, 1990), 210–11.
20. Donna Haraway, "Reading Buchi Emecheta: Contests for 'Women's Experience' in Women's Studies" (1988) in *Simians, Cyborgs, and Women*, 109–24, quotations at 121, 124; Richard J. Bernstein, "The Constellation of Hermeneutics, Critical Theory and Deconstruction," in *Cambridge Companion to Gadamer*, 267–82, also discusses whether "there is any 'reality' or 'text' beyond and below our interpretations" (279).
21. Haraway, "Situated Knowledges," 189; Michel de Certeau, *The Practice of Everyday Life*, trans. Steven Rendall (Berkeley: University of California Press, 1984), 91–95.
22. Georgia Warnke, "Hermeneutics, Ethics, and Politics," in *Cambridge Companion to Gadamer*, 79–101, quotation at 92.

23. See James Clifford, "On Ethnographic Authority" (1983) in *The Predicament of Culture: Twentieth-Century Ethnography, Literature, and Art* (Cambridge: Harvard University Press, 1988), 21–54; Peter Novick, *That Noble Dream: The "Objectivity Question" and the American Historical Profession* (Cambridge: Cambridge University Press, 1988).
24. See, for instance, Renato Rosaldo, *Culture and Truth: The Remaking of Social Analysis* (Boston: Beacon Press, 1989), esp. "After Objectivism," 46–67. Lawrence Osborne, "Letter from New Guinea: Strangers in the Forest," *The New Yorker* 81, 9 (April 18, 2005): 124–40, quotes the anthropologist Rupert Stasch: "often it's the urban Westerners who are 'uncontacted,' in the sense that they're stuck inside their own projected fantasies" (140).
25. Londa Schiebinger, *Nature's Body: Gender in the Making of Modern Science* (Boston: Beacon Press, 1993), 13, 38–39; Schiebinger, *Has Feminism Changed Science?* (Cambridge: Harvard University Press, 1999), 153.
26. Edward W. Said, *Orientalism* (New York: Pantheon Books, 1978), 5, 222, 272, 326.
27. Patrick Brantlinger, *Crusoe's Footprints: Cultural Studies in Britain and America* (New York: Routledge, 1990), 3.
28. Thomas S. Kuhn, *The Structure of Scientific Revolutions*, second edition, enlarged (Chicago: University of Chicago Press, 1970), 77–79; Fish, "Critical Self-Consciousness," 457; Nelson Goodman, *Of Mind and Other Matters* (Cambridge: Harvard University Press, 1984), 25.
29. For Gadamer on prejudice, see Wachterhauser, "Getting it Right," 72; Bernstein, "Hermeneutics," 272–73; Hans Albert, "Critical Rationalism and Universal Hermeneutics," in *Gadamer's Century: Essays in Honor of Hans-Georg Gadamer*, ed. Jeff Malpas, Ulrich Arnswald, and Jens Kertscher (Cambridge: MIT Press, 2002), 15–25, esp. 18–19.
30. Dewey, *Human Nature and Conduct*, 4: 24–25, 26, 55, 121. The structure of this last formulation, common in Dewey's writings ("the choice is not between a moral authority outside of custom and one within it. It is between adopting more or less intelligent and significant customs" (*Human Nature and Conduct*, 4: 58 [see also 51, 115]), organizes many of Stanley Fish's arguments: "The opposition is never between the rational and the irrational, but between opposing rationalities, each of which is equally, but differently, intolerant" ("Boutique Multiculturalism" [1997] in *Trouble with Principle*, 56–72, quotation at 70).
31. Hans-Georg Gadamer, "On the Scope and Function of Hermeneutic Reflection" (1967) in *Philosophical Hermeneutics*, 18–43, quotations at 27–33 and "Universality of the Hermeneutic Problem" (1966) in *Philosophical Hermeneutics*, 3–17, quotations at 5, 9; Dewey, *Human Nature and Conduct*, 4: 26, 123; Fish, "Critical Self-Consciousness," 455; Thomas McCarthy, *The Critical Theory of Jürgen Habermas*

(Cambridge: MIT Press, 1978), 173, 179. For the Gadamer-Habermas debate, see Bernstein, "The Constellation of Hermeneutics," in *Cambridge Companion to Gadamer*, 267–82.
32. Warnke, "Hermeneutics," 91.
33. Jürgen Habermas, *Between Facts and Norms: Contributions to a Discourse Theory of Law*, trans. William Rehg (Cambridge: MIT Press, 1996), 163.
34. Georgia Warnke, "Social Identity as Interpretation," in *Gadamer's Century*, 307–29, quotation at 312.
35. *Gadamer in Conversation: Reflections and Commentary*, ed. and trans. Richard E. Palmer (New Haven: Yale University Press, 2001), 43; David Detmer, "Gadamer's Critique of the Enlightenment," in *The Philosophy of Hans-Georg Gadamer (The Library of Living Philosophers, Volume XXIV)*, ed. Lewis Edwin Hahn (Chicago: Open Court, 1997), 275–85, quotation at 280.
36. Fish, "Critical Self-Consciousness," 467; Fish, "Prologue: Taking Sides," in *Trouble with Principle*, 1–15, quotation at 9; Fish, "The Dance of Theory," in *Trouble with Principle*, 115–50, quotation at 150; Fish, "Vicki Frost Objects," 159; Fish, "A Wolf in Reason's Clothing" (1997) in *Trouble with Principle*, 187–210, quotation at 206–207; Rorty, "Solidarity and Objectivity?," 24.
37. Anthony Giddens, *Central Problems in Social Theory: Action, Structure and Contradiction in Social Analysis* (Berkeley: University of California Press, 1979), 52; Paul Smith, *Discerning the Subject* (Minneapolis: University of Minnesota Press, 1988), 12, 17.
38. Dewey, *Human Nature and Conduct*, 4: 213. I have analyzed this separation between knower and known more fully in chapter 4.
39. John Locke, *An Essay Concerning Human Understanding*, ed. Peter Nidditch (Oxford: Clarendon Press, 1975), 118.
40. Thomas Reid, *An Inquiry into the Human Mind on the Principles of Common Sense*, ed. Derek R. Brookes (University Park: Pennsylvania State University Press, 1997), 69, 71, 74, 90. The best guide to Reid's thought is Nicholas Wolterstorff, *Thomas Reid and the Story of Epistemology* (Cambridge: Cambridge University Press, 2001).
41. Haraway, "Reading Buchi Emecheta," 115, 121, 123–24.
42. Francis Bacon, *De dignitate et augmentis scientiarum* (1623) in *The Works of Francis Bacon*, ed. James Spedding, Robert Leslie Ellis, and Douglas Denon Heath, 14 vols. (London: Longman, 1857–1874), 4: 275–498, quotation at 4: 327.
43. John Dewey, "The Influence of Darwinism on Philosophy" (1909) in *John Dewey: The Middle Works*, 4: 3–14, quotation at 4: 13.
44. John Dewey, "The Need for a Recovery in Philosophy" (1917) in *John Dewey: The Middle Works*, 10: 3–48, quotations at 10: 6, 16–17.
45. Dewey, "Need for a Recovery," 10: 38; Dewey, "Does Reality Possess Practical Character?" (1908) in *John Dewey: The Middle Works*, 4: 125–42, quotations at 4: 125, 129, 134.

46. Dewey, "Does Reality Possess Practical Character?" 4: 134; "Influence of Darwinism," 4: 13.
47. Dewey, *Human Nature and Conduct*, 4: 213.
48. Haraway, "Reading Buchi Emecheta," 124,
49. Jenkins, *Re-Thinking History*, 11, 25, 49, 57, 67; Dewey, *Human Nature and Conduct*, 4: 150.
50. Donna Haraway, "Modest Witness: Feminist Diffractions in Science Studies," in *The Disunity of Science: Boundaries, Contexts, and Power*, ed. Peter Galison and David J. Stump (Stanford: Stanford University Press, 1996), 428–41, quotation at 431–32; Haraway, "Situated Knowledges," 198, 201.
51. Richard Rorty, "Introduction: Pragmatism and Philosophy" in *The Consequences of Pragmatism: Essays, 1972–1980* (Minneapolis: Minnesota University Press, 1982), xiii–xlvii, quotations at xxx, xxxix; Rorty, "Solidarity or Objectivity?" 28; Nelson Goodman, *Ways of Worldmaking* (Indianapolis: Hackett, 1978), 14 and *passim*.
52. Jenkins, *Re-Thinking History*, 47–48; Michel de Certeau, "History: Science and Fiction," in *Heterologies: Discourse on the Other* (Minneapolis: University of Minnesota Press, 1986), 199–221, quotation at 206.
53. John Dewey, "What Pragmatism Means by Practical" (1908) in *John Dewey: The Middle Works*, 4: 98–115, quotation at 102.

Index

Aden, John, 106
Adorno, Theodor, 176
Algarotti, Francesco, 102
Alison, Archibald, 155
Alliston, April, 139
Aristotle, 31
Astley, Thomas, 29–30
Austen, Jane, 42, 124, 146, 169

Bacon, Francis, 14–22, 53, 135, 143, 156, 177, 182–4
Bahktin, Mikhail, 171
Barker, Jane, 39
Barnes, Barry, 105, 117
Barnett, Louise, 106
Barrell, John, 155–6
Barrett, Eaton Stannard, 9, 41, 42, 44, 49, 65, 202 n 15
Barthes, Roland, 105, 174
Battestin, Martin, 70, 71
Baudrillard, Jean, 168
Behn, Aphra, 71–2, 86, 88, 109, 110, 210 n 44
Bell, Michael, 171
Bentley, Richard, 102
Bersani, Leo, 24
"beyond quixotism," 5, 7–9, 96, 120, 167–85
    see also objective perception; prejudice; quixotism [cure]
bias, see perception; prejudice
blindness, see under quixotism
Bloom, Harold, 13
Bogel, Fredric, 99–100, 103, 105, 110
Bordo, Susan, 101

Bourdieu, Pierre, 112
Bowers, Toni, 87
Boyle, Robert, 80, 150–1
Braider, Christopher, 96–7
Brantlinger, Patrick, 175
Bredvold, Louis, 103
Bronte, Emily, 132
Brown, Gillian, 26, 45
Burke, Edmund, 17–18, 142, 145, 152–7, 199 n 90
Burleigh, Lord (William Cecil), 129
Burney, Frances, 79, 122, 204 n 40
Byrd, Max, 86
Byron, Lord (George Gordon), 102

Campbell, Colin, 36
Campbell, Jill, 111
Carter, Elizabeth, 102
Castle, Terry, 118, 156
Cecil, Robert, 129
Cervantes, Miguel de, 14
    see also Don Quixote, *Don Quixote*
Cherniak, Warren, 109
Cheynell, Francis, 28
Chloe Surpriz'd, 109–10
clear sight, see objective perception
Clery, E. J., 36
Cleveland, John, 28–9
Close, Anthony, 5, 12
Cohn, Dorrit, 120
Cole, Lorraine, 104
Colie, Rosalie, 13
Collier, Jane, 169–70

common sense, 1–3, 5, 11–13, 21, 24, 26–33, 42, 46–7, 50, 53, 63, 66, 135, 148–9
　see also objective perception; reality
Congreve, William, 17
coquet, 52, 59–62
Craciun, Adriana, 36–7
Craft, Catherine, 64–5
credit, 34, 36, 67–8, 71–2, 86–90
cure, see under quixotism
Curll, Edmund, 109

Darwin, Charles, 157
Daston, Lorraine, 20
Davidson, Donald, 172
Davys, Mary, 87–8
Dear, Peter, 31–2
Decartes, Rene, 181
de Certeau, Michel, 131, 173, 185
Defoe, Daniel, 30, 68
DeLamotte, Eugenia, 124–5, 145
delusion, 1–7, 13–14, 15–24, 27–31, 42–4, 47–8, 50–1, 53–5, 62, 65, 81–4, 96, 109–16, 124–32, 134–6, 144–9, 158, 176
　see also quixote trope
Detmer, David, 178–9
Dewey, John, 2, 21, 22, 157, 177, 180–3, 185, 230 n 30
disappointment poem, 9, 97, 109–16
Don Quixote, 4, 11, 12, 13, 14, 20, 21, 24, 26–7, 33, 34, 46, 58, 84, 96–7, 115, 145
　idealistic hero, 12–3, 38, 52, 69, 84–5
　satiric butt, 12–3, 26–7, 69, 84–5
Don Quixote, 4, 5, 6, 12, 13, 15, 22, 24, 27, 37, 65, 97
Doody, Margaret, 51, 64, 120
Dryden, John, 102, 152
Dulcinea, 4, 34, 84, 96

Edgeworth, Maria, 9, 11, 23, 41, 44, 65
Egerton, Sarah Fyge, 22–3, 40, 83
Elizabeth I, Queen of England, 117, 121, 125–9, 132, 141, 143
Ellis, Kate, 117, 118
Emecheta, Buchi, 173, 181–2
Enlightenment, 3, 4, 7, 11, 15, 30, 62, 167–8, 170, 177–9, 184
enthusiasm, 29, 31, 32, 33, 159–60, 163
Essex, Earl of, 117–19, 122, 128–31
Etherege, George, 109, 110
experience, 144
　basis for proper suspicion, 72, 77, 78–81
　and partial views, 160–1
　unreliable, 76–7, 79–80, 81, 83, 87–8, 90
　women's experience dismissed, 81
explained supernatural, 142–3

fact, 2, 20, 21, 43, 44, 57, 68, 97, 103–12, 115–16, 135, 171, 173–4, 184
female quixotes, 8–9, 33–40, 86–9
　see also imagination [and women]
Fergus, Jan, 36
Ferguson, Frances, 18
fetishism, 8, 29–31, 56, 151–2, 156–9, 168
fetishist, see fetishism
Feyerabend, Paul, 167–8
fiction, see genre; reading; romance
Fielding, Henry, 34, 37, 69, 70–1, 79–80, 81, 83–5, 86, 205 n 47
Fielding, Sarah, 9, 67–91, 113, 161
filter, 5, 13, 18–19, 22, 28–9, 46, 49, 53, 62, 72, 85–6, 96–7, 119, 121, 126–7, 132, 143–6, 149–55, 157, 166, 173
　see also genre
finding, see making versus finding

Fish, Stanley, 8, 23–4, 25, 50, 95, 151, 171–2, 176, 177–9, 230 n 30
Foucault, Michel, 51, 69
Fredrickson, George M., 25
Freedman, William, 99–100
French Revolution, 41–2
Freud, Sigmund, 30

Gadamer, Hans-Georg, 3–4, 135, 169, 172, 174, 176–9
Galileo, 32
Gallagher, Catherine, 63
Gay, John, 93
Gayton, Edmund, 27
genre, 1–2, 5, 6, 8, 9, 13, 18, 33, 36, 46–7, 72, 95–7, 110–16, 117–23, 138–40, 144, 146, 171
  see also filter
"Gentleman's Study, The," 108
Giddens, Anthony, 180
Gilliam, Terry, 4
Gilmore, Thomas, 98–9, 107
Gilpin, William, 149, 155–6
Godwin, William, 138, 140
Goldberg, Homer, 12
Goldsmith, Oliver, 120
Goldstein, Jan, 31
Goodman, Nelson, 8, 123, 176
Gossman, Lionel, 134–5
gothic fiction, 117–18, 124, 139
Graham, Kenneth, 145
Graves, Richard, 3, 30, 34
Gray, Arthur, 93–5
Greene, Donald, 98
Griffin, Dustin, 103
Grossman, Edith, 4
Grundy, Isobel, 94

habit, 123, 150–1, 166, 177
Habermas, Jürgen, 176–8
Haggerty, George, 51, 53, 63, 65
Hall, John, 29
Halsband, Robert, 94

Hamilton, Elizabeth, 3, 9, 11, 13, 19, 21, 37, 41–50, 170
Hammond, Paul, 24
Haraway, Donna, 8, 17, 116, 170–3, 181–4
Harding, Sandra, 115–16, 169, 171
Hartsock, Nancy, 169
Hawkesworth, Mary, 101, 114
Hayles, Katherine, 100–1
Hays, Mary, 42, 124
Haywood, Eliza, 30, 38, 78, 86–8, 210 n 44, 210 n 51
Hazlitt, William, 156
Henry, Prince, 132–6
history, 118–23, 132, 137–40, 172, 174
Hooke, Robert, 18, 102
Howells, Coral Ann, 145–6
Hulme, Peter, 15
Hume, David, 120, 129
Hussey, Christopher, 155
Hutchens, Eleanor, 70

idols, see delusion
imagination
  creative, 4–5, 13, 22, 36, 38, 42, 50, 55, 63, 66
  pejorative connotations of, 35–7
  rehabilitated, 36–7
  ungoverned, 21, 36, 43–4, 47, 50, 147–9, 162
  and women, 34–40, 42–3, 53, 86–8
  see also delusion; quixote trope; quixotism [and cure]
Ingrassia, Catherine, 35
interpretation, 12–13, 17, 20, 21, 135, 144, 156, 178
  improperly active, 13, 45–6, 48, 53–4, 65, 80, 136
  see also translation
Iser, Wolfgang, 70, 137–8

James I, King of England, 118, 121, 132–3, 135–6

Janeway, Elizabeth, 205 n 1
Jebb, Samuel, 143
Jenkins, Keith, 172, 183
Jhally, Sut, 168
Johnson, Barbara, 106
Johnson, Claudia, 37, 124
Johnson, Samuel, 11, 37, 39, 103, 122, 146
Jones, Ann, 112–13
Jordanova, Ludmilla, 15

Keller, Evelyn Fox, 100–1
Kellner, Hans, 126
Kelly, Gary, 44
Kermode, Frank, 134
Kimball, Roger, 1
Kinkead-Weekes, Mark, 70
Knight, Richard Payne, 154–5
Klein, Lawrence, 31
Kraft, Elizabeth, 53, 59
Kuhn, Thomas, 57, 175–6

Landry, Donna, 108
landscape
  obscure, 160–1, 163
  picturesque, 149, 153–6, 161
  prospects, 161, 163, 172
  spiritualized reading of, 149–52, 155, 165–6
  sublime, 142, 145, 152–4, 162–5
Langbauer, Laurie, 51–2
Laqueur, Thomas, 33–4, 35
Lee, Sophia, 9, 45–6, 117–40, 143, 145–6, 158
Lefkowitz, Mary, 111
Leicester, Earl of, 122, 125–31, 134
Leland, Thomas, 133
Lennox, Charlotte, 6, 9, 37, 38, 41–2, 49, 50–66, 71, 124
lens, *see* filter; genre
Levin, Kate, 53, 63
Lewis, Jayne, 118–19
Linnaeus, Carl, 174–5
Lithgow, John, 4
Locke, John, 17, 25–6, 33, 34, 58, 143, 171–2, 181

Longino, Helen, 173
Lorrain, Claude, 155–6, 165
Lowenthal, Cynthia, 95
Lukács, Georg, 5, 167–9
Lynch, Diedre, 156
Lynch, James, 61

madness, 14, 19, 25, 34, 43–4, 51, 53, 84, 96, 98, 113–14, 147
making versus finding, 1, 7, 9, 13, 14, 18–19, 21, 28, 30, 47, 53–4, 66, 83, 100, 103, 149–66, 173, 180–5
Malina, Debra, 6, 35
man of feeling, 37, 71
"Man of La Mancha," 4
Mandel, Oscar, 12, 22, 26–7
Mandeville, Bernard, 2, 3, 27
Manley, Delarivier, 38–9, 125
Mar, Lady, 93
Marshall, David, 52, 57
Mary, Queen of Scots, 117, 125–8, 132, 141–3
Marx, Karl, 30, 152, 168
Mason, William, 143
McCarthy, Thomas, 178
McKeon, Michael, 14, 54
Merchant, Carolyn, 101
Mercurius Britanicus, 28–9
Michasiw, Kim Ian, 145, 155
Milton, John, 26, 50, 95
"mists dispelled," 3–4, 30, 40, 62
  see also objective perception; quixotism [and cure]
Mitchell, Brian Stokes, 4
Montagu, Mary Wortley, 8, 9, 91, 93–7, 108–16, 169
More, Henry, 27
Motooka, Wendy, 1, 21, 46, 59, 120, 123, 135
Motteux, Peter, 34
Mundus Foppiensus, 105
Mundus Muliebris, 105
Murray, Griselda, 93–5

Newton, Isaac, 80, 102, 148, 150
Norton, Rictor, 156
novel, 33, 35–6, 38, 39, 42–4, 48–50, 64, 71, 94, 124
Nussbaum, Felicity, 89

objective perception, 1–8, 14–23, 27–33, 43–7, 72, 75, 68, 80–3, 98–104, 107, 114–16, 119–20, 130–1, 138–9, 145, 149, 167–73, 184–5
"opened eyes," 3, 19, 28, 46, 67, 75, 79–80, 83, 85, 90, 96, 110–11, 114, 116, 143, 174
  see also objective perception; quixotism [and cure]
overreading, 1, 13, 35, 91, 162, 187 n 3
  see also interpretation

Panza, Sancho, see Sancho Panza
Paracelsus, 19, 20
paradigm, 8, 57, 175–6
  see also filter; genre
paranoia, 4, 13–14, 23–4
Parker, Blanford, 33
Parker, Fred, 5, 14
Pascal, 32
passivity, see perception
Paulson, Ronald, 12, 57, 98
Pawl, Amy, 54, 57–8
Pearson, Jacqueline, 35
Pêcheux, Michel, 106, 107
perception, 1–2
  active, 7, 14, 17–22, 42, 53–8, 67, 80–1, 96, 119–23, 135–6, 143–4, 151–2, 155–6, 158–66, 175, 180–5;
    see also imagination [creative]; making versus finding
  mediated by texts, 5, 11, 15–16, 28–9, 33, 62, 72, 114, 119–22, 149, 160, 172–30;
    see also filter; genre
  objective, see objective perception

passivity of, 17–18, 19, 53, 56, 62, 105, 143, 154–6, 158, 160, 164, 180–1
two-step process, 16, 21, 46, 135, 143, 156
perspective, see filter; genre; quixotism [and competing perceptions]
Petrarch, 112–13
Pettit, Alexander, 89
Philips, John, 28
picturesque, see landscape
Pietz, William, 29, 168
Plato, 157
Pollak, Ellen, 48
Poole, Kristen, 31
Poovey, Mary, 25
Pope, Alexander, 36, 103, 104
postmodernism, 4–5, 8, 12, 167–85, 188 n 16
pragmatism, 151, 172, 179, 182–3
Predmore, Richard, 24
prejudice, 122, 131, 135, 153–4
  elimination of, 3–4, 8, 17, 34, 67, 167–72
  positive account of, 49–50, 172–9
  resilience of, 67, 172
prepossession, 7, 9, 40, 47, 55, 65, 116, 119–40, 146, 154, 180
Preston, John, 79
Price, Uvedale, 149, 153–5
Priestley, Joseph, 4
Proctor, Robert, 106, 111
prudence, 69–74, 79, 208 n 25
  see also suspicion
Punter, David, 137–9, 146

Quintana, Ricardo, 103
Quixote, see Don Quixote
quixote figures
  Abraham Adams (Parson Adams), 34, 72, 69, 70, 72, 88
  Angelina, 11, 23, 44, 49, 50, 65
  Arabella, 6, 9, 38, 41, 42, 49, 50–66, 71, 124

quixote figures—*continued*
  Bridgetina Botherim, 11, 13, 19, 37, 43–5, 48
  Catherine Morland, 42, 124, 169
  Cherubina, 42, 49, 202 n 15
  David Simple, 67–91, 113–14, 161
  Delia (*Secret Memoirs*), 38–9
  disappointed Dean, 9, 108–16
  Dorcas Sheldon, 39, 42–7, 49–51
  Dorinda (*Lining of the Patch Work Screen*), 39
  Edmund Burke, 199 n 90
  Ellinor, 117–40, 158
  Emily St. Aubert, 8, 9–10, 142–66
  Emma Courtney, 42, 124
  Imperia (*Rambler*), 39
  Julia Delmond, 43–4, 46–50
  Maria (*Wrongs of Women*), 119–20, 134
  Matilda, 117–40
  Projector, the (*Tale of the Tub*), 34
  Sidney Bidulph, 124
  Strephon, 34, 97–107
  Uncle Toby, 34
  Walter Shandy, 34
  Wildgoose, 3, 34
  see also enthusiasm; fetishism; rational individual
quixote narratives
  innovative, 5–10, 14, 22, 40, 41, 67–166 *passim*
  conventional, 3–14, 22, 22–6, 33, 38, 40–66, 67, 110, 114, 119–20, 128, 143–6, 160, 164–5, 180, 184
  recent retellings, 4
  and subversion, 5, 7, 9, 12–13, 26, 38, 51–3, 62–5
quixote trope
  appropriated by varied ideologies, 7, 28, 40, 168, 170
  separates deluded from accurate perception, 1–3, 12, 22–3, 25, 28, 30, 40, 47, 67, 90, 98, 114, 116, 119–20, 130–2, 138, 148–9, 159, 167–8, 171–6, 181, 184–5
  definitions, 1–2, 33, 40, 42, 120
quixotism
  blindness, 2, 46–8, 50, 54, 65, 77, 85–6, 114, 121, 128–9, 130–2, 138, 151–2, 167–70
  competing perceptions, 4–5, 6–7, 13, 22–7, 29, 33, 45, 47, 53, 86, 148, 153–8
  continued pejorative connotations, 38, 84–5, 199 n 90
  cure, 2–6, 9, 11, 13, 16–17, 20, 22–6, 30, 34, 38–9, 48–51, 61–6, 85, 96, 110–11, 119–21, 128, 130–1, 139, 143–52, 158–60, 163–8, 171–2, 178–9, 184–5
  definition, 1–2, 11, 15, 123
  inevitability of, 5, 7–8, 87, 111, 114–16, 122, 160–6, 172–9
  resilience of, 14, 15, 29, 32, 47–50, 56–7, 134–5, 139
  resistance to patriarchy, 9, 41, 51–3, 59, 62–5
  "Romantic" account of, 12–13, 164
  satirizes surrounding world, 9, 12–13, 42, 52, 67, 164
  scandal of, 11, 24, 31, 194 n 44
  universal occurrence of, 8, 34, 83, 85–6, 109–10, 122, 158, 172–9, 199 n 86
  unsociability of, 3, 27, 31–3, 45, 53, 196 n 65
  see also fetishism; making versus finding; paranoia; perception [active]

Rabb, Melinda, 106
Radcliffe, Ann, 8, 9, 118, 141–66
Rajan, Tilottama, 122, 138
rational individual, 1–3, 7, 25, 123, 147, 181

rationality, 2, 3, 8, 26, 88, 159, 164, 167–8, 170, 226 n 46
Rawson, Claude, 70–1, 103
Raymond, Joad, 29
reading
  colonizes minds, 1, 3, 11, 15, 21–2, 28–9, 33–5, 39, 59–61, 124–5, 154, 172–9
  dangers of, 20–1, 33–4, 38, 42–3, 64
  gendering of, 34–42
  see also romance
reality
  defined by quixote narratives, 22, 62, 142–3, 145
  preexisting observers, 1–2, 20–1, 30–1, 101–7, 111, 115–16, 142–3, 155, 157, 182–5
  shared by nonquixotes, 2, 5, 11, 22, 25–6, 30–3, 40, 45–6, 96–7, 148, 170, 181, 184–5
  see also common sense; delusion; objective perception; quixote trope
reality effect, *see under* satire
Reeve, Clara, 39, 133
Reid, Thomas, 181
Richardson, Samuel, 43, 146
Richetti, John, 13
Richter, David, 118
Riggin, William, 137
Riley, E. C., 96
Roach, Joseph, 102
Robertson, William, 120, 125, 129, 220 n 29
Rochester, Earl of (John Wilmot), 109, 110
romance, 20, 22, 28, 33, 35, 37, 42, 49, 53, 58, 94–5, 118–30, 132–6, 154
  and improper expectations, 38–9, 43, 46, 48–9, 51, 57, 59, 119–20, 124
  Laws of, 58, 204 n 39

  and virtue, 60–2
  and women's power, 51–2, 58–60, 62–6, 118–19
Rorty, Richard, 149, 160, 172, 179
Rosa, Salvator, 149–50, 155
Ross, Deborah, 52

Said, Edward, 175
Sancho Panza, 23, 84
satire, 6, 33, 36, 97, 108–9
  claims to objectivity, 99–100, 102–4, 107, 112–16
  reality effect of, 97, 102–7, 109, 111, 214 n 41
  views of women, 112–14
satirist, 99–100, 102–4, 112–13
  see also objective perception
Schaffer, Simon, 20, 68, 102
Schiebinger, Londa, 174–5
Schiller, Friedrich, 150
Schmidgen, Wolfram, 159
science, 57, 172–3
  and objectivity, 4, 100–4, 107, 110, 114, 175–6
  seventeenth and eighteenth century, 20, 31, 36, 58, 68, 80–1, 101–2, 104, 107, 150–1, 169, 174–5, 180–1
scientific method, 101
sectaries, 27, 29, 31, 32, 33
sensibility, 153–9
Shakespeare, William, 47, 126–7
Shapin, Stephen, 20, 32, 68, 81, 102
Shelley, Mary, 204 n 42
Sherburn, George, 70
Sheridan, Frances, 124
Sheriff, Mary, 36
Siddons, Sarah, 36
Sidney, Philip, 118, 122, 125
Silverman, Kaja, 136
Sinfield, Alan, 64
skepticism, 14
Smith, Adam, 88
Smith, Paul, 14, 180
Solomon, Harry T., 106

Spacks, Patricia Meyer, 59, 64, 79, 145
Spencer, Jane, 118
Spitzer, Leo, 6
Stallybrass, Peter, 112–13
standpoint theory, 168–72
Starr, G. A., 71
Staves, Susan, 11
Steele, Richard, 34
Sterne, Laurence, 34, 37, 85–6
Stevens, Anne, 123, 221 n 35
sublime, *see* landscape
supernatural, *see* superstition
superstition, 117–18, 142–4, 146–9, 154, 156, 162–6
suspicion, 9
   approved, 67, 69, 75–8, 86–8, 91
   critiqued, 67, 72–3, 76, 78–9, 82
   difficult to learn, 73–4, 77, 86–8, 129
   necessary, 67, 69, 72, 78, 82, 86–8, 91
   and prudence, 69–71, 79
   and quixotism, 81–3, 90–1
system, 14, 16, 18–19, 57, 80, 167–8, 176, 181, 192 n 30
Swift, Jonathan, 2, 9, 19, 34, 36, 80, 97–107, 108

Taylor, John, 27
Tenney, Tabitha Gilman, 9, 39, 41, 42–6
Thomson, James, 148–51, 165
Todd, Janet, 69, 88–9

Todorov, Tzvetan, 139
Tompkins, J. M. S., 118
transforming eye, 159–66
   see also perception [active]
translation, 13, 15, 19, 46, 57, 73, 150–1, 167–8, 190 n 11
   see also interpretation

W—, Miss, 108
Wachterhauser, Brice, 169
Walpole, Horace, 117, 133
Warner, William, 35
Warnke, Georgia, 174, 178
Warton, Joseph, 159–60
Watt, James, 166
Weinsheimer, Joel, 26
Weiskel, Thomas, 18
Welsh, Alexander, 13, 24
White, Hayden, 136
Willey, Basil, 105
Williams, Raymond, 23
Williams, Vanessa, 4
Wittgenstein, Ludwig, 172
Wollstonecraft, Mary, 40, 119–20, 122, 134
Woodward, Carolyn, 89
Wordsworth, William, 160
Wortley, Edward, 95
Wycherley, William, 40, 109

Zimbardo, Rose, 111–12, 214 n 41
Ziolkowski, Eric, 13
Žižek, Slavoj, 151–2

PR 113 .G67 2006
Gordon, Scott Paul, 1965-
The practice of quixotism

DEC 07 2007